MARX AND ETHICS

MARX AND ETHICS

PHILIP J. KAIN

CLARENDON PRESS · OXFORD

Oxford University Press, Walton Street, Oxford OX2 6DP
Oxford New York Toronto
Delhi Bombay Calcutta Madras Karachi
Petaling Jaya Singapore Hong Kong Tokyo
Nairobi Dar es Salaam Cape Town
Melbourne Auckland
and associated companies in
Berlin Ibadan

Oxford is a trade mark of Oxford University Press

Published in the United States
by Oxford University Press, New York

© Philip J. Kain 1988

First published 1988
First issued in paperback 1991

British Library Cataloguing in Publication Data
Kain, Philip J., 1943-
Marx and ethics.
1. Ethics. Theories of Marx, Karl, 1818–1883
I. Title
170'.92'4
ISBN 0–19–823932–7

Library of Congress Cataloging in Publication Data
Kain, Philip J., 1943-
Marx and ethics / Philip J. Kain.
p. cm. Bibliography: p. Includes index.
1. Marx, Karl, 1818–1883—Ethics.   I. Title.
B3305.M74K274 1988
171'.7'0924—dc19   88–8649   CIP
ISBN 0–19–823932–7

Printed and bound in
Great Britain by Biddles Ltd,
Guildford and King's Lynn

For Brother S. Robert Smith
my teacher and friend

Acknowledgements

I would like to thank Annette Aronowicz and Michael Brint for reading and commenting on an earlier draft of this manuscript, for many long and exciting discussions, and for their friendship.

Parts of Chapters 1 and 2 first appeared as 'The Young Marx and Kantian Ethics' in *Studies in Soviet Thought*, 31 (1986), 277-301. Copyright by D. Reidel Publishing Company. It is reprinted here by permission of the publisher.

Parts of Chapter 3 were first published as 'Marx and the Abolition of Morality' in *The Journal of Value Inquiry*, 18 (1984), 283-97. It is reprinted here by permission of the editor.

Parts of Chapter 4 were first published as 'Marx, Justice, and the Dialectic Method' in *The Journal of the History of Philosophy*, 24 (1986), 523-46. It is reprinted here by permission of the editor.

P.J.K.

Contents

Abbreviations

PH	Hegel, *Philosophy of History*
PP	Kant, *Perpetual Peace*
PR	Hegel, *Philosophy of Right*
PS	Hegel, *Phenomenology of Spirit*
'Reply'	Wood, 'Marx on Right and Justice: A Reply to Husami'
SC	Marx and Engels, *Marx Engels Selected Correspondence*
SCn	Rousseau, *Social Contract*
SW	Hegel, *Sämtliche Werke*
SWN	Schiller, *Schillers Werke: Nationalausgabe*
TF	Marx, 'Theses on Feuerbach'
TSV	Marx, *Theories of Surplus Value*
VPP	Marx, *Value, Price, and Profit*

Introduction

I have entitled this book *Marx and Ethics* rather than *Marx's Ethics* because I do not think that Marx has a single ethical theory that he sticks to throughout all periods of his thought. In the early writings, Marx's ethics are based on a concept of essence much like Aristotle's which he tries to link to a concept of universalization much like that found in Kant's categorical imperative. In the *German Ideology*, Marx develops a doctrine of historical materialism, abandons these Kantian and Aristotelian elements, and indeed rejects the very possibility of ethics altogether. In the later writings, he revives an ethical theory which, however, is different from that of his early works.

My interpretation of Marx differs quite sharply from that of most contemporary Marx scholars. Let me try to outline the current state of Marx scholarship and explain my views against this background.

It was not until the second quarter of the twentieth century that several of Marx's texts were discovered and published for the first time. The *Economic and Philosophic Manuscripts*, an early work written in 1844, and a complete edition of the *German Ideology*, originally written in 1845-6, were published for the first time only in 1932. The *Grundrisse*, a later work written in 1857-8, was published first in 1939 and 1941. The publication of these texts—all of them very important ones—seriously upset the traditional understanding of Marx's intellectual development. In particular, it produced a series of problems and disagreements in Marx scholarship over how the relationship of the earlier to the later Marx should be understood. Those scholars who concern themselves with these matters can be roughly divided into three schools.

The first school is made up of those who think that there is an essential unity to Marx's thought. These scholars usually focus on the philosophical and humanistic writings of the early Marx and argue that they give us the key to unlocking the later Marx. Their point is to show that Marx as a whole, even in his later scientific writings, is a thoroughgoing humanist.

The second school takes the opposite approach. It argues that there is a break in Marx's thought. The most interesting representative of this approach is Althusser, who wants to reject the early Marx and his humanism as pre-Marxist, and who thinks that the later scientific Marx is the true Marx. For Althusser, Marx's thought falls into four periods: (1) the early works of 1840-4, (2) the works of the break (the 'Theses on Feuerbach' and the *German Ideology* of 1845-6), (3) the transitional works of 1845-57, and (4) the mature works of 1857-83.[1]

The third school, in many cases, begins by assuming an essential unity to Marx's thought, then goes on to argue that fundamental contradictions run throughout it. Gouldner, for example, argues that there are 'two Marxes'. Scientific Marxism, for Gouldner, emphasizes objective conditions, blind impersonal laws, and determinism. In opposition to this, Critical Marxism emphasizes purposive action, voluntarism, human ideals, and freedom.[2] These contradictory tendencies, for Gouldner, can be found both in Marx and in the later Marxist tradition.

For the past fifteen years, I have been trying to work out my own interpretation of Marx's intellectual development and have argued that there are problems with each of these schools.[3] In *Schiller, Hegel, and Marx*, I studied Marx's views on the state, on society and labour, on alienation, and on the aesthetic ideal of ancient Greece. In *Marx' Method, Epistemology, and Humanism*, I extended my study to Marx's doctrine of nature and essence, his epistemology, and his method. In this present book, I would like to examine his views on ethics.

In my opinion, the main problem with the view of those who see an essential unity in Marx's thought, as usually argued, is its superficiality. In attempting to iron his thought into a smooth and unified whole, such theorists flatten out important shifts and developments to be found in it at various periods and ignore or underestimate the differences between these periods. To take one example, essential unity theorists rarely achieve an adequate understanding of the concept of essence which Marx employs in his early writings or of its radical implications for his social and political theory, his views on alienation, his method and epistemology, or his doctrine of nature. Moreover, essential unity theorists *must* refrain from a deep and adequate study of all that this concept implies if they are to avoid the conclusion that Marx abandons this understanding in the *German Ideology*, that his views then are altered fundamentally, and begin to develop in a new direction.

[1] L. Althusser, *For Marx*, trans. B. Brewster (London: NLB, 1977), 28-35.

[2] A. Gouldner, *The Two Marxisms* (New York: Seabury, 1980), 32-5, 58 ff.

[3] P. J. Kain, *Schiller, Hegel, and Marx* (Montreal: McGill-Queen's University Press, 1982) and *Marx' Method, Epistemology, and Humanism* (Dordrecht: D. Reidel, 1986).

In particular, those who follow the essential unity school make at least two errors when they come to the study of Marx's ethics. They dilute his early concept of essence and underestimate the determinism to be found in the *German Ideology*. I will argue that Marx's ethical views in the early writings, especially the *Economic and Philosophic Manuscripts*, are incompatible with the views of the *German Ideology*. In the early writings, Marx's concept of essence is the foundation of his ethics. In the *German Ideology*, he rejects this concept of essence, develops a doctrine of historical materialism which, at least at this point in his intellectual development, involves a form of determinism that makes ethics impossible, and he rejects morality as ideological illusion that will disappear in communist society.

A typical argument by essential unity theorists runs as follows. Marx's views are based upon an ethical conception of individuals and society. The key to this ethical approach is a theory of human nature or essence. In capitalist society, for Marx, we are alienated and thus cannot realize our essence. Communist society is conceived as one which overcomes alienation, provides the social relations and institutions which allow the human essence to be realized, and thus allows for the full and free development of the individual. Then it is often argued that this outlook is compatible with Marx's scientific approach to the study of society and thus that Marx combines facts with values.[4]

These claims are so general and unspecific that they actually do come close to being correct about Marx's thought as a whole, but at the same time they tell us very little. It is true that if one studies Marx's thought at a high enough level of abstraction and generality, one will find that there is some continuity to it. It is always Marx's view that society should be transformed to overcome alienation and realize the full development of the individual. But this is very superficial. At the heart of Marx's thought, we will see, if we study him carefully, such views are understood quite differently and have quite different implications in different periods of his thought. Essential unity theorists do not look this deeply. For example, it is not the case that Marx's theory of the overcoming of alienation and of the full realization of the individual is always based upon an ethical conception of individuals or on a concept of human nature or essence. This is not the case in the *German Ideology*, and, in that text at least, ethical conceptions are not compatible with

---

[4] e.g. see D. Kellner, 'Marxism, Morality, and Ideology', *Marx and Morality*, ed. K. Nielsen and S. C. Patten, *Canadian Journal of Philosophy*, supplementary vol. 7 (1981), 94-5. Also J. McMurtry, *The Structure of Marx's World-View* (Princeton University Press, 1978), 6-7 n., 20 ff., 29, 32-3, 34 n., 53, 170, 222-3, 233.

science. If we study the early Marx's concept of essence in detail and in depth, we shall see, as I shall argue in Chapters 1 and 2, that this is the key to his concept of freedom. Freedom as self-determination is possible for the early Marx when our essence has been objectified in existence; then, as we seek existing objects, these objects cannot be seen as alien or heteronomous—they have become parts of our essence and thus our relations to them are free and self-determined. In the *German Ideology*, this concept of essence, and indeed even freedom understood as self-determination, is rejected. Again, it is Marx's concept of essence which explains how facts imply values. It allows us to treat things or facts descriptively. We can describe objectively what things are in essence. But at the same time things can be treated prescriptively. We can say how they ought to develop if they are to realize their essence fully. This approach is certainly abandoned in the *German Ideology* as, I think, is the general attempt to combine facts and values.

Moreover, when essential unity theorists begin to discuss the *German Ideology*, they usually argue for a very soft version of historical material-ism and play down the amount of determinism involved. They often avoid difficult passages which count against their interpretation and misread others.[5] Frequently, they provide us with their own arguments for the compatibility of ethics and determinism rather than those of Marx.[6] Furthermore, in discussing freedom, almost all such comment-ators fail to recognize that Marx rejects freedom as self-determination in the *German Ideology*. In short, I will argue for a very different inter-pretation of Marx's historical materialism than that of the essential unity theorists.[7]

There are other scholars who do take seriously Marx's historical materialism and the degree of determinism it involves in the *German Ideology*. They conclude that Marx rejects ethics.[8] However, they often

[5] e.g. see G. G. Brenkert, *Marx's Ethics of Freedom* (London: Routledge & Kegan Paul, 1983), 25 ff., 27.

[6] Ibid. 35-6, 42 ff.

[7] There are some scholars who might be mentioned in passing. Some of them discuss essential unity and mention morality only briefly. Others discuss Marx's ethics in detail and seem to accept an essential unity but do not dwell on it. See A. Schaff, *Marxism and the Human Individual* (New York: McGraw Hill, 1970). S. Stojanović, *Between Ideals and Reality*, trans. G. S. Sher (New York: OUP, 1973). I. Fetscher, 'The Young and the Old Marx', *Marx and the Western World*, ed. N. Lobkowicz (Notre Dame: University of Notre Dame Press, 1967), 19-39. M. Marković, 'Marxist Humanism and Ethics', *Inquiry*, 6 (1963), 18-34.

[8] D. C. Hodges, 'Historical Materialism in Ethics', *Philosophy and Phenomenological Research*, 23 (1962-3), 1-22. L. S. Feuer, 'Ethical Theories and Historical Materialism', *Science and Society*, 6 (1942), 242-72.

do not discuss the moral views found in Marx's early writings, nor the absence of such strict determinism there and in later writings like the *Grundrisse* and *Capital*, as I will argue in Chapter 4.

The general point I am trying to make and will argue is that since there actually are shifts in Marx's intellectual development, anyone committed to its essential unity will tend to ignore, dilute, or misinterpret some part of Marx's thought. Moreover, a commitment to essential unity will tend almost inevitably to blind one to the deeper significance of one issue or another in Marx's thought. For example, the *German Ideology* so clearly attacks and rejects Kantian morality that anyone committed to essential unity is not likely to perceive that the ethical views of the early writings are influenced deeply by Kant, and, indeed, in many respects are Kantian. The abandonment of a commitment to essential unity makes it easier to notice such things. I will argue, in Chapters 1 and 2, that in his early writings Marx tries to combine a doctrine of essence much like Aristotle's with a concept of universalization not unlike that found in Kant's categorical imperative.

Althusser's views are quite different from those of the essential unity theorists. He argues that there is a break in Marx's thought which occurs in the *German Ideology* and wants to separate the philosophical and humanistic writings of the early Marx from the scientific writings of the later Marx; for Althusser, the science of the later Marx is not humanist, but anti-humanist. My views are closer to those of Althusser than to the essential unity theorists in that I too think there are shifts in Marx's thought. There are several respects, however, in which I sharply differ from Althusser. In the first place, I do not think that these shifts amount to a 'break' or 'coupure epistémologique', which, for Althusser, means a total shift in a whole pattern or frame of reference such that any element in the first pattern must have a totally altered or different meaning in the second.[9] For example, I argued in *Marx' Method, Epistemology, and Humanism* that Marx's development should be understood as a rather ordinary evolution. The method which Marx first develops in the *Grundrisse* and employs in *Capital* is a new method. But in putting it together, Marx modifies his earlier views in a rather ordinary way. He drops some elements, keeps others, adds new ones, and moulds them into a new method.[10]

Moreover, despite his emphasis on a break, Althusser finds more unity between the works of 1845–6 and the mature works (the *Grundrisse*

[9] *For Marx*, pp. 198-9, 244, 249. L. Althusser and E. Balibar, *Reading Capital*, trans. B. Brewster (London: NLB, 1970), 148-57.

[10] *Marx' Method, Epistemology, and Humanism*, ch. 3.

and *Capital*) than I do. For Althusser, the period after the break is a relatively steady movement to maturity. In my view, there is more than one shift in Marx's thought. After the *German Ideology*, another change occurs, in the *Grundrisse*. The method outlined there is quite different from those set out in either the *Economic and Philosophic Manuscripts* or the *German Ideology*. I read the *German Ideology* as an overreaction to the views of the early writings which had to be corrected later in the *Grundrisse*.

However, my main disagreement with Althusser concerns his claim that the scientific approach of the later Marx is anti-humanist. Let us try to understand what this claim means. For Althusser, humanism involves ethics, and both humanism and ethics are ideological, not scientific;[11] ideology represents the imaginary relationship of individuals to their real conditions of existence. In other words, ideology does not correspond to reality. As Collier, who follows Althusser in this respect, puts it, humanism, ideology, or value judgements are not a sound basis for scientific theories. Ideology, for Althusser, does not give us scientific knowledge.[12]

I must point out that Althusser's theory of ideology is different, as he himself admits, from the theory of ideology that Marx outlines in the *German Ideology*. In that text, as I will argue in Chapter 3, ideology is seen as something that must be pierced through and overcome in communist society. It is Althusser's view, however, that while particular ideologies, say capitalist or feudal ideologies, can be overcome, ideology in general cannot be. It is omni-historical, eternal, and will exist even in communist society.[13] In this sense, humanism and ethics do have a place in communist society, but only at the ideological, not the scientific, level.[14]

I must say that I disagree with Althusser. I do not think that the later Marx is an anti-humanist and I do not think that humanism is ideological. Althusser's opposition to humanism is based on his view that humanism reduces the forces and relations of production to objectifications of the human essence. For the early Marx, the forces and relations of production and their development are explained in terms of relationships and interactions between human individuals. For Althusser,

---

[11] *For Marx*, pp. 11-12, 45, 222 ff., 229-34. Also L. Althusser, *Lenin and Philosophy*, trans. B. Brewster (New York: Monthly Review Press, 1971), 38, 134, 155.

[12] *For Marx*, p. 233. *Lenin and Philosophy*, pp. 162, 164-5, 173. A. Collier, 'Scientific Socialism and the Question of Socialist Values', *Marx and Morality*, pp. 124-5.

[13] *Lenin and Philosophy*, pp. 159-61.

[14] *For Marx*, pp. 232, 235. *Lenin and Philosophy*, p. 161.

ideology constitutes individuals as subjects. The science of the mature
Marx, however, does not study ideological appearances, nor subjects,
nor even individuals. Moreover, it does not reduce the forces and
relations of production to relations between individuals. Instead,
science studies reality; it studies social structures—forces and relations
of production, which, far from being the outcome of relations between
individuals, structure those relations.[15]

I do not think that Althusser has characterized correctly the method
of the mature Marx. In my view, Marx's science confines itself to a
study of social structures only due to the fetishism that is present in
capitalist society. Fetishism causes what are actually relationships
between human beings to appear as relationships between things. It is
the task of science to pierce through this fetishized surface appearance
of society and to aid practice in transforming society so as to end
fetishism. Then, according to Marx, we will see clearly that social
relations *are* in fact relations between human beings, and at that point
theoretical science will wither away.[16] Althusser is right to insist that the
later Marx rejects the concept of human essence which informed his
early writings. He is correct in claiming that the forces and relations of
production, once fetishism is overcome, are not to be reduced to the
human essence, but incorrect in claiming that they are not to be reduced
to human relations. That *is* Marx's goal and it is a *humanistic* goal. In
the *German Ideology*, morality was viewed as ideological illusion
destined to disappear in communist society. I will argue in Chapters 4
and 5 that, in the *Grundrisse* and *Capital*, morality is not ideological
illusion and it does not disappear under communism. When fetishism
and ideology are overcome, we will appear again as what we are, as
individuals, who far from being dominated by social structures will
control our forces and relations of production for our own benefit. This
humanism is not ideological; it is a reality which ought to be realized.

Thus, I am opposed both to the essential unity theorists who reduce
Marx's thought to a uniform consistency which ignores important shifts
and developments and equally to Althusser's attempt to force Marx's
thought into rigid and radically distinct periods which serve to deny his
humanism. I see the humanism of his later writings as different from,
but an outgrowth of, the humanism of his early writings. In all periods
of his thought, it is Marx's goal to bring about a society which will

---

[15] *Reading Capital*, pp. 139-41, 180. *Lenin and Philosophy*, pp. 170-3. L. Althusser,
Essays in Self-Criticism, trans. G. Lock (London: NLB, 1976), 200-6.

[16] For an extended discussion of this point, see *Marx' Method, Epistemology, and
Humanism*, ch. 3.

realize the highest development of the individual, but in these periods we find different understandings of morality and the way in which it is connected with and contributes to this human development.

The third school often assumes that there is or ought to be an essential unity to Marx's thought, but then goes on to argue that fundamental contradictions run throughout it. For this school there are two strands in Marx's thought which he is unable to reconcile. On the one hand, his science claims to be descriptive and objective. However, it also attempts to be prescriptive and to deduce moral norms. Kamenka, for example, argues that Marx in an uncritical and illogical way attempts to give ethical judgements the objectivity of scientific descriptions.[17] For Kamenka, 'good' can be treated in two ways. It can be treated as a quality—an intrinsic property—which can be described scientifically and objectively, but, if so, ethics is shorn of its advocative and normative pretensions. Or 'good' can be treated as a relation—something demanded or pursued, something it is wrong to reject—but, if so, 'good' is not an objective property and cannot be treated objectively. Marx, in Kamenka's view, illegitimately attempts to combine scientific description and advocacy, facts and values, by treating relations as constituting the character or quality of things. For Kamenka, things cannot be constituted by their relations. A thing must have qualities before it can enter into relations.[18]

In Chapter 2, I will argue that it is not Marx's view that things are constituted by their relations: things do have qualities before they enter into relations, but relations transform those qualities. In this way, Marx avoids, I think, some of the problems that Kamenka raises.

Stanley Moore also argues that there is a contradiction running throughout Marx's thought between a scientific and descriptive sociology of change, which arises from Marx's doctrine of historical materialism, and a prescriptive and ethical dialectic of liberation, which stems from his early writings.[19] Moore admits that a shift occurs in the *German Ideology*, but claims that it is less radical than it appears. In the *German Ideology*, Marx does reject the premises of his early writings, but not the conclusions he drew from them.[20] According to Moore,

[17] E. Kamenka, *The Ethical Foundations of Marxism*, 2nd edn. (London: Routledge & Kegan Paul, 1972), 3, 89.

[18] Ibid. 89-90.

[19] S. Moore, 'Marx and Lenin as Historical Materialists', *Marx, Justice, and History (MJH)*, ed. M. Cohen, T. Nagel, and T. Scanlon (Princeton University Press, 1980), 213, 216-17.

[20] S. Moore, *Marx on the Choice between Socialism and Communism* (Cambridge, Mass.: Harvard University Press, 1980), 19-20, 24.

Marx adopted communism on moral grounds before developing his doctrine of historical materialism in the *German Ideology*. There Marx drops his original moral arguments, but keeps communism as his goal, despite the fact that he is unable to defend it on historical materialist grounds.[21] Moore argues that, in the 'Critique of the Gotha Program', Marx only gives a moral reason for moving from socialism to full communism, whereas only a historical materialist one would be sound.[22] I will try to argue in Chapter 5 that this is neither objectionable nor a contradiction because it is Marx's view that in socialist society human beings will gain control over the forces and relations of production which hitherto in history have dominated them. Freedom will replace determinism. Thus, moral reasons for moving on to full communism would be perfectly good reasons for doing so—they would no longer be incompatible with historical materialist determinism.

But, even if specific difficulties like those raised by Kamenka and Moore can be solved, there still remains the general problem of whether in other areas of Marx's thought there is an ongoing contradiction between science and ethics. Acton thinks so, as does Habermas and Wellmer.[23] And Gouldner is even willing to argue that there are 'two Marxes'. I certainly do not want to assert that there are no contradictions in Marx's thought. In fact, I have argued elsewhere that there are.[24] But I have tried to show that, while Marx's thought is not absolutely free of inconsistencies, we do not find ongoing and uniform contradictions running throughout it. We must study contradictions, when they exist, within the specific periods of Marx's thought. They may be very different in different periods or they may simply be absent in some periods and more or less intense in others. Moreover, I think that if the periods of Marx's thought are studied carefully, we find shifts or changes of mind, rather than 'two Marxes'.

I have said that the moral theory of the early Marx is built around a concept of essence much like Aristotle's and that Marx tries to reconcile this with a concept of universalization much like that found in Kant. In the *German Ideology*, he rejects this attempt and argues that morality is

---

[21] Ibid. 89-90.

[22] Ibid. 36 ff., 44-5. 'Marx and Lenin as Historical Materialists', pp. 230-3.

[23] H. B. Acton, *The Illusion of the Epoch* (Boston: Beacon, 1957), 191-2. J. Habermas, *Knowledge and Human Interests*, trans. J. Shapiro (Boston: Beacon, 1971), 43-4, 52-3. J. Habermas, *Theory and Practice*, trans. J. Viertel (Boston: Beacon, 1974), 195-252 *passim*. A. Wellmer, *Critical Theory of Society*, trans. J. Cumming (New York: Herder and Herder, 1971), 70-5.

[24] P. J. Kain, 'Estrangement and the Dictatorship of the Proletariat', *Political Theory*, 7 (1979), 509-20.

ideological illusion destined to disappear in communist society. In the *Grundrisse* and *Capital*, however, Marx again begins to argue for morality which is not ideological illusion and which will not disappear in communist society.

However, there has been a good deal of controversy over the way in which Marx's ethical views in the later writings should be interpreted. Allen Wood, for example, argues that, for Marx, the concept of justice belonging to any society is rooted in, grows out of, and expresses that particular society's mode of production in such a way that each social epoch gives rise to a different standard of justice and must be judged by this standard alone. It is Wood's view that capitalism, for Marx, generally lives up to its own standards and thus is perfectly just. Furthermore, for Wood, slavery must be accepted as perfectly just within the context of ancient society, and so also, for Marx, socialist society will not be able to condemn capitalist society as unjust because its standards would not be rationally applicable to capitalism.[25] Other writers, like Husami, sharply disagree with Wood and hold that Marx does morally condemn capitalist society, from the perspective of a higher socialist morality.[26]

In my view, both writers are in some respects correct and in others quite wrong. But, more importantly, neither seems to understand the new method for the study of the social world which Marx outlines in the *Grundrisse* and employs in *Capital*, nor that it is quite different from the historical materialist method sketched in the *German Ideology*. A correct understanding of this new method, as I argue in Chapters 4 and 5, will show that the paradigm which allows us to understand highly developed society also will give us an insight into earlier societies such that we can judge them by later standards. Moreover, a correct understanding of this new method will show us that we must operate with a distinction between essence and appearance. I will try to show, then, that Wood *is* correct in arguing that capitalist society is perfectly just, but, for Marx, this is *only* the case at the level of surface appearance. And, on the other hand, Husami is also correct in arguing that capitalist society is unjust, but, for Marx, this is so only at the level of essence; it is something we can discover only when science has allowed us to pierce through surface appearance. Thus, it is my view that the later Marx, after having rejected his earlier concept of essence in the

---

[25] A. W. Wood, 'The Marxian Critique of Justice', *MJH*, pp. 3, 13, 15-16, 18-19. A. W. Wood, 'Marx on Right and Justice: A Reply to Husami', *MJH*, pp. 107-9, 131-2.
[26] Z. I. Husami, 'Marx on Distributive Justice', *MJH*, pp. 43 ff., 47-51, 53-4, 60.

German Ideology, begins to employ a very different concept of essence again in the *Grundrisse* and *Capital*.

Thus, I hope to show that by establishing the claim that there are shifts in Marx's thought we can free ourselves and make possible a much deeper and more careful analysis of its different periods. An interpretation of the method of the later Marx which is not restrained by a desire to preserve an essential unity between it and the method of the *German Ideology*, I hope to show, will resolve neatly one of the major recent debates over the nature of the ethical views of the later Marx.

What is the point of arguing for shifts and development in Marx's thought? It certainly is not to fragment Marx's thought into little pieces that simply lie scattered like the shards of a broken pot, though it may seem that way to some. The point is to reach a clearer understanding of the later Marx. I do not think that Marx's thought ought to be forced and stretched into a mould that will preserve its essential unity. I think this will cause us to miss rich and interesting developments. Nor do I agree with those essential unity theorists who tend to argue that the early Marx is the 'true' Marx, or who try to reduce the later Marx to the early Marx, or who claim that the essence of the later Marx is to be found in the early writings. Like Althusser, I see shifts in Marx's thought, that his later writings are the culmination of a development, and that the later Marx is the more interesting and valuable. However, I understand these shifts and developments in a very different way from Althusser, and I certainly do not agree that the later Marx is an anti-humanist. In this respect, with the essential unity theorists, I think that the early writings give us a key to the later writings. The later Marx is a humanist and his humanism is an outgrowth of, but different from, the humanism of his early writings.

Most scholars would admit that Marx's humanism is most visible in the early writings. Althusser thinks that it is only there that humanism can be found. The essential unity theorists would reject this, but they would admit that in the early writings Marx's humanism is clearer, sharper, and more explicit. In Chapter 5, I propose something which I think no one has noticed and which many will not agree with immediately, namely, that at least in one respect the later Marx is *more* of a humanist than the early Marx. In the early writings, Marx completely rejects civil rights as a means of protecting the individual. In his view, a concern with rights would feed self-interest and lead to isolated egotism in opposition to the community. But in his later writings, especially in the 'Critique of the Gotha Program', Marx aims to realize rights in the socialist stage, the first stage of communist society, but to transcend rights in the second and higher stage of communist society, and to transcend them in a way which, I think, would preserve them in custom and tradition. His initial rejection of rights even as a transitional measure for the early stage of an ideal society, was, I will argue, due to their incompatibility with his concept of human essence. When he dropped this concept he made possible a deeper humanism by allowing for the protection of individuals through rights and then through rights transcended but preserved in custom and tradition.

Nor do I agree with the contradiction theorists, many of whom seem to imply that the 'true' Marx is the scientific or historical materialist Marx and who understand his historical materialism on the model of the *German Ideology* where it was incompatible with ethics. Many of those who write on Marx, including contradiction theorists, seem to assume, implicitly if not explicitly, that Marx is primarily a theorist of revolution, that revolution is the goal of Marx's thought, and that all other elements of it must support and lead to revolution. If one believes that ethics will not promote revolution, then where Marx makes an ethical judgement, or uses an ethical argument rather than a historical materialist one, Marx is seen to have contradicted himself, or else there is a problem to be solved, or another interpretation is needed to avoid such problems.

On my reading of Marx, in the early writings he believes in ethics; he thinks morality can play a real role in transforming the world; and his theory of revolution is grounded on his ethical theory. In the *German Ideology* and the *Communist Manifesto*, he changes his mind. Here he does not think that morality can transform the world or lead to revolution, and he rejects morality as ideological illusion. In the *Grundrisse* and *Capital*, he shifts again. Morality is no longer ideological illusion, but nevertheless in capitalist society it is incapable of transforming the world or promoting revolution. However, despite this, it still has a necessary and important place in his theory. Many cannot accept this as Marxist because they assume that Marx is primarily or exclusively a theorist of revolution. Certainly Marx's theory of revolution is a very important part of his overall theory, but his doctrine of historical materialism is a much broader theory than his theory of revolution. It claims that there is a certain relationship between material conditions and all forms of consciousness—politics, law, aesthetics, religion, *and ethics.* Moreover, the doctrine of historical materialism contains, at least implicitly, the demand that theories of aesthetics, law, religion, ethics, and so forth, be worked out. It does not follow at all that each and every form of consciousness will serve to promote revolution. Some forms may hinder revolution or simply be neutral. Nevertheless, Marx must have theories of these forms of consciousness and it is his view that historical materialism gives us the key to these theories. The way in which he understands historical materialism in the *German Ideology* leads him to develop a theory of ethics in which morality is ideological illusion. Later, due to his changed views on historical materialism, his theory of ethics holds neither that morality is ideological illusion, nor that morality promotes revolution. One can object to this only if one holds to the primacy of revolution and to the notion of the incompatibility of historical materialism and ethics as outlined in the *German Ideology*.

Let us now proceed to the details of our study of Marx's ethical views.

1

Aristotle, Kant, and
the Ethics of the Young Marx (1835–1843)

I would like to argue in this chapter that the young Marx's ethical views have been influenced not only by Hegel but even more so by Aristotle and Kant. Marx draws away from Hegel's concept of essence towards one in some ways more like Aristotle's and he operates with a concept of universalization similar to that found in Kant's categorical imperative. At the same time, Marx's task is to reconcile these Aristotelian and Kantian elements. Eventually, as we shall see in Chapter 3, Marx's doctrine of historical materialism leads him to abandon these elements and indeed to reject all morality as ideological illusion.

To claim that the young Marx was influenced by Aristotle is not new and some scholars admit that there is a relationship between the young Marx and Kant or that Marx has been influenced by Kant.[1] But very few would admit that the young Marx has been influenced by Kantian ethics to the extent to which I will claim. However, Marx cannot simply be called a Kantian. At most, he uses parts of Kant for his own purposes, rejecting others, for example, significant parts of Kant's concept of freedom. Nevertheless, I hope to show that in many ways Kant and Marx agree and that in a very significant sense Marx is Kantian in his use of the categorical imperative. I must point out from the start, however, that Marx does not accept many of the assumptions in Kant's discussion of the categorical imperative as it appears in Kant's ethical writings—the *Foundations of the Metaphysics of Morals* and the *Critique of Practical Reason*. There Kant focuses primarily on what it means to be moral and he seems to assume that morality has exclusively to do with the individual. The individual is free and thus should act

---

[1] For examples of those who see a relationship between Marx and Kant or who think Marx has been influenced by Kant, see Max Adler, *Kant und der Marxismus* (Berlin: E. Laub'sche Verlagsbuchhandlung, 1925); Otto Bauer, 'Marxismus und Ethik', *Die Neue Zeit*, 24 (1905-6), 485-99; Karl Vorländer, *Kant und der Sozialismus* (Berlin: Reuther und Reichard, 1900); L. Colletti, *Marxism and Hegel*, trans. L. Garner (London: NLB, 1973); L. Althusser, *For Marx*, trans. B. Brewster (London: NLB, 1977), 35, 158, 223-44; J. Habermas, *Knowledge and Human Interests*, trans. J. Shapiro (Boston: Beacon, 1971).

morally, no matter what.[2] But these are not Kant's assumptions in his writings on politics and philosophy of history. In these texts things are not just left to the individual. Individual choice is not enough to produce morality. The historical development of culture and social institutions is a necessary presupposition for the possibility of morality—for acting in accordance with the categorical imperative. This is where we find the similarity between Marx and Kant. Marx is seeking a historical agent that will make possible the realization of morality and in doing so is influenced by what Kant has to say about this sort of agency.

Marx's main concern is not simply to explain what morality is but to explain how it can be realized in the world. For us to understand his views we first must gain at least a basic understanding of what morality means for the young Marx. To do this we must examine several concepts and the way in which they are connected to each other: his concepts of freedom, essence, and the state. Then we will be able to understand his concept of universalization and will begin to see how it is like Kant's concept of a categorical imperative. This will be the task of section i. Once we have taken these preparatory steps, we can begin to talk about what really interests Marx, namely, how morality can be realized in society and here we will come to see even more clearly the influence of Kant. This will be the task of section ii. Let us begin by discussing Marx's concepts of the state and freedom.

I

In his very earliest writings, by which I mean those written before the *Critique of Hegel's Philosophy of Law* of 1843, Marx accepts a Hegelian form of state.[3] For Marx, the state should be an organic unity which

---

[2] e.g. see *Critique of Pure Reason* (*CPR*), A 555 = B 583; references to the *Critique of Pure Reason* are to the standard 1st (A) and 2nd (B) edn. pagination. I have used the N. Kemp Smith English translation and, for the German, *Kant's gesammelte Schriften* (*KGS*), ed. Royal Prussian Academy of Science (Berlin: Reimer, 1910-). It is true that in other places Kant speaks of serious conflict between duty and inclination and even admits that perhaps there never has been a pure example of acting for the sake of duty. But in so far as we do act morally or in so far as we are concerned with what it would mean to act morally, it is simply up to the individual to choose to do so (*Foundations of the Metaphysics of Morals* (*F*), trans. L. W. Beck (Indianapolis: Bobbs-Merrill, 1959), 22-4, and *KGS* IV. 406).

[3] In this period Marx is not yet a communist (see 'Communism and the Augsburg *Allgemeine Zeitung*', *Marx Engels Collected Works* (*MECW*) (New York: International, 1975-), I. 220, and for the German, *Marx Engels Werke* (*MEW*) (Berlin: Dietz, 1972-), I. 108. 'Marx to Ruge on 30 Nov. 1842', *MECW* I. 394, and *MEW* XXVII. 411). He

moulds its members and institutions into a spiritual whole. It transforms individual aims and particular interests into general aims and universal moral concerns. It transforms 'natural independence into spiritual freedom, by the individual finding his good in the life of the whole, and the whole in the frame of mind of the individual'.[4]

Morality, for the young Marx, as for Hegel, Aristotle, and others, only arises in a state, and moral theory is inseparable from social and political theory.[5] Morality involves obeying universal rational laws, but it is not enough that these laws be subjectively rational, that is, based upon the rationality of the individual. These laws and their rationality must be objective. They must be the public laws of the state, and reason must be objectified in the state's institutions. Only in this way can freedom be objective. It is only the state which is 'the great organism, in which legal, moral, and political freedom must be realized, and in which the individual citizen in obeying the laws of the state only obeys the natural laws of his own reason, of human reason'. The state must be the realization of reason; then morality will be the 'principle of a world that obeys its own laws'.[6]

We can begin to understand this by looking at Hegel. He distinguished between *Moralität*, which is usually translated as 'morality', and *Sittlichkeit*, which is usually translated as 'ethics' or 'ethical life'. *Moralität*, which begins with Socrates and reaches its high point in Kantian morality, is individual, reflective, and rational. It is based upon

clearly rejects Hess's notion of overcoming the state ('Question of Centralization', *MECW* I. 183, and *MEW*, suppl. I. 380). He even claims that his journal, the *Rheinische Zeitung*, has not opposed monarchy ('Marginal Notes to the Accusation of Ministerial Rescript', *MECW* I. 363, and *MEW*, suppl. I. 422). He also holds that the state should protect private property and trade ('Law on Theft of Wood', *MECW* I. 256-7, and *MEW* I. 141-2; 'Industrialist of Hanover', *MECW* I. 286, and *MEW*, suppl. I. 398).

[4] 'Debates on Freedom of the Press', *MECW* I. 135, and *MEW* I. 31. 'Leading Article in No. 179 of the *Kölnische Zeitung*', *MECW* I. 193, and *MEW* I. 95. 'Wood Theft', *MECW* I. 236, and *MEW* I. 121. 'Commissions of the Estates in Prussia', *MECW* I. 295-6, and *MEW*, suppl. I. 409-10.

[5] Aristotle, *Nicomachean Ethics* (*NE*), 1103[b], 1179[b]-1180[a]; *Politics*, 1337[a]. I have used the McKeon edn. of Aristotle's works but cite the column pagination. G. W. F. Hegel, *Philosophy of History* (*PH*), trans. J. Sibree (New York: Dover, 1956), 38, 41, 48, and for the German, *Sämtliche Werke* (*SW*), ed. H. Glockner (Stuttgart: Frommann, 1927-), XI. 70, 74, 82. At the time of Marx's first contact with Hegel's writings, he becomes critical of Kant (see 'Marx to his Father on 10-11 Nov. 1837', *MECW* I. 17-18, and *MEW*, suppl. I. 7-8. *Dissertation*, *MECW* I. 104, and *MEW*, suppl. I. 370-3. Also *MECW* I. 577, and *MEW*, suppl. I. 608). Then, I hope to show, Marx moves increasingly closer to Kant until 1845-6 when he finally rejects him.

[6] 'Free Press', *MECW* I. 162, and *MEW* I. 58. 'Leading Article', *MECW* I. 202, and *MEW* I. 104. 'Latest Prussian Censorship Instruction', *MECW* I. 117-18, and *MEW* I. 12.

the autonomy of individual self-consciousness, on personal conviction and conscience, and is a relatively late development in history. *Sittlichkeit*, best represented perhaps in the Greek *polis* before Socrates, is ethical behaviour governed by natural custom and tradition. It is based on habit in accordance with the objective laws of the community. Personal reflection and analysis have little to do with ethical life.[7]

Clear and simple examples of the difference between *Moralität* and *Sittlichkeit* can be found in Plato. Euthyphro, for example, when he is asked to explain the meaning of a moral notion, is quite able to expound at length on the customs, traditions, and myths which exemplify and underlie the notion—traditions, which it has never occurred to Euthyphro to question, analyse, or reflect upon. This is *Sittlichkeit*. Socrates, on the other hand, forces Euthyphro to analyse and reflect. Socrates asks how we know that something is moral, why it is moral, what makes it moral, and it is clear that for Socrates only our own rationality can decide such questions. This is *Moralität*. Again, in the 'Myth of Er' at the end of the *Republic*, we meet a man who is about to select his next reincarnated life. We are told that in his previous life he had been a good man but only because he had been brought up in a good city. His ethical behaviour had been based upon custom, tradition, habit, and upbringing, not upon philosophy, reason, and reflection. He had behaved properly, but not because he knew what morality was. Consequently, possessing *Sittlichkeit* but lacking *Moralität*, he chooses the life of a grand tyrant before noticing that it will involve eating his own children.[8]

The task of the modern ethical theorist, for Hegel, is to reconcile *Sittlichkeit* and *Moralität*. *Sittlichkeit* without *Moralität* is inadequate. And, for Hegel, *Moralität* without *Sittlichkeit* is impossible, as can be seen in Hegel's critique of Kantian morality—the highest form of *Moralität*. In the *Phenomenology*, Hegel argues that it is impossible to discover one's moral duty simply by analysing abstract principles to see if they are universal and non-contradictory. For example, both private property and its opposite, common ownership or the absence of private property, are equally universalizable and non-contradictory. Without *Sittlichkeit*—without an objective, immediately given, ethical substance embedded in custom and tradition, which actually *is* rather than merely

---

[7] *PH* 39-40, 104, 251-3, 269, and *SW* XI. 71-2, 150-1, 328-31, 350. G. W. F. Hegel, *Philosophy of Right* (*PR*), trans. T. M. Knox (Oxford: OUP, 1967), 36, 91-2, 103-9, and for the German *Grundlinien der Philosophie des Rechts* (*GPR*), ed. J. Hoffmeister (Hamburg: Felix Meiner, 1955), 49-50, 122-3, 140-8.

[8] Plato, *Euthyphro*, 4 B-16 A; *Republic*, 619 B-619 C (I have used the Bollingen edn. of the complete dialogues, but cite the column pagination).

ought to be—it is impossible to discover one's moral obligation through analysis.[9] *Moralität* gets it content from *Sittlichkeit*. Moreover, *Moralität* without *Sittlichkeit* would leave us with an inadequate form of freedom. Certainly for Kantian *Moralität*, the individual is free; in fact, morality is based upon freedom. But it is individual subjectivity alone that is free, the individual will deciding its action in accordance with reason. The individual is not necessarily free to realize the moral action. The world may well present obstacles to its execution without, for Kant, affecting the individual's moral freedom in the slightest.[10] For Kant, such empirical factors, whether they be obstacles or aids, are irrelevant to freedom. Nor do feelings play a role. They need not agree with the action for it to be moral and free. Nor is our freedom affected if our feelings are opposed to the moral action.[11] But for Hegel and Marx, freedom is realized only when the objective external world and our feelings fit, agree with, and support the subjective rational freedom of the individual. Laws and institutions, feelings and customs, as well as the rationality of the individual, must form a single organic spiritual unity.

This is the basis for Hegel's rejection of 'ought' in favour of 'is'. *Moralität* tells us what we ought to do; it is morality which has not yet been realized. *Sittlichkeit* does not involve an 'ought'. It is ethical life which exists—which has been realized. Even Kant said that for a holy will, an 'ought' would be out of place because volition would already, in itself, be in union with the moral law.[12]

Thus, for Hegel and Marx, freedom demands three things: (1) that the individual be self-determined by universal and rational principles, (2) that the laws and institutions of the state also be rational so that in obeying civil laws you obey the laws of your own reason, and (3) that feeling and custom have been moulded so as to agree with and support these rational laws.[13]

[9] G. W. F. Hegel, *Phenomenology of Spirit (PS)*, trans. A. V. Miller (Oxford: OUP, 1978), 257-61; for the German see *Phänomenologie des Geistes (PG)*, ed. J. Hoffmeister (Hamburg: Felix Meiner, 1952), 306-11.

[10] *F* 10, 16, 66, 80-1, and *KGS* IV. 394, 399-400, 448, 461; *Critique of Practical Reason (CPrR)*, trans. L. W. Beck (Indianapolis: Bobbs-Merrill, 1956), 3-4, 71, and *KGS* V. 3-4, 68-9.

[11] *F* 10, 13-17, 44, 53-4, 60-1, and *KGS* IV. 394, 397-401, 426, 435, 442. *CPrR* 28, 31, and *KGS* V. 28-9, 31.

[12] *PH* 35-6, and *SW* XI. 66-7. *PR* 11-13, and *GPR* 15-17. *PS* 255-6, 260, and *PG* 304-5, 310. See also 'Marx to his Father on 10-11 Nov. 1837', *MECW* I. 11-12, and *MEW*, suppl. I. 4-5. *F* 31, and *KGS* IV. 414.

[13] *PH* 38-9, and *SW* XI. 70-1. *PR* 160-1, and *GPR* 214-15. These three characteristics also can be found in Aristotle, though he is discussing virtue not freedom; *NE* 1179b-1180a.

For Kant, the possibility of freedom required that the transcendental self not be located in the natural, causally determined, phenomenal world. A noumenal realm, apart from the natural, was necessary as the source of self-determined free action. Many German philosophers after Kant, including Marx and Hegel, in rejecting the existence of an unknown thing-in-itself,[14] reject the existence of this noumenal realm and thus must have a different model of freedom. Rather than locate a transcendental self in a realm apart, they deny that there are such different realms and they view reality as a single field with two elements reacting against each other such that ultimately the natural objective element is absorbed into the conscious subjective element. In this way the object is no longer alien or other. They argue in various ways that the subject is the essence of the object—that it finds itself, its own rationality, in the object. Thus, the object is not heteronomous but compatible with the subject's freedom. For Hegel, this requires an Absolute Spirit or God, responsible for creating and moulding the natural and social world through history. Ultimately, for the young Marx, the human species, through its labour, constitutes, moulds, and purposively controls the objective social and natural realm.[15] The subject exists and develops within the natural and social realm, but it also constitutes and comes to control it. The subject constitutes the object, objectifies itself in it, finds itself at home with it, and thus is free.

The human species works on its world through history and transforms it to conform with its own essence, such that in confronting the world the human species discovers itself and becomes conscious of the power of its own rationality objectively embedded in that world. Freedom, in short, is this development and objectification of reason in the world. Realizing this and living accordingly is morality. We shall return to this later.

For Marx, in his earliest writings, 'morality is based on the autonomy of the human mind' and freedom is 'the generic essence of all spiritual existence'. To understand Marx's ethics we must begin to understand

[14] *F* 69-73, and *KGS* IV. 450-4. *CPrR* 28, 50, and *KGS* V. 28-9, 48. That Marx rejects an unknown thing-in-itself, see *Dissertation*, *MECW* I. 39-40, 63-5, and *MEW*, suppl. I. 271-2, 294-7. Also see the *German Ideology* (*GI*), *MECW* V. 264 n., 273-4, 292, and *MEW* III. 247 n., 254-5, 273, where Marx rejects Fichte's version of the thing-in-itself.

[15] *PH* 17, 438-9, and *SW* XI. 44-5, 549. *PR* 30-1, 35, and *GPR* 41-3, 47. *PS* 479, 481, and *PG* 549, 551. *Dissertation*, *MECW* I. 52, and *MEW*, suppl. I. 284. For a fuller discussion of Marx's position see my *Marx' Method, Epistemology, and Humanism* (Dordrecht: D. Reidel, 1986), ch. 1.

his concept of essence and how it is linked to freedom and the state. In the first place, for Marx, essences develop. Freedom, for example, much as for Hegel, develops from being the special privilege of particular individuals to being a universal characteristic of all human beings.[16] Each sphere or institution in the state has its own essence which develops according to the inner rules of its life. This is its particular freedom, and it must be allowed to develop in its own particular way. For Marx, 'only that which is a realization of freedom can be called humanly good'.[17] Moral good, for Marx, is the realization of freedom. Freedom does not mean being unhindered in any and all ways, but it means the unhindered development of what is the essence of the thing. The realization of the thing's essence—its nature, what it inherently is—is the thing's good.

As we shall come to see even more clearly, Marx's concept of essence is in many ways like Aristotle's. For Aristotle, the essence of a thing is formulated in its definition. The essence cannot be independent of its matter or substratum, but neither can it be defined in terms of its matter alone. The definition grasps the form of the thing.[18] For Aristotle, the thing is more properly said to be what it is when it has attained to the fulfilment of its form than when it exists potentially. The essence of the thing is exhibited in the process of growth or development by which the form or essence is attained. Each thing has a process, activity, or function and when it fully achieves its proper activity or function, when it has realized its essence, it achieves its end or good. For human beings, their proper activity—their end, their essence—is activity in accordance with reason, and the realization of this end implies happiness.[19] In certain ways Marx's concept of essence is closer to Aristotle's than to Hegel's. For Marx and Aristotle, things exist on their own and have their own essence. For Hegel, at least ultimately, there is a single essence and this essence is identified with the Idea or God.[20] While individual

[16] 'Prussian Censorship', *MECW* I. 119, and *MEW* I. 13. 'Free Press', *MECW* I. 151-3, 155, 158, and *MEW* I. 47-9, 51, 54. *PH* 103-4, and *SW* XI. 150-1.
[17] 'Free Press', *MECW* I. 159, 173-4, and *MEW* I. 54, 69-70.
[18] Aristotle, *Metaphysics*, 983ᵃ, 996ᵇ, 1017ᵇ, 1031ᵃ; *Physics*, 194ᵃ.
[19] *Physics*, 193ᵇ; *Metaphysics*, 1013ᵃ-1013ᵇ, 1014ᵇ, 1015ᵃ; *NE* 1098ᵃ.
[20] This is suggested in 'Free Press', *MECW* I. 173-4, and *MEW* I. 69-70. It is quite clear in the *Critique of Hegel's Philosophy of Law* (*CHPL*), *MECW* III. 7-9, 39, and *MEW* I. 205-8, 240-1. Also see the *Holy Family* (*HF*), *MECW* IV. 57-61, and *MEW* II. 60-3, where Marx rejects Hegel's concept of essence but not all concepts of essence. However, in 1837 and at certain points thereafter, Marx seems to hold Hegel's concept of a single essence; see 'Marx to his Father on 10-11 Nov. 1837', *MECW* I. 18, and *MEW*, suppl. I. 9; 'Leading Article', *MECW* I. 195, and *MEW* I. 97. *PH* 9-10, 27, and *SW* XI. 35-6, 56. G. W. F. Hegel, *Science of Logic*, trans. W. H. Johnston and L. G.

things, for Hegel, do have essences, they are not independent of the Idea. For Hegel, individual empirical things are products, manifestations of the Idea. Marx, following Feuerbach, criticizes Hegel for turning things into attributes, predicates, of the Idea. Marx argues that this robs individual things of their own reality.[21] We shall return to this later.

On the other hand, Marx does not accept Aristotle's notion that the form or end of a thing is fixed and unchanging.[22] For Marx essences change and develop through history. Furthermore, Aristotle does not have much to say about a link between freedom and essence, whereas, for Marx as for Hegel, there is an intimate connection between freedom, the laws of the state, and essence.

In his earliest writings, Marx has not rejected law as we shall see he does later. Freedom exists in the state as law; in fact, 'A statute-book is a people's bible of freedom'. Laws are the positive universal norms in which freedom, the development of essence, acquires a theoretical existence independent of the arbitrariness of individuals. Universal laws embody essence; on the other hand, the particular interests of individuals are unessential, arbitrary, and accidental. To be led by particular interest rather than universal rational law is to be immorally, irrationally, and slavishly subordinated to a particular object. Laws cannot be subordinate to wishes; wishes must be subordinate to laws.[23] Echoing Rousseau's claim in *Émile* that subordination to persons is slavery while subordination to rational law is freedom, Marx holds that persons must not stand above laws nor can persons be a guarantee against bad laws or the misuse of laws. Instead, laws must be the guarantee against persons and their particular interests. For Marx, unconscious natural laws of freedom are formulated as conscious laws of the state. Laws are thus the reflection of actual life in consciousness. Since laws embody essence, which is to say, since they are natural, when the individual ceases to obey these laws of freedom, the state can

Struthers (London: Allen & Unwin, 1966), II. 15, 162, and for the German, *Wissenschaft der Logik*, ed. G. Lasson (Hamburg: Felix Meiner, 1969), II. 3-4, 158-9.

21 *PH* 50-1, and *SW* XI. 84-5. Moreover, for Hegel, the Idea manipulates the historical conflict of particular interests in order to realize itself; *PH* 20, 22-3, 25, 33, and *SW* XI. 48, 50-1, 54, 63. L. Feuerbach, 'Preliminary Theses on the Reform of Philosophy', in *The Fiery Book: Selected Writings of Ludwig Feuerbach*, trans. Z. Hanfi (Garden City, NY: Doubleday, 1972), 154 ff.; for the German see *Sämtliche Werke*, ed. W. Bolin and F. Jodl (Stuttgart-Bad Cannstatt: Frommann, 1959-), II. 223 ff.

22 *Physics*, 198b-199b. *Metaphysics*, 1033b, 1039b. *Politics*, 1256b.

23 'Free Press', *MECW* I. 162, and *MEW* I. 58. 'Wood Theft', *MECW* I. 262, and *MEW* I. 147. 'Divorce Bill', I. 308, and *MEW* I. 149. See also *PH* 39, and *SW* XI. 71.

compel the individual to obey the law and thus, as for Rousseau, it compels the individual to be free. A civil law is like a law of nature. For example, it is like the law of gravity in that it confronts the individual as something alien and restrictive only when the individual attempts to violate or ignore the law. The laws of the state are the conscious expression of natural laws; they express the essence of things. The laws of the state do not regulate the legal nature of things; rather the legal nature of things regulates the laws of the state.[24]

For Marx, there are two interconnected sides to any moral or political reality—an objective and a subjective side. To understand the objective side a scientific study of the concrete empirical object itself is necessary. The subjective side requires the formulation of the essence of the object as a conscious, universal, and recognized law. On the objective side, instead of attributing everything to individual will, one must study the actual nature of the circumstances as these can independently determine the actions of individuals. Moreover, Marx thinks that such study can bring about the same degree of certainty as that achieved in natural science. He argues that the legislator, in order to formulate laws, should be a natural scientist. Civil laws are not made or invented any more than the law of gravity is, the actual inner laws of social relations are discovered and consciously formulated as civil laws.[25]

Marx is willing to say that 'In the political sphere, philosophy has done nothing that physics, mathematics, medicine, and every science, have not done in their respective spheres'. Just as science emancipated itself from theology and established its own independent sphere, so modern political theorists proceed by deducing the natural laws of the state from reason and experience, not from theology.[26]

Once this objective concrete study of the particular essence of a specific object has been carried out, then, on the subjective side, the essence must be formulated conceptually and rationally as a universal law which becomes an ideal self-conscious image of reality and can be recognized as such. This subjective formulation is just as important as the objective study. As Kant said, freedom consists not in acting in

[24] J. J. Rousseau, *Émile*, trans. B. Foxley (New York: Dutton, 1966), 49, and for the French, *Oeuvres complètes* (*OC*) (Paris: Gallimard, 1959–　), IV. 311. 'Free Press', *MECW* I. 162, and *MEW* I. 58. 'Wood Theft', *MECW* I. 227, 243, and *MEW* I. 112, 128. 'Divorce Bill', *MECW* I. 308, and *MEW* I. 149.
[25] 'Marx to his Father on 10-11 Nov. 1837', *MECW* I. 12 and *MEW*, suppl. I. 5. 'Free Press', *MECW* I. 167, and *MEW* I. 63. 'Divorce Bill', *MECW* I. 308, and *MEW* I. 149. 'Justification of the Correspondent from Mosel', *MECW* I. 337, and *MEW* I. 177.
[26] 'Leading Article', *MECW* I. 200-1, and *MEW* I. 103.

accordance with law but in accordance with the *concept* of law.[27] Rational laws *must* be consciously recognized. Recognition is a most important category for both Hegel and Marx. For Hegel, no entity, whether natural or social, can become actual unless it comes to be recognized consciously. This is not merely to point out the obvious fact that an unrecognized thing remains unknown. Rather, for an idealist, it is to say that an entity is only constituted, only becomes an actual thing, by being recognized. Recognition plays this role throughout Hegel's thought.[28] Marx, who in this early period is still in many ways an idealist, holds a very similar position, as we shall see.

Marx tells us that we must measure existence by essence. We must evaluate any particular reality by measuring it against its idea or concept.[29] An essence is grasped abstractly and conceptually; it is the idea or concept of a thing—its definition, Aristotle would say—as opposed to its sensuous empirical existence.[30] Moral evil is the outcome of a state of affairs in which an empirical existent is shut off from and fails to live up to its essence. Marx later calls this failure alienation. On the other hand, moral good is the result of existence conforming to essence.[31] Thus, for example, we can evaluate the moral worth of a state

[27] 'Free Press', *MECW* I. 162, and *MEW* I. 58. 'Divorce Bill', *MECW* I. 308, and *MEW* I. 149. *F* 29, 45, and *KGS* IV. 412, 427.

[28] See esp. *PS* 111, 113, 116, and *PG* 141, 143-4, 147. *PR* 45, 57, and *GPR* 62, 78-9.

[29] *Dissertation, MECW* I. 85, and *MEW*, suppl. I. 326-9. 'Free Press', *MECW* I. 154, and *MEW* I. 50. 'Liberal Opposition in Hanover', *MECW* I. 264, and *MEW*, suppl. I. 387. 'Divorce Bill', *MECW* I. 308-9, and *MEW* I. 149-50.

[30] 'Estates in Prussia', *MECW* I. 295, and *MEW*, suppl. I. 409. 'Divorce Bill', *MECW* I. 309, and *MEW* I. 149-50.

[31] *Dissertation Notes, MECW* I. 448-9 and *MEW*, suppl. I. 106-7. 'Free Press', *MECW* I. 158-9, and *MEW* I. 54. 'Divorce Bill: Criticism of a Criticism', *MECW* I. 274, and *MEW*, suppl. I. 389. 'Divorce Bill', *MECW* I. 307-9, and *MEW* I. 148-50. In some discussions of Marx's early ethical views it is primarily his concept of freedom that is addressed as if that were his only or main concern and as if he had no interest in discussing what sorts of acts are moral and which are not (e.g. see B. Ollman, *Alienation: Marx's Conception of Man in Capitalist Society*, 2nd edn. (Cambridge: CUP, 1976), 42; E. Kamenka denies that Marx has a theory of obligation: *The Ethical Foundations of Marxism*, 2nd edn. (London: Routledge & Kegan Paul, 1972), 96). Marx has both a theory of moral good and one of obligation, and, as we shall see, the latter holds, much as for Kant, that only those acts are moral which can be universalized. On the other hand, it may not appear as if Marx has a theory of obligation because he never puts any emphasis on fulfilling burdensome duties. This, I think, is because morality, for Marx, at least in one respect, is not understood as it is for Christian morality or as for Kant, but more as it was for Aristotle. Morality is not seen as a burden which we naturally tend to shun. Marx rejects the notion of an unhappy consciousness—the Christian notion of a dual nature where the human essence involves an opposition between a physical-natural and a spiritual-supernatural principle. For Christianity, to seek our highest realization, which is supernatural, is to deny the physical and natural, while to seek to satisfy our physical and natural drives is to abandon our higher spiritual and

by examining its essence and asking whether or not the actual state fulfils, lives up to, or can be derived from and justified by this essence.[32]

When we turn to a consideration of the human essence, we must add another concept. Anything, for Marx, is an aspect of the human essence if that thing is *needed* by the human being. The presence of need indicates that an existent is essential to a being—without it the being cannot have a full, realized, and satisfied existence.[33] If this need is frustrated, if it cannot be satisfied, or if its satisfaction frustrates other needs, existence is out of accord with essence and alienation is present.

We have already said that for Marx the human essence develops. Marx's concept of need is an important tool for understanding this development. New needs arise and are transformed in the context of evolving social conditions and relations. Moreover, new needs set the individual specific tasks and thus require transformation of the world if the need is to be satisfied. By following and understanding the reciprocal transformation of needs and of the world we can chart the development of the human essence. Needs, for example for food, human interaction, or education, are not satisfied in the same way and through the same cultural processes at all times. They have different contents and objects, and their satisfaction involves different sorts of activities. Thus for Marx the needs are different needs.[34] Even basic needs are different

supernatural destiny. The individual is eternally caught in a situation where every satisfaction is a loss and where every duty is resisted as a burdensome self-denial (see Hegel, *PS* 126-38, and *PG* 158-71). For Marx as for Aristotle, the human being is exclusively natural and morality or virtue is the perfection of our nature. Thus, virtue is something we naturally seek. If duty appears as a burden, this is not due to an essential opposition between physical and supernatural natures, but due to an opposition, or alienation, which has arisen within the natural-social realm itself. If this opposition is removed, we will naturally seek virtue. Aristotle spends a good deal of time describing the conditions (the advantages, the opportunities, the social and personal circumstances like upbringing and education) necessary to allow this natural tendency to manifest itself (e.g. *NE* 1179ᵃ).

[32] 'Leading Article', *MECW* I. 199-200, and *MEW* I. 102-3.

[33] 'Free Press', *MECW* I. 137, and *MEW* I. 33. Also 'Comments on Mill's *Elements of Political Economy*' (CM), *MECW* III. 218-20, and *MEW*, suppl. I. 452-4.

[34] Marx makes this point most clearly in the *Grundrisse*, though he would agree with it in the early writings: 'Hunger is hunger, but the hunger gratified by cooked meat eaten with a knife and fork is a different hunger from that which bolts down raw meat with the aid of hand, nail, and tooth. . . . Production thus creates the consumer . . . Production not only supplies a material for the need, but it also supplies a need for the material', *Grundrisse* (G), trans. M. Nicolaus (London: Allen Lane, 1973), 92, and for the German *Grundrisse der Kritik der politischen Ökonomie* (GKPO) (Frankfurt: Europäische Verlagsanstalt, n.d.), 13. Despite the fact that I wish to argue that there are fundamental shifts to be found in Marx's thought, I definitely do not think he changes his mind about everything: his theory of need is one of the things that remains relatively unchanged.

needs in different historical periods.[35] By understanding what at a particular historical point is experienced as a need, its specific quality, and the processes required to satisfy the need, we then can understand the level to which the human essence has developed and the degree to which existence has been transformed to fit the level which essence has reached. We then can evaluate the situation morally. For example, by determining the specific character of needs generated in a particular society and the productive forces and social processes available for satisfying these needs, we can begin to discover to what extent needs are satisfied, and we can measure this against the degree to which needs can be satisfied, or should be satisfied. We can discover to what extent existence corresponds to essence.

Moreover, existing needs always point not merely to the past but to the future. They continually indicate how existence must be further transformed to meet our needs and further realize our essence. The successful transformation of existence to satisfy a need will transform the need or allow new needs to be felt. This will give rise to a demand for a further transformation of existence. Humans always have a moral goal; they always are involved in transforming existence to fit their essence.

This concept of need is developed fully only in the writings of 1844. In the earliest writings, without referring to needs, Marx discusses the development of essence in a similar but less concrete and more metaphysical way. Here he holds that when theory is developed fully it inevitably turns to practice. When the essence of a thing has developed to the point where it can be grasped conceptually and formulated universally it then turns against the world in the form of practical activity. Here Marx has in mind the essence of a state or of a people in a given historical epoch. When this essence is developed fully, it is grasped as a philosophy, a total world outlook, the spirit of a people. When this theoretical level is reached, theory begins to measure all particular existents against the essence—it criticizes them and sets about

[35] In the *Economic and Philosophic Manuscripts* (*EPM*), Marx says that the relationship, the felt need, between men and women indicates the level to which the human essence has developed; see *EPM*, *MECW* III. 295-6, also 300-2, and *MEW*, suppl. I. 535-6, 540-2. In a passage crossed out in the final draft of the *German Ideology*, Marx says, 'some of these desires—namely desires which exist under all relations, and only change their form and direction under different social relations—are merely altered by the communist social system; but others—namely those originating solely in a particular society, under particular conditions of |production| and intercourse—are totally deprived of their conditions of existence', *German Ideology* (*GI*), *MECW* V. 256 n., and *MEW* III. 238-9 n.

the practical task of transforming them to fit the essence. The result, Marx says, is that the world is made philosophical—it is transformed in accordance with theory. And philosophy becomes worldly—it engages and works in the world.[36]

This process also results in the development of subjectivity. The subject internalizes theory, engages in criticism, and transforms the world. The individual no longer finds a simple unity of theory and reality. Rather the individual actively turns theory against the world.[37] In doing so both the subject and the world develop. The concept of individuality that we find in Hegel and Marx is quite different from that which we find in the Anglo-American liberal tradition. Individuality is not a natural and original characteristic of human beings. We simply do not find ready-made individuals with developed needs, interests, and characteristics, either in a state of nature or in early society. Individuals are produced historically; they are created by culture. Human beings internalize the spirit of their time—the values, philosophy, outlook, aims, and aspirations of their world. They are educated and cultured socially. Individuality is a crystalization of the objective world in subjectivity. The individual then begins to live and act in the world, even to act against it, judge it, evaluate it, criticize it, and transform it. Moreover, the individual can remould these internalized cultural values, modify them, develop them, or give them a new direction or significance. The individual may then express something new and deposit it in the common culture such that it becomes a part of the developing spirit of the time and can be internalized by others. Thus the thought and action of individuals produce and transform the culture which produces and transforms them. Each can develop and become richer through interaction with the other.[38]

How do we judge, once we have grasped the objective nature of a thing and formulated it conceptually as law, whether essence and existence are in accord? Here Marx has been strongly influenced by

[36] *Dissertation*, *MECW* I. 85-6, and *MEW*, suppl. I. 326-31. *Dissertation Notes*, *MECW* I. 491-3, and *MEW*, suppl. I. 214-19. 'Leading Article', *MECW* I. 195, and *MEW* I. 97-8. This view is similar to that found in Kant's 'What is Enlightenment?' in *On History*, ed. L. W. Beck (Indianapolis: Bobbs-Merrill, 1963), 3-10, and *KGS* VIII. 35-42 and also to that found in 'Absolute Freedom and Terror' of Hegel's *PS* 356 ff., and *PG* 414 ff.

[37] *Dissertation*, *MECW* I. 85-6 and *MEW*, suppl. I. 326-31. *Dissertation Notes*, *MECW* I. 491-3, and *MEW*, suppl. I. 214-19.

[38] *Dissertation*, *MECW* I. 85 and *MEW*, suppl. I. 326-9. *Dissertation Notes*, *MECW* I. 435-41, 491-3, 506, and *MEW*, suppl. I. 78-91, 214-19, 246-9. 'Leading Article', *MECW* I. 195, and *MEW* I. 97-8. *EPM*, *MECW* III. 298-9, and *MEW*, suppl. I. 538-9. *PS* 297-9, and *PG* 350-3.

Kant and we can begin to see how Marx's concepts of essence and freedom are linked to his concept of universalization. Marx holds that the test of whether existence measures up to essence is to compare form and content. The content of the law must not contradict the form of the law. The objective content of law arises from the particular nature, the actual life, of the thing in question. On the other hand, for Marx as for Kant, universality is the proper form which any law must have.[39] The content of the law must be capable of being given a universal form without contradiction. The state and its laws must represent universal ends, not private or particular interests. If laws represent private interest, the interest of a special group or class opposed to others, the state becomes a mere means to further this private interest[40] and the content of the law contradicts the universal form of law.

This concept of universalization can go some way towards distinguishing true from false needs—essential needs as opposed to mere whims that it would be foolish to take as essential.[41] Needs which we could will that all human beings would develop and satisfy would be true needs. However, unlike Kant, universalization does not seem to be the sole criterion for Marx. We will see that, in the *Economic and Philosophic Manuscripts* of 1844, his goal is to develop a human being rich in needs—a human being with as wide as possible a range of needs and the highest possible development of each need (as well, of course, as the means of satisfying them). It would also seem likely, since he is opposed to levelling and homogenization, that he is after diversity of needs.[42] Thus it would not make sense to limit true needs to those needs we would will that all human beings develop. Marx operates not just with a Kantian categorical imperative[43] but with an Aristotelian

---

[39] 'Marx to his Father on 10-11 Nov. 1837', *MECW* I. 15, and *MEW*, suppl. I. 5-6. 'Prussian Censorship', *MECW* I. 121, and *MEW* I. 15. 'Wood Theft', *MECW* I. 231, and *MEW* I. 116. *CPrR* 26-9, and *KGS* V. 27-9.

[40] 'Wood Theft', *MECW* I. 241, 245, 259, and *MEW* I. 126, 130, 143-4.

[41] For an e.g. of the distinction between true and false needs see *EPM*, *MECW* III. 324-6, and *MEW*, suppl. I. 564-7.

[42] *EPM*, *MECW* I. 294-6, 304, and *MEW*, suppl. I. 534-6, 544.

[43] It is often argued that Kant's categorical imperative, being formal and contentless, cannot give us specific moral laws. Hegel was one of the first to make this criticism. He argued that the purely formal procedure of universalization, which abstracts completely from all empirical content, will not indicate our duty. He points out that private property and the absence of property are both perfectly universalizable. The categorical imperative alone is incapable of telling us which is right. It can tell us that theft is wrong but not what constitutes an act of theft. Removing an article for personal use from a market stall without paying for it would be theft in a market economy with private property but not in a communist society based on the principle 'to each according to need'. Hegel's point is that without some objective way to decide which concrete

concept of essence and the realization of one's essence calls for the development of needs which might not be universalizable. However, the principle of universalization can still operate here in a negative way. It can tell us that those needs whose satisfaction would contradict, hinder, or frustrate the development and satisfaction of the needs of others must be ruled out. Any needs which would not be objectionable in this way, though we would not will that everyone develop them, would be true needs in the sense that they develop the human essence.[44]

In further agreement with Kant, Marx holds publicity to be a test of laws. He holds that private interest 'cannot bear the light of publicity'. For Kant, any action that would be frustrated by publicly proclaiming it beforehand is to be considered illegal. This principle functions in the legal sphere much as the categorical imperative does in the moral sphere. Marx and Kant agree that only what is universal can stand the light of publicity; particular interests which contradict the general interest cannot—form and content would be in contradiction. For Marx, when laws are formulated, material content is idealized and raised to the conscious level of public universality such that a people can see itself, its essence, reflected as in a mirror.[45]

At this point it should be clear that Marx in many ways agrees with the natural law tradition: (1) He holds that there is an independent moral ground from which to judge the validity or justice of civil laws; laws are not valid simply because they have been properly instituted.

customs are right, i.e. without *Sittlichkeit*, the categorical imperative is empty (*PS* 257-9, and *PG* 306-9. *PR* 89-90, and *GPR* 120-1). Marx does not have this problem. The principle of universalization serves to tell us whether existence accords with essence. The essence itself is revealed by study of the existing world, of needs, and their development.

[44] Thus, we might distinguish between: (1) needs common to all, whose denial we could not universalize, e.g. the need for food, (2) needs of particular individuals, groups, or classes whose satisfaction would frustrate the satisfaction of needs of others—that is, needs whose satisfaction we could not universalize, e.g. needs involved in pursuing economic exploitation, and (3) particular, even unique needs not opposed to the needs of others whose denial or satisfaction it does not make sense to universalize, e.g. a scholar's need for unusual MSS (also see W. K. Frankena, *Ethics*, 2nd edn. (Englewood Cliffs, NJ: Prentice Hall, 1973), 32-3). However, it is not clear that Kant would be unable to accommodate this third category. He argues that an individual cannot without contradiction will to leave a talent undeveloped (*F* 40-1, and *KGS* IV. 422-3). Even if such an accommodation could be worked out, for Marx unlike Kant, there are still two factors present: the principle of universalization and the realization of essence, and these two converge. All of this, of course, assumes a society *able* to satisfy needs. In a society of scarcity we might not even be able to satisfy those universalizable needs (even needs for food) we would will to satisfy.

[45] I. Kant, *Perpetual Peace* (*PP*) in *On History*, pp. 129-30, and *KGS* VIII. 381-2. 'Wood Theft', *MECW* I. 261, and *MEW* I. 145. Also 'Prussian Censorship', *MECW* I. 121, and *MEW* I. 15. 'Free Press', *MECW* I. 164-5, and *MEW* I. 60-1.

(2) He sees this normative criterion of civil law as rational and rooted in nature, and like many natural law theorists sees a close relationship between descriptive laws of nature and laws as prescriptive social norms. (3) Finally, as does much of this tradition, Marx holds a doctrine of essence—one very much like Aristotle's.

I hope to show in Chapter 3 that in the *German Ideology* of 1845-6 Marx moves away from the natural law tradition. He abandons completely the first and third of the above positions, and while he does think that social laws are like natural laws (the second position), he does not think that this can serve as a basis for objective moral judgements. It must be said that even in his earliest writings Marx diverges from the natural law tradition in holding that essences, and thus the criteria of just civil laws, change through history. They develop and unfold; they are not eternal and unchanging.

Marx's concept of nature is an unusual one, and is quite different, say, from Kant's. Laws of nature and civil laws which are like laws of nature are not opposed to freedom as 'phenomena' is opposed to 'noumena'. Such civil laws are laws of freedom given three conditions: that these laws embody our essence (and our essence is natural; we are parts of nature); that these laws are universal and rational (not based upon particular interest); and that the unconscious essential laws of the object have been consciously recognized and publicly instituted as universal norms such that we act in accordance with the *concept* of law, not just in accordance with law.[46] Marx is not confusing facts with values. It is not enough simply to follow nature or one's essence. One must rationally know what this essence is and act accordingly, in the sense that one's act is regulated by conscious, publicly recognized, universal principles. Yet in doing so, one's act does not stem from a realm outside of nature, as for Kant, nor is the act contrary to nature. The human being, including consciousness and reason, is a part of nature for Marx.[47]

Marx's concept of essence makes possible the transition from fact to value. Much as for Aristotle, discovering the essence of a thing is to discover what it is in fact and this tells us what particular individuals of that species can become. It allows us to identify the range of possible development and the fullest development of the thing in a factual way. With human beings, reason can then seek to realize these possibilities. But why ought reason to seek this end? Why should it value such a goal?

[46] 'Free Press', *MECW* I. 162, and *MEW* I. 58.

[47] *Dissertation*, *MECW* I. 65, and *MEW*, suppl. I. 297. *EPM*, *MECW* III. 275-6, 336, and *MEW*, suppl. I. 515-16, 579.

Reason must do so to realize itself. It too is a part of nature and has an essence to realize. If it does not do so, if it does not unfold itself, which is its natural course, we can say that it has been frustrated and is unfree. But this is still to say that it merely *must* or *can* realize itself, not yet that it *ought* to. If an acorn succeeds or fails in becoming an oak tree, we do not speak of the presence or absence of moral freedom. But if a human being, if reason, succeeds or fails in realizing itself, we do. Reason aims at its realization because of its nature. But this aim is not impressed on it from outside, nor is its aim imminent but unconscious. Because of its particular nature, reason can achieve its realization only in a particular way—*consciously* and freely. Here we can say legitimately that reason *ought* to realize itself, because it can realize itself only by acting consciously and freely, and yet we also can say that it is its nature to do so.

Marx's view, however, is even more complex than this. If to be actual, objects must be constituted and recognized, then facts are not simple givens. Natural objects, for Marx (and recall that the essences of natural objects are the basis for the formulation of civil laws), are not given factually but constituted. Furthermore, our consciousness, our needs, and thus values, play a role in determining this constitution. Thus, we cannot have a neat distinction between facts and values. Nature is transformed and developed by human beings. This process is directed by their needs which in part are needs for given natural objects, but labour, in satisfying need, transforms both the natural object and our needs and consciousness, and reciprocally our needs and consciousness play a part in constituting facts—natural objects. Thus, when we study natural objects, which already are value-embedded, in order to grasp their essence and derive civil laws, we cannot say that we deduce moral conclusions from non-moral premises. Facts and values interpenetrate all along the way.

This would also be true for human beings. We have said that they are formed by their culture—by other human beings. The human essence, then, is not just factually given; it is constituted and developed by the social and cultural activity, the labour, of other human beings who form the culture we internalize. Moreover, since values and needs would obviously play a part in constituting culture, as we internalize this culture, our essence would be formed by these values and needs. Values then would be embedded in our essence. Facts and values would interpenetrate here too. So again, when we study the human essence so as to formulate universal moral laws, we would not be deducing moral conclusions from non-moral premises.

It is true to say that we cannot deduce moral conclusions from non-moral premises. But it does not follow from this that we cannot derive values from facts. If a set of abstract premises could be exclusively factual and truly contain or imply no values, then we could not deduce moral conclusions from them. But if real world facts—especially if they are constituted by us—already have values embedded or implied in them, we can derive values from these facts.

Thus, to say that morality means realizing one's essence, does not mean that morality is being reduced to merely acting in accordance with nature or being determined by our nature. This alone would not make us moral or free. Our essence, it is true, is to be part of nature, but nature, existence, has been transformed to accord with it. Our essence has also developed, and consciousness was the most important factor in this development. As we have seen, in transforming our existence to suit our essence, we transform our world and thus ourselves in accordance with our needs and values. This is a process in which facts and values inevitably interpenetrate, mutually influence each other, and thus develop. To fully realize our essence, this process finally must take place consciously and freely. We must discover and bring to consciousness the values that have been objectified in our world and formulate them as universal rational laws. If we regulate our actions in accordance with these laws, then we have realized our essence and are free and moral.

Kamenka discusses these matters in a particularly clear way. His book on Marx's ethics, especially chapter 9, is most impressive, though I am not in agreement with everything he says. In connection with the fact-value controversy, he points out that 'good' has been treated both as a quality and as a relation. A scientific or an objective form of ethics can be established most easily if 'good' is treated as a quality. Here, 'good' is taken to be a characteristic which can be investigated in a factual way. Such an approach, however, destroys the illusion that there is anything about the good which logically implies or requires that we seek or support it. On the other hand, a traditional advocative conception of ethics is most easily established by treating 'good' as a relation. Here, 'good' is something for-us, something demanded, required, or pursued which it is wrong to reject. However, Kamenka suggests that, if 'good' is treated as a relation and not a quality, there can be nothing objective about claiming that the good should be sought.

For Kamenka, ethics can be advocative or objective, but not both, as that would mean that 'good' had to be both a quality and a relation.

Kamenka thinks such an amalgamation is confused and would lead to treating relations as constituting the qualities of things. This position follows from a doctrine of internal relations, as Ollman points out.[48] Kamenka argues that things cannot be constituted by their relations because a thing must have qualities before it can enter into relations. It must be something before it can be commended, rejected, or pursued. Qualities do not depend logically on relations, nor do qualities by themselves imply relations.

Thus Kamenka rejects a strict doctrine of internal relations of the sort that Ollman attributes to Marx.[49] Gould has shown that Marx does not hold such a strict doctrine of internal relations in the later writings.[50] Even in Marx's early writings, it seems to me that relations do not constitute qualities, though they do *transform* pre-existing qualities. In particular, our most essential relation to things, labour, transforms the qualities of natural objects, of our needs, our senses, and our consciousness. This is not, prima facie, an illegitimate way to link qualities and relations, facts and values.

Kamenka seems to understand what Marx is trying to do and he argues that to accomplish it Marx is driven to absorb all differences into a strict monism. Since Kamenka thinks that the only way to amalgamate qualities and relations, facts and values, is to hold that relations create or constitute qualities, he holds that Marx is driven to the untenable position that all qualities must be absorbed into relations, *all* differences between subject and object, the human being and nature, must disappear—they must be totally obliterated. The object must be totally absorbed into the human subject.[51] But this is not Marx's position. Marx holds very clearly in the *Economic and Philosophic Manuscripts* that an objective being, a human being, must be related to independent objects outside itself.[52] Labour does constitute or absorb but only by transforming the pre-existing qualities of the object. Thus, it does not obliterate all distinction between subject and object. It only unifies subject and object *in essence*. It overcomes the alienness of the object, not all difference.[53]

[48] See Ollman, *Alienation*, pp. 45-9.
[49] Kamenka, *Ethical Foundations of Marxism*, pp. 89-94.
[50] C. Gould, *Marx's Social Ontology* (Cambridge, Mass.: MIT Press, 1978), 38, 40, 87, 184 n.22.
[51] Kamenka, *Ethical Foundations*, pp. 95, 99, 110.
[52] *EPM, MECW* III. 336-7, and *MEW*, suppl. I. 578-9.
[53] For a discussion of related issues, see my *Marx' Method, Epistemology, and Humanism*, ch. 1.

II

We have said enough about Marx's concepts of freedom, essence, and universalization for us to have at least a basic idea of what morality means to him and begin to discuss what he sees as most important, namely, how such morality is to be realized in the world. We have seen that we must grasp the essence of particular objects, formulate them as rational and universal laws, and then measure existence against essence—the particular content against the form of universality. However, Marx does not think this merely a process of individual subjective analysis. The universalization of the content does require this subjective component, but it is also, indispensably, an actual process going on in the social world which to reach its highest development must appear to subjective consciousness.[54]

It is the nature of this objective process of development (how it occurs and how it can be understood, controlled, and guided) that most interests Marx and is at the heart of his early ethical theory. In fact, it can be said that the major aim of Marx's early political and ethical thought, from 1843 on, is to explain how this objective development to universality occurs and to locate the concrete agent capable of realizing it in the modern world. First, Marx thinks that he has found it in the free press; then he thinks that the poor can also be taken as such an agent; finally, in 1843, he decides that it is the proletariat.

Marx is seeking an agent with certain characteristics—an agent capable of transforming society in a revolutionary way because that agent's natural course, its essence, leads it towards the universal. Its activity and goal are moral because it is capable of reconciling essence and existence and thus of realizing freedom.

In his first attempt to locate this agent, Marx argues that the spirit of an age is captured, expressed, and produced by a free press. The press will play an important part in any revolution and the revolution will be reflected in the press. A press transforms material struggles into intellectual struggles; it idealizes the struggle. It links individual and particular interest with the general and the universal, and it is a most powerful lever of culture. The motive force of revolution begins as mere need or interest, but through the mediation of the press the aim or goal

---

[54] We can now see how custom and feeling fit into this process. Just as the legislator can give the law of an entity the form of civil law, so existing unwritten customs and customary rights can be formulated as civil laws if their content does not contradict the form of law. Law is thus reinforced by custom and feeling, and custom becomes universal and rational ('Wood Theft', *MECW* I. 231-4, and *MEW* I. 116-9. See also *PR* 135, and *GPR* 181).

is given a universal and rational form. The individual interests of scattered groups are recognized as common interests. Needs felt as particular needs are recognized as essential human needs. The press is an important means of giving *recognition*, that is to say, reality and power, to needs and interests.[55] It causes us to recognize publicly needs and interests which are universalizable.

In his article, 'Debates on the Law on Theft of Wood', Marx reformulates his argument and in certain respects carries it further when he discusses the rights of the poor or propertyless. It is not at all clear that he means to replace the free press with the poor as the agent of revolution, since he continues to talk of the free press as such an agent in later articles. Perhaps he has in mind a combination of the poor and the press. At any rate, what he has to say of the poor prefigures what he will later say of the proletariat. He argues that in the Sixth Rhine Province Assembly's debate on a new law concerning wood theft, the aristocracy had tried to establish its own particular interests as law, the result being that the content of the law contradicted the form of law. Their private interests could not be publicly accepted as the universal. On the other hand, Marx argues that the particular interests of the poor are importantly different from those of the aristocracy: the interests, the needs, the customary rights of the poor to gather fallen wood do in fact agree with the form of law and can be universalized because the needs of the poor are natural, essential needs—needs common to all human beings.[56] Here form and content are not in contradiction. In this case particular and universal, need and right, coincide.

In both cases, that of the free press and that of the poor, Marx finds a group which links the particular with the universal so that particular interest is channelled towards the universal. In this way philosophy can turn to practice such that the world becomes philosophical and philosophy becomes worldly.

We now turn to Marx's discussion of the proletariat. But first we must notice that Marx rejects some of his earlier views and that he makes his disagreement with Hegel even clearer. In the *Critique of Hegel's Philosophy of Law*, written in 1843, Marx finally rejects the Hegelian concept of the state which he had accepted and employed in

[55] 'Free Press', *MECW* I. 143-5, 164-5, and *MEW* I. 39-40, 60-1. 'Estates in Prussia', *MECW* I. 292, and *MEW*, suppl. I. 405. 'Ban on the *Leipziger Allgemeine Zeitung*', *MECW* I. 312-13, and *MEW* I. 153-4.

[56] 'Wood Theft', *MECW* I. 230-4, and *MEW* I. 115-19. Also, compare to Hegel's discussion of world-historical individuals and the cunning of reason; *PH* 30-3, and *SW* XI. 60-3.

his earliest writings.[57] Marx has several objections to it. First, he thinks that Hegel inverts in a mystical and idealistic way the real relation between the Idea of the state and concrete institutions like the family and civil society. The latter for Hegel, as Feuerbach pointed out, are mere attributes, products, phenomenal appearances of the Idea. For Marx and Feuerbach it is the reverse. The state arises from concrete institutions which are the real driving force. One must start from real, concrete subjects and view the state as their objectification. The state is the outcome, the product, the actualization of concrete human beings in civil society.[58]

Second, though Marx does not give up his concept of essence, he does insist much more clearly and sharply on a point suggested earlier, which he now develops in explicit opposition to Hegel, namely, that each concrete empirical entity has its own essence. The essence is located in concrete empirical entities which are not the appearance of a single alien essence—the Idea—as for Hegel. Empirical existents have their own reality.[59] Moreover, it is still Marx's view that laws are discovered and formulated, not made or invented.[60] Civil laws are the laws of reason, conscious formulations of the essence of concrete relations.

Thirdly, Marx rejects Hegel's concept of the political state. For Marx, the political state is an estranged entity dominating civil society. He also rejects Hegel's preference for monarchy and advocates a radical form of democracy capable of overcoming the difference between the political state and civil society.[61]

[57] It is clear that even in the *Critique of Hegel's Philosophy of Law* (*CHPL*) Marx is not yet a communist. S. Avineri is wrong in claiming that he is (*The Social and Political Thought of Karl Marx* (Cambridge: CUP, 1970), 34). The *CHPL* was written in the spring and summer of 1843. In a letter written in Sept. 1843, Marx remains critical of communism ('Marx to Ruge in Sept. 1843', *MECW* III. 142-4, and *MEW* I. 344-5). Neither the concept of classes in general nor the proletariat in particular play a significant role in the political theory of the *CHPL*.

[58] *CHPL*, *MECW* III. 8-9, 11, 23, 39, and *MEW* I. 206-7, 209, 224, 241. One can find tendencies in this direction in Marx's earlier writings but the opposition to Hegel had not been emphasized; see 'Estates in Prussia', *MECW* I. 296, 306, and *MEW*, suppl. I. 409, 419.

[59] 'Free Press', *MECW* I. 173-4, and *MEW* I. 69-70. 'Divorce Bill: Criticism of a Criticism', *MECW* I. 274, and *MEW*, suppl. I. 389. *CHPL*, *MECW* III. 7-9, 15, 17-18, 39, 81, and *MEW* I. 205-7, 213, 215-16, 241, 285.

[60] *CHPL*, *MECW* III. 58, 119, and *MEW* I. 260, 325.

[61] *CHPL*, *MECW* III. 30-1, 77-8, 121, and *MEW* I. 232-3, 281-2, 326-7. By 'civil society' Marx means the everyday realm of economic exchange and private interest. By the 'political state' he means the governing apparatus whose concerns are public and universal. The political state dominates civil society.

Marx, it is clear, thinks that Hegel has correctly described the actual empirical relation of the political state to civil society as it exists in the modern state. What Marx rejects is Hegel's acceptance of this relation and Hegel's claim to have overcome the estrangement involved while preserving the difference between the political state and civil society.[62]

But Marx's rejection of Hegel's concept of the state is not as simple and complete as it might at first appear. Though opposed to a dominating *political* state, Marx is not against the state as an organic community of free individuals where there is no political state estranged from society. In fact, following Feuerbach, he thinks that in a democratic state the essence of a people truly manifests itself in existence such that existence is made to correspond to essence. The constitution of such a state will appear as the work of the people and the state will appear as the objectification of the human being. The state will be the self-determination of the people, not an abstract, distant, other-worldly realm beyond the control of citizens.[63] This is not a simple and outright rejection of the political state. Marx agrees with Hegel that the political state is, in fact, the realm of universality and equality. The political state is the realization of species-being, community, and ethical life.[64] The trouble is that the political state embodies these characteristics in an estranged form. Just as in Feuerbach's concept of religion, where God is the alienated projection of the human essence, so the political state is the alienated embodiment of the human essence lost to the citizen in a distant, other-worldly realm. Thus simply to reject or negate the political state would be to totally cut oneself off from one's essence. Instead, the political state, like Feuerbach's God, must be brought down to earth. Its estrangement from the everyday realm of human activity and existence must be eliminated. The political state must be *aufgehoben*, transcended and preserved, not simply negated. Only in democracy is content adequate to form; only here does the realm of the universal, the state and its laws, appear as the objectification of particular individuals and their interests.[65]

---

[62] *CHPL, MECW* III. 50-1, 75, 79, and *MEW* I. 253, 279, 283.

[63] *CHPL, MECW* III. 29-31, and *MEW* I. 230-3. 'Marx to Ruge in May 1843', *MECW* III. 137, and *MEW* I. 338-9. L. Feuerbach, 'The Necessity of a Reform of Philosophy', in *The Fiery Brook: Selected Writings of Ludwig Feuerbach*, pp. 150-1, and *Sämtliche Werke*, II. 220-1. Also, 'Preliminary Theses on the Reform of Philosophy', pp. 172 and *Sämtliche Werke*, II. 224.

[64] *CHPL, MECW* III. 31, 107-8, and *MEW* I. 233, 312-13. 'Marx to Ruge in Sept. 1843', *MECW* III. 143-4, and *MEW* I. 344-6. 'On the Jewish Question' (*JQ*), *MECW* III. 153-5, and *MEW* I. 354-6.

[65] *CHPL, MECW* III. 29-30, 39, and *MEW* I. 230-2. *JQ, MECW* III. 152-4, and *MEW* I. 353-5. L. Feuerbach, *The Essence of Christianity*, trans. G. Eliot (New York:

How then, more specifically, is the political state to be overcome and particular interest reconciled with the universal? Marx points out that one of the ways in which Hegel in the *Philosophy of Right* tried to reconcile universal and particular was by locating a 'universal class'—a class whose nature was such that its particular interests led it to promote the universal. Indeed, Marx's identification of the free press, and then of the poor, as such a universal class, followed Hegel's argument. For Hegel, this universal class was the class of Civil Servants—the bureaucracy. The task of this class was to tend to the universal concerns of the state. Since Civil Servants would be relieved of the necessity of direct labour to satisfy their needs, since they would receive a salary from the state, their private interests (the satisfaction of their needs) would be achieved in work for the universal (the state).[66] Their particular interest would be the universal. While Marx himself is clearly looking for such a universal class, he finds it ludicrous to think that the bureaucracy could fill that role. Rather than find the satisfaction of their particular interests in working for the universal, Marx thinks it more likely that bureaucrats would tend to subordinate the universal to their particular interests. The universal, the state, which should be an end, would be turned into a means to advance the career of the bureaucrat.[67] For Marx, particular interest must realize the universal, not realize itself by subordinating the universal.

In his 'Introduction to the Critique of Hegel's Philosophy of Law', written just after the *Critique of Hegel's Philosophy of Law*, Marx finally decides that the proletariat, not the free press or the poor, is the historical agent he is looking for—the universal class. In doing so, Marx develops a theory of revolution whose function is to realize essence in existence, link particular to universal, reconcile content with form, and overcome the opposition between state and society. It is designed to solve these ethical problems. Thus, I would suggest that Marx's theory of revolution is more an outgrowth of his ethics than his ethics are an outgrowth of, or an attempt to justify, revolution (though he certainly does want to give a moral justification for revolution). His ethical concerns at this point are basic and primary. His theory of revolution,

Harper & Row, 1957), 26, 29-30, 195, 197, 271-2, and *Sämtliche Werke*, VI. 32, 37, 235-6, 238, 326-8; 'Necessity of a Reform of Philosophy', pp. 150-1 and *Sämtliche Werke*, II. 220-1.

66 *PR* 132, 189, 191, 197-8, and *GPR* 177, 253, 256, 264. See also Avineri, *Social and Political Thought of Marx*, pp. 57 ff.

67 *CHPL*, *MECW* III. 45-8, and *MEW* I. 247-50. Echoing his earlier claim that laws must be given a universal form, Marx argues that Hegel's bureaucracy is the formalism of the state and involves a false categorical imperative.

certainly proletarian revolution, while most important, is derivative. Moreover, the ethical views which underlie this theory of revolution are in many ways closer to Kant's views, especially in his 'Idea for a Universal History', than to Hegel, though of course there are definite similarities between Kant and Hegel.

Marx begins by telling us that, just as Feuerbach's critique of religion concludes by holding that the human essence, which has been alienated and projected into a distant heavenly realm, must be brought down to earth and realized in actual life, so, going beyond religion, the task of philosophical criticism is to overcome alienation in the political sphere, to overcome the estrangement of the citizens from the state.[68]

In Germany, philosophical criticism will take a particular form. In Marx's view, Germany in comparison to the rest of Western Europe was at this time extremely backward socially, economically, and politically, while at the same time extremely advanced philosophically. This gap between philosophy and the real world must be closed, Marx says, by realizing philosophy. Philosophy must turn to practice,[69] so that, to use his earlier formulation, philosophy can become worldly and the world philosophical. This criticism from the perspective of the ideals of German philosophy gives rise, Marx says, to a 'categorical imperative' to overthrow all relations in which man is not 'the highest being for man'. Just as for Kant, human beings must be treated as ends in themselves. All institutions which treat humans merely as means must be transformed in a revolutionary way. If this revolution is to realize the categorical imperative that humans be treated as ends in themselves, then theory, the philosophical ideals of German philosophy, must become a material force. To do this, philosophical theory must grip the masses.[70] This can only happen if theory matches and realizes the *needs* of the masses. A fit between theory and need will close the gap between philosophical ideals and the world—between essence and existence. Philosophy will become worldly and the world philosophical. Or, as Marx puts it here, thought will strive towards realization and reality will strive towards thought.[71] The universal—freedom and the categorical imperative—and particular needs will accord and promote each other.

In one sense, for any revolution to succeed, it must bring universal

[68] 'Introduction to the Critique of Hegel's Philosophy of Law' (*CHPLI*), *MECW* III. 175-6, and *MEW* I. 378-9.
[69] *CHPLI*, *MECW* III. 177-81, and *MEW* I. 380-4.
[70] *CHPLI*, *MECW* III. 182, 187, and *MEW* I. 385, 391.
[71] *CHPLI*, *MECW* III. 183, and *MEW* I. 386.

and particular interests into agreement at least temporarily. In the bourgeois revolution, which Marx calls a partial or political revolution, a particular class emancipated itself and achieved political domination. To accomplish this, the particular class interest of the bourgeoisie had to appear as a general or universal interest. The bourgeoisie had to appear as the general representative of society against another class which appeared as a general oppressor, such that the liberation achieved appeared to the rest of society as a universal liberation from the oppressing class.[72] However, soon after the revolution, the particular class interest of the bourgeoisie ceased to represent the general interest. It soon came into conflict with the interests of other lower classes.

A proletarian—a radical or universal—revolution would differ in important ways. Marx tries to argue that the particular class interest of the proletariat truly accords with the universal—it accords with the categorical imperative. The proletariat is 'a class of civil society which is not a class of civil society, an estate which is the dissolution of all estates, a sphere which has a universal character by its universal suffering and claims no particular right because no particular wrong but wrong generally is perpetrated against it; which can no longer invoke a historical but only a human title'. Marx's point is a very interesting and ingenious one. Because the proletariat is so oppressed, so deprived and degraded, its particular class interest, its selfish needs, are so funda- mental that they could hardly be viewed as demands for special privil- eges. Such needs and interests would be the basic needs and interests of any and all human beings. They would be essential needs—needs for decent food, clothing, shelter, education, normal human development, and so forth—needs we would demand be satisfied for anybody. These would be needs which the categorical imperative would demand be satisfied for all. Because the proletariat is so oppressed, its particular interests correspond with the categorical imperative.

Thus Marx thinks that the proletariat 'cannot emancipate itself without . . . emancipating all other spheres of society'. The proletariat 'is the complete loss of man and hence can win itself only through the complete rewinning of man'.[73] Since the proletariat's needs are essential needs, needs in accordance with the categorical imperative, if we can satisfy them, if we realize the universal, we emancipate humankind generally.

    72 *CHPLI*, *MECW* III. 184-5, and *MEW* I. 388-9.
    73 *CHPLI*, *MECW* III. 186-7, and *MEW* I. 390-1. See also *HF*, *MECW* IV. 36-7, and *MEW* II. 37-8.

Marx does not side with the proletariat due to a sentimental sympathy for the underdog. He is led to the proletariat for philosophical and moral reasons. The proletariat is more of a universal class than the free press, the poor, or Hegel's bureaucracy. Social revolution need not depend on altruism or even highly developed consciousness. Simple interest and need drive the proletariat towards revolution. But at the same time the proletariat is driven towards universal principles in accordance with the categorical imperative. The proletariat's motives—its interests and needs—are not moral in Kant's sense, but its ends are those demanded by the categorical imperative. Thus, in time, the proletariat's motives also could become moral.

Philosophy is the head of this revolution and the proletariat is its heart. Philosophy turns to practice, it becomes worldly, by finding its material weapon in the proletariat. So also, the world becomes philosophical as the proletariat finds its spiritual weapons in philosophy.[74]

In a later article, 'Critical Notes on "The King of Prussia and Social Reform"' of 1844, Marx ties his theory of revolution even more clearly to his concept of essence. He argues that all revolution breaks out in 'isolation of man from the community'. For Marx, as we soon shall see more clearly, human nature, much as for Feuerbach, is communal. Thus, in saying that revolutions occur in isolation from the community, Marx is saying that they occur in isolation from the human essence. It follows from this, for Marx, that no matter how small a proletarian uprising might be, it contains within it a movement towards universality—towards the realization of the human essence.[75]

In the *Holy Family*, written in 1844 and published in 1845, Marx says, 'It is not a question of what this or that proletarian, or even the whole proletariat, at the moment regards as its aim. It is a question of what the proletariat is, and what in accordance with this being it will historically be compelled to do.'[76] This implies that an objective study can ascertain the essence, the objective needs, of the proletariat, needs which they may well not be aware of yet, but which will move them. However, these needs must be brought to consciousness and recognized as universal if essence and morality are to be realized.

Marx's argument in the 'Introduction to the Critique of Hegel's

[74] *CHPLI, MECW* III. 187, and *MEW* I. 391. See also L. Feuerbach, 'Preliminary Theses on the Reform of Philosophy', pp. 164-5, and *Sämtliche Werke*, II. 236-7.

[75] 'King of Prussia and Social Reform', *MECW* III. 204-6, and *MEW* I. 407-9; L. Feuerbach, 'Principles of the Philosophy of the Future', in *The Fiery Brook*, p. 244, and *Sämtliche Werke*, II. 318.

[76] *HF, MECW* IV. 37, and *MEW* II. 38.

Philosophy of Law' bears a remarkable resemblance to the views of Kant, despite the fact that in the *Foundations of the Metaphysics of Morals* and in the *Critique of Practical Reason* Kant explicitly denies that morality can be determined by anything empirical—by interest, need, or inclination, even when these agree with what morality demands.[77]

In morality, at least for Kant and for certain other traditions, an act cannot be motivated by self-interest if it is to be moral. Nevertheless, in moving from ethics to political theory, or when considering the connection between ethics and philosophy of history, no serious modern political theorist, Kant included, simply assumes that people behave morally. People will not always refrain from self-interest or act in accordance with a categorical imperative. If all that you have to say in political theory, no matter how complex you make it sound, reduces to arguing that to have a good society people first must learn to behave morally, then you have little to say. This would not even be utopian. It would just be naïve and would be to avoid the first and most basic step of political theory. A realistic modern political theorist, and Kant is a realistic theorist, must assume, at least to some extent, that people will behave immorally, selfishly, or in their own interest. The first task of modern political theory—I do not say the *only* task—is to explain how agents who are not moral, or who often fail to be moral, can produce the common good. Starting with humans as they actually exist, a great many modern political theorists try to work out a model for redesigning social institutions or for understanding their changing structure such that self-interest can be channelled to produce order and security, and eventually, if possible, morality. As Rousseau says, we must take men as they are and laws as they might be made.[78] Marx too does not assume that humans are good. He argues that class interest and need will lead to a society in which morality will begin to be possible.

Marx's argument, as well as Kant's, is a transformed version of Adam Smith's theory of an 'invisible hand', a theory which explains how a common good arises out of a series of selfish acts. In a market economy, for Smith, each attends only to their own selfish interest—their own profit. But given the structure of this society, namely, that due to division of labour no one is self-sufficient or produces all that they need, but must rely upon others in hundreds of ways (to buy from, sell to,

[77] *F* 5, 28, and *KGS* IV. 389, 411-12; *CPrR* 34-5, and *KGS* V. 34. But see *CPrR* 8-9, and *KGS* V. 8.

[78] J. J. Rousseau, *The Social Contract*, in *The Social Contract and Discourses*, trans. G. D. H. Cole (New York: Dutton, 1950), 3 and *OC* III. 351.

work for, employ, and so forth), given this thoroughgoing interdependence of each upon all, aggressive self-seeking, through an invisible
hand, that is, unconsciously, will produce, more effectively than if it
had been sought consciously, a common good—national wealth—without
which each would have no chance of realizing a personal profit.[79]

A similar argument is embedded in most social contract theories
where aggressive and selfish conflict in a pre-social state of nature
eventually drives individuals to common agreement through a social
contract, and the theory of checks and balances found in the *Federalist
Papers* involves a similar argument.[80] We also find a metaphysical
version of this model in Hegel's concept of the cunning of reason,
where conflict between particular interests or passions allows the Idea
to realize the universal historically.[81]

A similar argument is to be found in Kant. Despite his rejection of
particular interest in his writings on ethics, when he turns to political
theory and philosophy of history, particular interests are essential to the
realization of morality. In *Perpetual Peace*, he says, 'A good constitution
is not to be expected from morality, but a good moral condition of a
people is only to be expected under a good constitution', and also,

The problem of organizing a state, however hard it may seem, can be solved for
a race of devils, if only they are intelligent. The problem is: 'given a multitude
of rational beings requiring universal laws for their preservation, but each of
whom is secretly inclined to exempt himself from them, to establish a constitution in such a way that, although their private interests conflict, they check each
other, with the result that their public conduct is the same as if they had no such
intentions.'[82]

Similarly, Kant develops a philosophy of history in his 'Idea for a
Universal History' and in *Perpetual Peace* in which 'Each according to
his own inclination, follows his own purpose, often in opposition to
others; yet each individual and people, as if following some guiding
thread, go toward a natural but to each of them unknown goal; all work
toward furthering it, even if they would set little store by it if they did
know it.'[83]

[79] A. Smith, *The Wealth of Nations*, ed. E. Cannan (New York: Random House,
1937), 423. See also Hegel, *PR* 124-33 and *GPR* 167-9.
[80] A. Hamilton, J. Jay, and J. Madison, *The Federalist* (New York: Random House,
n.d.), nos. 48, 51, 73.
[81] *PH* 20, 32-3, and *SW* XI. 47-8, 63.
[82] *PP* 112-13, and *KGS* VIII. 366-7.
[83] 'Idea for a Universal History' (*IUH*) in *On History*, pp. 11-12, and *KGS* VIII. 17.
PP 106, and *KGS* VIII. 360-1.

The key to this development, for Kant, is 'unsocial sociability'. Individuals have both a strong propensity to associate with others in society and at the same time a selfish desire to isolate themselves and to have everything go according to their own wishes. This antagonism, propelled by vainglory, lust for power, and avarice, activates us and causes us to develop our powers and capacities. In time, Kant thinks, such a society will be transformed into a moral whole.[84]

The highest development of humankind, the complete realization of their powers and capacities, can only be attained in a society with a civil constitution that allows for the greatest freedom of each consistent with the freedom of all. This ideal constitution, Kant argues, will be produced through the very antagonism which arises from unsocial sociability. War will drive us to what reason would have told us at the beginning—to a league of nations, to just legal relations between states, and through this league, eventually, to just internal constitutions in each state. Put a bit differently, war produced by the conflicting particular interests of nations will lead to what the categorical imperative would have demanded in the first place.[85]

Given the growth of commerce, and thus ever increasing inter-dependence between nations, war will come to be perceived as a threat to the commercial interests even of nations not involved in the war. Such nations will be forced to intervene as arbiters and thus prepare the way for a league of nations.[86]

For Marx, the antagonists are not nations as for Kant but classes and the moral end is to be achieved by a single class rather than a league of nations. But aside from this (and, of course, many other differences between them), the notion of a conflict of particular interests leading towards what would be demanded by the categorical imperative is much the same for both Kant and Marx. Marx, however, does not employ this model in a state of nature, which he rejects totally, nor in his ideal society, but only in his theory of revolution.

Kant sees two factors at work in history, both converging towards the same end. The first is our own rationality—the moral commands of the categorical imperative. The second is a natural historical movement produced by conflict, which, as it becomes more threatening, forces us

---

84 *IUH* 15, and *KGS* VIII. 20-1. *PP* 111, and *KGS* VIII. 365.

85 *IUH* 16-19, and *KGS* VIII. 22-5. *PP* 112-13, and *KGS* VIII. 366-7. *Critique of Judgment* (*CJ*), trans. J. H. Bernard (New York: Hafner, 1966), 282-4, and *KGS* V. 432-4.

86 *IUH* 23, and *KGS* VIII. 28. *PP* 114, and *KGS* VIII. 368.

The Ethics of the Young Marx   45

unconsciously toward the very same rational ends which morality
would have demanded in the first place.[87]

The second factor, for Kant, is not to be taken as an actual purpose
known to be inherent in history, but as an idea, or what in the *Critique
of Pure Reason* he called a regulative idea—an idea whose reality we can
never establish but whose reality we must accept as if it were the case so
as to be able to find enough unity within the totality of phenomena for
our understanding to carry out its legitimate tasks.[88] Despite the fact
that it cannot actually be known, such an idea for a universal history
allows our rational activity to assist and hasten the historical process.[89]
For Kant, human beings must produce for themselves everything that
goes beyond the mechanical ordering of their animal existence. They
can achieve no other happiness or perfection than what they create
through their own reason.[90] This idea, then, is also similar to a
postulate of practical reason as we shall see later.

Certainly, Kant does not think that historical conflict can actually
produce morality. But it can produce legality; it can force us into a
situation in which our external action at least accords with our moral
duty. From there, the step to acting for the sake of the moral law can be
made only by us.[91]

Without a doubt, there is a certain tension between Kant's views on
morality and his views on politics and history. In his ethical writings he
says that any individual at any time is capable of acting morally and
freely. In his writings on politics and history he holds that moral
behaviour in general is made possible by history and culture.[92]
Moreover, it is the clash of particular interests which leads towards a
moral society and to the widespread possibility of individual morality.
Yet acting on particular interest is not moral.

Thus Marx's use of the concept of a categorical imperative is quite
similar to Kant's concept as found in his writings on politics and
philosophy of history. Nevertheless, one might object that there

[87] *IUH* 18-19, and *KGS* VIII. 24. *PP* 100, and *KGS* VIII. 355-6.

[88] *IUH* 24, and *KGS* VIII. 29. *PP* 107-8, and *KGS* VIII. 362. *CPR* B 373-5, A 323,
A 326-7, A 509-B 537, A 644-B 672, A 647-B 675, A 670-B 699. For a detailed
treatment of this issue see Y. Yovel, *Kant and the Philosophy of History* (Princeton
University Press, 1980), 29 ff.

[89] *IUH* 22, and *KGS* VIII. 27. *PP* 112, and *KGS* VIII. 366.

[90] *IUH* 13, and *KGS* VIII. 19.

[91] 'An Old Question Raised Again' in *On History*, p. 151, and *KGS* VII. 91-2. *Religion
Within the Limits of Reason Alone*, trans. T. M. Greene and H. H. Hudson (New York:
Harper & Row, 1960), 89-90, and *KGS* VI. 97-8.

[92] *CPrR*, 38, and *KGS* V. 36. *IUH* 21, and *KGS* VIII. 26. *PP* 112-13, and *KGS* VIII.
366. *Cf* 283-4, and *KGS* V. 433-4.

remains a very fundamental difference between Kant and Marx. For Marx, it is revolution which realizes morality, while, for Kant revolution is rejected as immoral. This would seem to make their views quite dissimilar. But even here, if we carefully study Kant's views on revolution, we will find less of a difference from Marx than we might expect. Speaking of the French Revolution, Kant says, 'If a violent revolution engendered by a bad constitution, introduces by illegal means a more legal constitution, to lead the people back to the earlier constitution would not be permitted; but, while the revolution lasted, each person who openly or covertly shared in it would have justly incurred the punishment due to those who rebel.' All revolutionary action is immoral and illegal. Yet revolutionary action can produce just constitutions and then it would be immoral and illegal to try to remove them.[93]

Kant is willing to accept the gains made by revolution, but he does not think revolution is moral and he does not want to encourage revolution, at least not revolution from below. He wants a monarch who would be an autocrat, but an enlightened autocrat who would give the sorts of laws that a people would choose themselves if they were able.[94] He wants an autocrat, one can say, who would give laws in accordance with the categorical imperative. The sole means of reform open to the ordinary citizen, Kant tells us in 'What is Enlightenment', is public criticism. The citizen may rationally examine and publicly speak out against unjust laws and institutions, but meanwhile the citizen must obey. Criticism alone, it seems, will eventually lead the autocrat towards enlightenment.[95]

Kant develops what he calls a 'principle of publicity', which he thinks shows that revolution is illegal. The principle of publicity functions for legality much as the categorical imperative functions for morality. Any action which would be frustrated if it were revealed publicly beforehand, Kant holds, must be considered illegal. The principle, as stated here, is negative. It will tell us that actions incompatible with publicity should be illegal, but, on the other hand, it is not the case that all actions compatible with publicity should therefore be considered legal. For example, a powerful government with a sufficiently strong army

---

[93] *PP* 120, and *KGS* VIII. 372-3. Also see *The Metaphysical Elements of Justice: Part I of the Metaphysics of Morals*, trans. J. Ladd (Indianapolis: Bobbs-Merrill, 1965), 86-9, and *KGS* VI. 320-3. However, Kant adds here that a monarch has an unchallenged right to try to regain a kingdom taken from him by insurrection.

[94] 'Old Question', *On History*, pp. 145-6 n. 146-7, and *KGS* VII. 86-87 n., 88.

[95] 'What is Enlightenment?', pp. 5-10 and *KGS* VIII. 37-41. However, the enlightened autocrat seems to be a transitional stage to republicanism, *PP* 95-7, and *KGS* VIII. 351-3.

may well be able to reveal publicly an oppressive plan without at all risking its failure.[96] The principle will indicate some but not all acts which should be illegal.

Thus, for Kant, the principle of publicity shows revolution to be illegal.[97] However, as we noticed earlier, Marx employs a principle of publicity to *support* revolution. How is this disagreement possible? The answer, it seems to me, is that Kant has made a mistake. He confuses a revolution with a coup. His principle would show a coup to be illegal— the plans of a small conspiratorial band planning to topple the government would almost certainly be frustrated if they were revealed beforehand. But a popular revolution supported by the majority may well gain from publishing 'the maxim of its intention to revolt upon occasion'. Often, the most serious obstacle to such revolutions, far from being publicity, is lack of access to the means of publicity. Revolutions which promote improved conditions often thrive on publicity. Nevertheless, the principle of publicity is negative for Kant. Mere compatibility with publicity does not establish the legality of an act. Unjust acts of a powerful political force, we have seen, are compatible with publicity but not legal. However, at the end of *Perpetual Peace*, Kant gives us an affirmative principle of publicity. He says that, 'All maxims which *stand in need* of publicity in order not to fail of their end', in other words, acts which actually require publicity, 'agree with politics and right combined'.[98] Thus, despite Kant, mass popular revolutions, but not coups, could well be just.

It would still be true, however, that any popular revolt might be opposed by the government. The extent to which the government could frustrate the revolution thus would turn upon the relative strength of the government *vis-a-vis* the revolutionary forces. But to allow legality to be determined in this way seems to make right dependent on might, whereas the principle of publicity offered a higher rational criterion of what ought to be legal. It thus might be argued that empirical issues like relative strength should play no role in determining legality. Perhaps Kant's meaning is that revolution is illegal simply because it would call forth opposition, whether effective or not, from the government. But if the publication of intent to revolt calls forth opposition from a repressive and unpopular government while it receives support from the population, why then should we take it that the government's opposition proves illegality rather than that the populace's support

[96] *PP* 129-131, 133, and *KGS* VIII. 381-3, 384-5.
[97] *PP* 130, and *KGS* VIII. 382.
[98] *PP* 134, and *KGS* VIII. 386.

(assuming that it is also needed) proves legality? To side with the government seems to be to move towards a positivistic conception of law—where the main criterion of the validity of laws is that laws have been instituted through valid procedures. The principle of publicity as originally stated was clearly intended, as in the natural law tradition, to be a higher rational criterion of the legitimacy of existing laws.[99]

It still might be argued that the violence involved in a revolution would contradict the categorical imperative never to treat anyone only as a means but always as ends in themselves. But Kant himself does not seem to think that violence is necessarily ruled out by this formulation of the categorical imperative. He does reject standing armies on these grounds when he says that 'to pay men to kill or to be killed seems to entail using them as mere machines and tools in the hands of another (the state), and this is hardly compatible with the rights of mankind in our person'. But, on the other hand, in the passage which immediately follows, he seems to approve of a defensive citizen militia.[100]

If all violence does not necessarily involve illegitimately treating others as means, and if majority revolutions against a repressive government pass the principle of publicity, a case might well be made more in accordance with Marx that popular revolutions against an oppressive authority could be willed as a universal law.[101]

In Hegel's discussion of the cunning of reason, we find an argument similar to that found in Kant's philosophy of history. For Hegel, too, the motive force of history is the clash of passions and private interests. This conflict is necessary for the universal, the Idea, to be realized. The Idea and the passions are the warp and the woof of human history. For Hegel, the Idea—the World Spirit or God—is understood as a reality which uses human passions as the means and instrument for realizing its own universal end. What for Kant was merely a regulative idea, an

99 Both of these tendencies seem to be present in Kant. He operates with two sorts of principles—principles of right (the principle of publicity and the categorical imperative) and a principle of authority (the autocrat). Kant's hope is that these two principles will agree. If they do not, then the principle of authority takes precedence; see 'What is Enlightenment?', pp. 5–6, 10, and *KGS* VIII. 37–8, 41. 'Old Question', *On History*, pp. 145-6 n., 146-7, and *KGS* VII. 86-7 n., 88.

100 *PP* 87, and *KGS* VIII. 345. Also *Metaphysical Elements of Justice*, pp. 118-19, and *KGS* VI. 346. Both Rousseau and Marx also advocated citizen militias instead of standing armies; see J. J. Rousseau, *The Government of Poland*, trans. W. Kendall (Indianapolis: Bobbs-Merrill, 1972), 80 ff., and *OC* III. 1013 ff. Marx, *Civil War in France*, in *Writings on the Paris Commune*, ed. H. Draper (New York: Monthly Review Press, 1971), 73-4, and *MEW* XVII. 338-40.

101 Kant seems to come very close to holding this in 'Old Question', *On History*, pp. 143-5, and *KGS* VII. 85-6.

'as if', becomes for Hegel the Absolute Idea working itself out with necessity. For Hegel, this is a process which at least in retrospect can be known completely.[102] Kant's regulative idea cannot actually be known but, if assumed, human reason would be able to guide and hasten history. For Hegel, in as much as the Idea is identified with God, we can neither anticipate nor guide its development. Philosophy can understand how the past produced the present, but it cannot look to the future.[103] For Kant, while it is true that history heretofore has proceeded unconsciously, nevertheless, there comes a point where to proceed further, historical development must become conscious, and from that point on human reason must take responsibility for guiding history. For Kant, the human being is the ultimate purpose of history and this purpose must be realized by humans themselves.[104]

In this respect, Marx is closer to Kant than to Hegel. Marx too makes it clear that we cannot predict or know the future:

we do not dogmatically anticipate the world . . . Hitherto philosophers have had the solution to all riddles lying in their writing desks, and the stupid exoteric world had only to open its mouth for the roast pigeons of absolute knowledge to fly into it . . . constructing the future and settling everything for all times are not our affair . . .

Instead, through 'ruthless criticism' of the 'forms peculiar to existing reality', we can 'develop true reality as its obligation and its final goal'.[105] Marx's emphasis on criticism echoes Kant's discussion of criticism in 'What is Enlightenment?'. In fact, in his earliest writings, Marx held that ideas were more powerful than mass action.[106] By 1843, however, he does not think criticism alone sufficient to produce social transformation; it must lead to revolutionary practice. On the other hand, Marx's concept of an essence realized through the transformation of existence does involve more than a regulative idea. His concept of essence allows him to talk of realizing true reality as an obligation and final goal. Nevertheless, as in Kant, this process is a purely human and

[102] *PH* 14-16, and *SW* XI. 41-3.
[103] *PR* 12-13, and *GPR* 16-17.
[104] *CJ* 279, 281, 285-6, and *KGS* V. 429, 431, 435-6. *IUH* 13-14, and *KGS* VIII. 19.
[105] 'Marx to Ruge in Sept. 1843', *MECW* III. 142-4, and *MEW* I. 344-6. For further discussion of the claim that Marx does not intend his science to predict, see my *Marx' Method, Epistemology, and Humanism*, ch. 2, sect. ii, and ch. 3, sect. iv; *PP* 114, and *KGS* VIII. 368. However, see 'Old Question', *On History*, pp. 137, 139, and *KGS* VIII. 79, 81.
[106] 'Communism and the Augsburg *Allgemeine Zeitung*', *MECW* I. 220-1, and *MEW* I. 108.

social one. There is no Hegelian God manipulating passions to realize its universality such that it is impossible for humans to anticipate or guide historical development.[107]

It is also a frequently heard slogan, based on an 1837 letter to his father, that Marx rejects the idealistic opposition between what is and what ought to be,[108] and in this sense is more Hegelian than Kantian. What this is usually taken to mean is that Marx rejects the sheer abstract 'ought' of the categorical imperative. Instead, values and behaviour must *be*—they must exist in and be reinforced by concrete institutions. What we must notice, however, is that for Hegel the rejection of 'ought' in favour of 'is' meant two things. First, it was an affirmation of *Sittlichkeit* and a rejection of sheer *Moralität*.[109] In this sense, Marx accepts that 'is' is preferable to 'ought', but unlike Hegel he does not think that this ideal *Sittlichkeit* has already been achieved in the modern world. Second, Hegel's rejection of 'ought' is a rejection of revolution and, in general, of comparing things as they are to things as they ought to be.[110] This Marx rejects totally. Things are not as they ought to be. Society must be transformed through revolution and this definitely involves moral criticism, a categorical imperative, an 'ought'. Thus, it is not at all surprising that in Marx's early writings after the letter of 1837 the 'is-ought' slogan is not repeated.

In the following chapter, we must say more about Marx's relation to Kant and to Aristotle, and we must discuss his attempt to synthesize their views.

107 Earlier, however, Marx's views were closer to Hegel's; see 'Marx to his Father on 10-11 Nov. 1837', *MECW* I. 18, and *MEW*, suppl. I. 9. Also 'Leading Article', *MECW* I. 195, and *MEW* I. 97.

108 'Marx to his Father on 10-11 Nov. 1837', *MECW* I. 11-12, and *MEW*, suppl. I. 4-5. For examples of Marx's later use of a moral 'ought' see *Dissertation Notes*, *MECW* I. 438, and *MEW*, suppl. I. 84. Also 'Marx to Ruge in Sept. 1843', *MECW* III. 143, and *MEW* I. 345.

109 *PR* 11-13, also p. 212, and *GPR* 16-17, 284. *PS* 255-6, 260, and *PG* 304-5, 310.

110 *PH* 35-6, and *SW* XI. 66-7. *The Logic of Hegel*, trans. W. Wallace (London: OUP, 1968), 11-12, and for the German *Enzyklopädie der philosophischen Wissenschaften*, ed. F. Nicolin and O. Pöggeler (Hamburg: Felix Meiner, 1969), 39. Kant rejected revolution but accepted, more so than Hegel, that society ought to be criticized and transformed.

2

The Synthesis of Kantian
and Aristotelian Ethics (1844)

In this chapter, we must explain how Marx reconciles his Aristotelian concept of essence with his Kantian concept of a categorical imperative. We will have to begin by examining the concepts of community, consciousness, and objectification. For Marx, essence is realized, and thus morality is possible, only in a consciously organized community, not in an alienated exchange economy. We will discuss these matters in section i. In section ii, we will consider Marx's concept of objectification and its importance for the realization of essence, freedom, and community. We will then be in a position to explain Marx's reconciliation of the Kantian and Aristotelian elements of his thought.

I

Marx, in his 'Comments on Mill's *Elements of Political Economy*' of 1844, begins to examine exchange. This, for the young Marx, is marked necessarily by estrangement. In general, estrangement means that a social phenomenon or institution, produced by the activity and interaction of individuals in society, but which appears to be independent, objective, and autonomous, turns upon and dominates those individuals. In an exchange economy, human beings produce, put their products onto a market, and independent market laws set in—market laws which cannot be controlled by any individual. Since human beings need these products but do not control them, they come to be dominated by the process of exchange. They are estranged. Moreover, since need indicates essence, the inability to satisfy need indicates that one's existence is estranged from one's essence.[1]

Again, since human beings need other human beings in many ways (to carry on production at anything more than the most minimal level, even to develop language, and, in short, to develop as human beings), then, given that need indicates essence, it follows, for Marx, that we are

[1] *CM, MECW* III. 212, 218, 220, and *MEW*, suppl. I. 446, 452, 454.

related essentially to others—the human essence is social. In an exchange economy these essential social relationships, Marx thinks, are estranged. Exchange and money, as they develop, stand between human beings and mediate, indeed, control their interaction. This is quite visible during economic crises but occurs at all times. Humans are not free; their essential relations are controlled by an alien power.[2]

Moreover, like Aristotle, Marx thinks that exchange perverts human virtue. Moral virtues no longer appear as ends to be sought but as means we are forced to use to achieve ends determined by the market. For example, in the relationship between lender and borrower, which Marx discusses at some length, normal human virtues are calculated in terms of potential credit risk. Trustworthiness, for example, no longer appears as a value or a virtue which is an end in itself, but, for the borrower, it becomes a means to gain credit, and, for the lender, it appears as a means to ensure the likelihood of repayment. The value of a human being is estimated in money. Credit standards become the standards of morality and human beings are viewed as elements, means, in an impersonal and alien process. Given the existence of human need and the lack of control over the products necessary to satisfy these needs, human morality will almost inevitably be shaped, dominated, and distorted by market forces.[3]

So also, in a developed exchange economy, the essential activity of human beings, which for Marx is their labour, no longer aims at producing products directly needed by the labourer. It no longer serves to realize the human essence. Labour and its product become a mere means to be exchanged for a wage to guarantee bare existence. Existence is not transformed and made a means to realize essence; rather, essence, essential human activity, becomes a means to preserve a minimal existence. For Marx as for Aristotle, production or 'wealth-getting' directed towards the satisfaction of basic needs and the preservation of life or existence is, of course, necessary. But such activity is not properly one's highest end. It should be seen as the necessary basis for allowing one to proceed on to the sorts of activities involved in the good life—a life involving activities which are ends in themselves—and thus the highest realization of one's essence.[4] To turn these activities into

[2] *CM, MECW* III. 212-13, 217-20, and *MEW*, suppl. I. 446-7, 451-4.

[3] *CM, MECW* III. 214-16, and *MEW*, suppl. I. 448-50. Aristotle, *Politics*, 1258ª.

[4] *CM, MECW* III. 219-20, and *MEW*, suppl. I. 453-4. Aristotle, *Politics*, 1257ᵇ-1258ª. Unlike Aristotle, Marx in the early writings does not distinguish labour from leisure as he later will in the *Grundrisse*. The good life, for Marx, the realm of ends in themselves, is to take place within a transformed and humanized labour time; see *CM, MECW* III. 227-8, and *MEW*, suppl. I. 462-3.

means to preserve mere existence is to turn things upside down and to fail to realize one's essence.

Again like Aristotle, Marx thinks that, without exchange, humans would produce no more than they needed. The limit of need would form the limit of production. Production would be measured by need and thus by the human essence. This, for Marx, is *real* exchange—the exchange of labour for the product. In a market economy with wage labour, what is produced is not controlled by the wage worker. Here, need no longer measures production, but production, or the ownership of the product, is the measure of how far needs will be satisfied. Independent and alien forces determine the distribution of the product and thus the extent to which need and essence are satisfied.[5]

There is another problem involved in exchange. Adam Smith, as we have seen, and Hegel as well, argue that in an exchange economy a common good is produced unconsciously through an invisible hand. Each seeks only their own self-interest, but, given the complex interdependence of each upon all, self-seeking produces the common good more effectively than if individuals had sought it consciously.

It is quite clear that Marx completely rejects the Smith-Hegel model for society. Moreover, his objection is in large part a moral one. As far back as Socrates, and certainly for Aristotle as well as for Kant, simply to produce a good, or to act merely in accordance with given moral expectations, does not amount to morality. To act morally, one must know rationally what the good is, and the act must be motivated by this rational knowledge. To act selfishly and allow a good to come about behind your back, no matter how effective it might be, is not moral. Morality requires conscious intent. We have already seen that to realize one's essence requires that this essence be grasped consciously and that one should set about transforming existence accordingly. The same applies at the social level.[6]

It is true that Marx relies on self-interest rather than morality as the

[5] *CM, MECW* III. 224-5, and *MEW*, suppl. I. 459-60. *Politics*, 1256ᵃ-1258ᵇ. Marx also argues that in a developed exchange economy, money replaces need as the mediator between human beings and the object. If I have a real need or talent, but no money, the need or talent may well remain unrealized and even may appear unreal and imaginary. On the other hand, if I have money but no true talent or need, I can easily realize my slightest whim. Thus, money distorts reality; it turns essential reality into an unreal dream, and mere whims into reality. Essence is not realized in existence and existence is made inessential; see *EPM, MECW* III. 324-5, and *MEW*, suppl. I. 565-7.

[6] *CM, MECW* III. 217, and *MEW*, suppl. I. 451. See also *CHPL, MECW* III. 56-7, 119, and *MEW* I. 259, 324. 'Marx to Ruge in Sept. 1843', *MECW* III. 144, and *MEW* I. 345-6. Plato, *Republic*, 619 B-619 C. Aristotle, *NE* 1105ᵃ, 1139ᵃ, 1169ᵃ. Kant, *F* 6, 13, 29, 45, and *KGS* IV. 390, 397, 412, 427.

motive force of revolution (though morality and interests do converge). An invisible hand argument has a legitimate place in explaining how it is possible to move from existing society to an ideal society because it allows us to avoid simply positing that people first must become ideally moral in order to realize the ideal society. This would be to abandon serious political theory. But invisible hand arguments have no place, for Marx, when discussing the ideal society itself. This society must be consciously and purposively directed. In fact, even when Marx does use an invisible hand argument, we must see that his approach is different from that of Adam Smith for whom competitive self-seeking *unconsciously* produces a common good. For Marx (as well as for Kant), while interests do unconsciously tend towards the common good or the ideal society, to move effectively towards this ideal society we must become aware of this tendency and assist it consciously. In his discussion of such an ideal society, Marx says,

Let us suppose we had carried out production as human beings. . . . (1) In my production I would have objectified my individuality, its specific character, and therefore enjoyed not only an individual manifestation of my life during the activity, but also when looking at the object I would have the individual pleasure of knowing my personality to be objective, visible to the senses and hence a power beyond all doubt. (2) In your enjoyment or use of my product I would have the direct enjoyment of being conscious of having satisfied a human need by my work, that is, of having objectified man's essential nature, and of having created an object corresponding to the need of another man's essential nature. (3) I would have been for you the mediator between you and the species, and therefore would have become recognized and felt by yourself as a completion of your own essential nature and as a necessary part of yourself, and consequently would know myself to be confirmed both in your thought and your love. (4) In the individual expression of my life I would have directly created your expression of your life, and therefore in my individual activity I would have directly confirmed and realized my true nature, my human nature, my communal nature.

Our products would be so many mirrors in which we saw reflected our essential nature.[7]

Social relationships, for Marx, should be direct and conscious. The common good should not be produced through an invisible hand; the needs of others should be satisfied consciously and purposefully. Exchange should not be allowed to operate independently of human beings, out of their control, dominating and frustrating their needs,

---

[7] *CM, MECW* III. 227-8, and *MEW*, suppl. I. 462-3.

subverting human values and virtue, standing between human beings and dominating their interaction. Humans should consciously and purposefully direct their own interaction.

We have said that, since need indicates essence, the fact that humans need each other indicates that their essence is social. It is true that human need will produce social interaction whether human beings consciously regulate it or not. Humans must interact socially in order to produce, distribute products, and develop. If not consciously directed, this interaction will take the form of exchange, and market forces will come to dominate individuals and produce estrangement. If this inter-action is co-operative, consciously controlled, and purposively directed, then society (*Gesellschaft*) is transformed into a community (*Gemeinschaft*). Conscious, co-operative, and purposive control of social interaction produces community. Marx clearly is arguing that a community, a communal organization of society, is the only sort of society that can realize the human essence; it is the only moral society. The human essence is communal. In general, essence is only fully realized if it is brought to consciousness and if existence is transformed to fit essence. To realize fully the human essence, social interaction must be understood consciously and directed purposively. Society must be transformed consciously.[8] In short, human interaction must be communal if existence is to accord with essence.

Thus, Marx envisions a society in which need directly regulates production. Individuals work not merely as a means to exist, but in order to satisfy and develop needs, that is, to realize their essence. The distribution of products in this society should take the form of direct communal sharing purposively designed to satisfy the needs of others such that a conscious bond is formed. In such a society each would recognize consciously as well as feel the power and importance of others who satisfy and develop one's essence and one's own power and importance in satisfying the essence of others. Social relations would be moral relations. Relationships between individuals would be like the community of friends which Aristotle thought necessary for a good state.[9]

Furthermore, community, for Marx, replaces the existing alienation of civil society from the political state. It transforms unconscious civil society into a consciously controlled and purposively directed economic community and eliminates the dominating estranged political state by

[8] *CM*, *MECW* III. 217-18, 227-8, and *MEW*, suppl. I. 451, 462-3.
[9] *NE*, 1155ᵃ, 1159ᵇ-1160ᵃ; *Politics*, 1280ᵇ.

making the universal elements of community and co-operation operative in day-to-day life.

Marx claims that the human essence is *social* whereas Aristotle claims that humans are *political* animals. These claims may appear incompatible but they are not. Aristotle does not make a distinction between the social and the political. Marx does distinguish between the two, but when he claims that the human essence is social, he is not opposing the social to the political, as he does when he opposes civil society to the political state. For Marx, both state and society are to be absorbed into community. We certainly cannot say that the human essence, for Marx, is social *as opposed* to political or communal. The highest realization of society is community and the political state involves community in an alienated form along with domination. To realize the human essence means to overcome the isolation of society as well as the domination and estrangement of the political state by realizing community. The realized human essence is communal. For Aristotle, we can say that the 'political' involves both communal interaction and domination—certainly the domination of slaves.[10] Thus, both thinkers hold that realized human beings require community. The difference between Marx and Aristotle, then, is that Marx wants community without domination. However, at points, this even seems to be Aristotle's ideal. He says,

if . . . every tool, when summoned, or even of its own accord, could do the work that befits it, just as the creations of Daedalus moved of themselves, or the tripods of Hephaestos went of their own accord to their sacred work . . . then there would be no need either of apprentices for the master, or of slaves for the lords.[11]

II

In the 'Comments on Mill' and especially in the *Economic and Philosophic Manuscripts* of 1844, we find clearly presented the very important concept of objectification (*Vergegenständlichung*), which allows Marx to formulate many of his views in a sharper and clearer way. An object, for Marx, is the result of an objectification: it is an entity necessary to maintain the existence and to satisfy the essence of another being. For Marx, much as for Feuerbach, the object is the

---

[10] *Politics*, 1252ª, 1253ª, 1280ª.
[11] Quoted from Marx, *Capital*, ed. F. Engels (New York: International, 1967), I. 408, and *MEW* XXIII. 430. Also see *Politics*, 1253ᵇ.

subject's own essence. Objectification, for Marx, is the expression, manifestation, or realization of the powers of an entity in an object. For example, Marx says the plant has the sun as its object—the plant *needs* the sun to exist and grow. And reciprocally, the sun has the plant as its object—the sun realizes, *objectifies*, its life-developing powers in the growth of the plant. For humans, an object is something needed by the human being to satisfy its essence and maintain its existence—food, for example, is the object of hunger. Humans also need objects in which they can objectify their powers—for example, raw material on which to work. Human beings must labour upon nature and transform it in order to satisfy their needs.[12] They transform existence to suit their essence. The existing natural world is thus rearranged and formed through labour, fashioned into the sorts of objects that can satisfy the existing level of needs and essence. The need-satisfying object is the outcome, the product, of a process of objectification. Objectification begins with a subject whose powers, capacities, and ideas have developed historically to a given level as conditioned by the subject's social world—its specific level of technology, organization of production, culture, and so forth. For these subjective factors (these powers, capacities, and ideas) to be objectified, that is, realized and developed, they must be set to work and produce an object. If they are not set to work, not exercised, they certainly do not develop, and, in fact, they really do not exist except in potential. One can identify the level to which these subjective factors have developed by studying the sorts of objects human beings are capable of producing. Furthermore, with the production of a new object, say, a tool, new powers and capacities will be called into play, exercised, and developed in using the tool; these then can give rise to new ideas and needs which can call for further new objects and thus again new powers, capacities, and ideas to produce and use them. Needed objects promote the development of objectification, and objectification promotes the development of needed objects. Existence is transformed and needs and essence develop.

To realize the human essence, for Marx, it is not only necessary to realize and to satisfy the needs of human beings but it is also necessary to develop their powers. In fact, there is an intimate connection between powers and needs for Marx. The ability to realize any power would involve certain needs, as, for example, when workers need raw material in which to realize their labour. The satisfaction of any need

[12] *EPM, MECW* III. 272, 336-7, and *MEW*, suppl. I. 511-12, 578-9. L. Feuerbach, *The Essence of Christianity*, pp. 4-6, and *Sämtliche Werke*, VI. 5-7.

would imply the maintaining, reinforcing, or realizing of a power, as, for example, the satisfaction of the need for food sustains workers' abilities to manifest their power through labour. Furthermore, the drive to realize any power, for Marx, would be felt as a need—not as a basic need, but as a higher need.[13]

It is important to notice that in the early writings the entire natural and social world is seen as the outcome of objectification; it has been progressively transformed by human labour into need-satisfying objects. Raw, untransformed nature, Marx thinks, no longer exists, nor could it satisfy human need.[14]

It follows from this concept of objectification, for Marx, that humans can contemplate themselves in their object. They can view their entire world as something produced by themselves—the realization of their powers and ideas. They find the world to be a place which satisfies their needs and thus confirms and reinforces them.[15] Their existence has been transformed to correspond with their essence. Their objects are not alien and other; they are their essence.

Moreover, for Marx, individuals should have the same relation to other human beings. Other humans are the individual's objects; they are needed by the individual. In a very interesting way Marx is trying to rid the terms 'object' and 'need' of their usual meaning. To say that humans are objects is *not* to say that they are things, or that they are needed as we need things, or that they are to be used as things. Objects, for Marx, are not means; they are ends. Objects are part of our essence. To say that other human beings, humankind, or the human species are our object is to say that we need them. They are part of our essence. Without them any complex production would be impossible; language would not exist; and individuals would not develop as human beings. Moreover, the human species is an object in the sense that human beings become what they are at any point in history by internalizing culture and society which have been produced as the objectifications of other human beings. We are thus the products of the objectifications of the human species. So also we become what we are by exercising and objectifying the powers and capacities which have been produced in us and thus again influence and produce others.[16] The products of objectification satisfy and develop not just the individuals

13 *EPM, MECW* III. 304, 336, and *MEW*, suppl. I. 544, 578.
14 *EPM, MECW* III. 273, 303-5, 345-6, and *MEW*, suppl. I. 512-13, 543-6, 587-8.
15 *EPM, MECW* III. 277, and *MEW*, suppl. I. 517.
16 *EPM, MECW* III. 278-9, 298-300, and *MEW*, suppl. I. 519, 537-40. *CM, MECW* III. 227-8, and *MEW*, suppl. I. 462-3.

who produced them but others in society. Objects produced by others free us from the domination of need and allow us to pursue higher needs and thus develop higher powers, capacities, and ideas which, in turn, make possible higher forms of objectification and thus a higher development of others as well as ourselves. The development of the individual's needs and powers, the individual's essence, both is dependent upon and contributes to the development of the species' powers and needs—the species' essence. Thus we can contemplate ourselves, our essence, in other human beings and the species in ourselves. The species is the product of our objectification and we are a product of its objectification.

We have already seen that Marx wants social interaction to be communal, that is, conscious and purposive. To be free, individuals must consciously and purposively make the species their object or end. Marx, following Feuerbach, claims that the human being is a species-being and that a species-being is a being capable of making its species the object of its theory and practice. This means that the individual is capable of conceiving a universal or general idea, that is, the idea of the species. Animals, unlike humans, can only conceive particulars. The human essence is identified by locating the characteristics that distinguish humans from animals—the species from the genus. It is much like the Aristotelian notion that humans are rational animals. On the other hand, to make the species the object of practice means to make the species the end or goal of practical activity.[17] Thus, to realize one's essence one must make the species the conscious object of theory and practice. Since the human essence only develops through the collective process of transforming existence to suit need and the objectification of its powers and capacities through labour, and since the development of the powers and capacities of the species is the outcome of the objectification of individuals whose powers are developed due to the objectification of the species, and since the realization of essence requires consciousness, it follows that the individual's fullest and highest development is dependent upon individuals making the development of the species their conscious and purposive goal.

Thus, to say that human beings are species-beings, that they have a species essence, or that human labour is species activity is a way of saying that the human essence is communal, that is, that social interaction must be conscious and purposive. Individuals are in essence what

[17] *EPM, MECW* III. 275-7, and *MEW*, suppl. I. 515-17. L. Feuerbach, *The Essence of Christianity*, pp. 1-2, and *Sämtliche Werke*, VI. 1-2.

they become through interaction with others. To make the development of the species one's end or object is to make the development of one's own essence one's end or object.

Pursuing private interests, that is, selfish or egotistical ends, in isolation from or in opposition to others, is not, as in the liberal tradition, a form of freedom nor a means of developing individuality. In one sense, for Marx, the liberal ideal is an illusion. Its model of the individual is not a true picture of the individual in all times and places, but simply the product of the way in which individuals have been socialized in a particular form of society. Individuals separately pursuing their particular interests are not part of the eternal and natural state of things, but a historical outcome produced by a certain form of competitive exchange society. In another sense, this form of socialization simply hinders and frustrates freedom, development, and true individuality by turning the individual's theoretical and practical effort away from what is essential towards mere appearance.[18]

We must also notice that Marx employs the concept of 'need' in an unusual way. A good deal of what Marx would call needs, we would ordinarily call wants or desires. Needs, for Marx, are definitely not limited to 'basic' needs; there are also higher needs—an example would be the 'need' for art or the 'need' to develop higher powers. Such higher needs are most important. For Marx, at least some wants and desires can be historically transformed into directly felt needs from what, under certain conditions, might even have been perceived as ideals so impossible to achieve that they could have been considered mere fantasies (for example, airplanes or submarines earlier in history). Such needs are valuable in themselves. Marx's ideal is a human being rich in needs. He wants the development of as wide a range of needs and powers, especially higher needs and powers, as possible, the qualitative development of each need, and, of course, their satisfaction.[19] Wants and desires which could not be universalized and which would contradict, hinder, or frustrate the development and the satisfaction of the needs of others would, of course, be ruled out, as we saw in Chapter 1, section i.

Humans always have needs. However, this is not to say that they must always be driven and dominated by need. For the process of objectification to be conscious and purposive, humans must be in a position to satisfy their needs regularly and smoothly. Need must not

---

18 *CM*, *MECW* III. 216-17, and *MEW*, suppl. I. 450-1. 'Philosophical Manifesto of the Historical School of Law', *MECW* I. 203-4, and *MEW*, I. 78-9.

19 *EPM*, *MECW* III. 300-4, 307-8, and *MEW*, suppl. I. 540-4, 547-8. See also *G* 92, and *GKPO* 13.

determine objectification. Rather, consciousness must determine our objectification, our needs, and the development of new higher needs.[20]

So far I have only described the ideal form of objectification. However, objectification can be alienated. If individuals do not consciously control their object, the need-satisfying product of labour, if it is controlled by another or by the alien laws of the market, then the product certainly cannot be consciously controlled and directed towards the good of the species. The product simply will benefit a particular individual—its owner (the capitalist). Nor will the need of the worker directly regulate the production of the product. Since the worker needs the product but does not control it, the individual will become a slave to the product. Since the entire social and natural world is the outcome of objectification, the entire world will be lost, estranged from, the worker.[21]

Secondly, if the worker is not in conscious control of the process of production, the activity of objectification, then neither can this activity be consciously directed towards the good of the species. Moreover, the activity of objectification, labour, will not be free species activity. This activity which should be an end in itself, the objectification of the species, will just be a means to benefit a particular individual—it will produce a wage to preserve the bare existence of a worker driven by need. The work in itself will be meaningless and coerced.[22]

These two forms of alienation, alienation from the product and in the process of production, produce alienation from the species. Neither the product nor the activity are directed consciously or purposively towards the species; the species does not develop; and thus neither does the individual. Since this activity is not directed consciously, it is not free. Nor does the species confront a world in which it finds itself reflected and confirmed. Its world does not appear as its work and reality. It confronts an alien object.

Such estrangement also produces, Marx says, the estrangement of 'man from man'. Since individuals are not organized consciously into a community, their interaction will be mediated and dominated by alien forces. Their relations will become competitive and antagonistic.[23]

Thus, we can say that to be moral, for existence to accord with essence, alienation (especially from the species) must be overcome.

[20] *EPM, MECW* III. 276-7, and *MEW*, suppl. I. 516-17.
[21] *EPM, MECW* III. 272-3, and *MEW*, suppl. I. 511-13.
[22] *EPM, MECW* III. 274-5, and *MEW*, suppl. I. 514-15.
[23] *EPM, MECW* III. 277-8, and *MEW*, suppl. I. 517-18.

Moreover, working for the benefit of a particular individual (for one's own wage or for the benefit of the owner) rather than for the species or the community, is neither a form of freedom nor a development of the individual. It alienates and impoverishes the individual. One must overcome alienation from the species and make the species the object of the individual. Far from being the denial of the individual, as the liberal tradition has it, this realizes the individual.

Marx's concepts of objectification and of species essence involve a view of freedom which in many ways is like that of Kant. Unalienated human beings are self-determined in the sense that they are not driven by need but regulate the satisfaction of need consciously. They are not dominated by alien market forces, but control their social interaction themselves. Such human beings are not determined heteronomously. Their activity is not determined by particular interests or individual needs, but is directed consciously towards the realization of the human essence, that is, towards the satisfaction of needs common to all, needs which can be universalized, needs whose satisfaction would be demanded by the categorical imperative.

We must say a bit more about the relationship between needs and the categorical imperative. Kant, at least in the *Critique of Practical Reason*, admits that inclinations, interests, or needs are embedded in the content of any maxim. But to act morally and freely we must will to carry out the maxim not because of these interests, needs, or inclinations, but solely because the maxim is universalizable and thus rational. In other words, Kant has no objection to the fact that ends, interests, needs, goods, or purposes will be embedded in our maxims. They are expected to be there, but they must not be the elements that determine our will; only the possibility of universalizing the maxim without contradiction can do that if the act is to be free and moral. Perhaps the clearest example of this can be found in Kant's claim that the categorical imperative requires us to seek our own happiness. It is at least an indirect duty to seek happiness, not because we desire it (though, of course, we do desire it), but because it is impossible to universalize not seeking it. This too, I think, is Marx's view. We do not seek the object because it satisfies a particular need or interest of the individual (though, of course, it does so). That would be to be need-driven and dominated by the object. That would be heteronomy. We seek an object because to do so is universalizable, because the need for the object is common to all human beings, because it would be impossible to universalize not seeking the object, all of which is also to say that the object realizes the essence of the species.[24]

The categorical imperative applies to powers as well as needs. Even for Kant the categorical imperative would require individuals to develop their talents.[25] But, for Marx, powers are not important merely for the individual. The powers of individuals affect and transform the socio-cultural world which other individuals internalize. The entire socio-cultural world is the outcome of what individuals have contributed to it through the manifestation of their powers, and this socio-cultural world moulds all individuals and makes possible the development of their powers. Thus, for individuals to seek their own realization they must seek the full realization of the powers of other individuals—the powers of the species as a whole.[26] This would require that we act on the universal—in accordance with the categorical imperative, which would demand the realization of quite specific powers of any particular individual, since such powers could contribute to the development of the species. It would be society's obligation to provide the conditions under which such powers could be realized. Moreover, as we saw earlier with respect to needs (in Chapter 1, section i) Marx operates not just with a Kantian categorical imperative but with an Aristotelian concept of essence, and the latter would call for the development of powers which we might not be able to will that all human beings develop but which nevertheless would develop the essence of the individual and conceivably contribute to the enrichment of the human species. The categorical imperative would, of course, also demand that those powers that would harm others should not be realized.

Furthermore, despite the importance of objects, needs, and powers, Marx implies that it is species activity itself which is our highest goal. Much as for Aristotle, activities can have their ends or objects outside themselves or the activity itself can be our highest end.[27] For Marx, it is

[24] *CPrR* 34-5, 72-6, and *KGS* V. 34, 69-73. *F* 15, and *KGS* IV. 400. *Religion Within the Limits of Reason Alone*, trans. T. M. Greene and H. H. Hudson (New York: Harper & Row, 1960), 4, and *KGS* VI. 4. For a good discussion of these matters see J. Ebbinghaus, 'Interpretation and Misinterpretation of the Categorical Imperative', *Kant: A Collection of Critical Essays*, ed. R. P. Wolff (Garden City, NY: Doubleday, 1967), 220-7. See also A. C. Ewing, *Ethics* (New York: Free Press, 1953), 56-7, and L. W. Beck, *A Commentary on Kant's Critique of Practical Reason* (University of Chicago Press, 1960), 96, 162. *EPM, MECW* III. 275-7, and *MEW*, suppl. I. 515-17.

[25] *F* 40-1, and *KGS* IV. 422-3. Feuerbach does not mention the categorical imperative, yet morality for him means acting for the benefit of the species and thus acting on the universal; see *The Essence of Christianity*, p. 158, and *Sämtliche Werke*, VI. 191.

[26] *EPM, MECW* III. 333, and *MEW*, suppl. I. 574.

[27] *CM, MECW* III. 228, and *MEW*, suppl. I. 463. *EPM, MECW* III. 276, and *MEW*, suppl. I. 515-17. Aristotle, *Metaphysics*, 1048b; *NE* 1094a, 1097a–1098a, 1176a–1176b.

true that objects are ends not means and activity cannot occur without objects and the satisfaction of needs, but it is the *activity* of producing objects and satisfying needs that is the highest end and not the objects of particular interests or individual needs themselves. The end is a certain form of activity—activity which is free, that is, conscious and purposively directed towards the realization of the species' essence. Achieving such activity would be the realization of the species; it would not be a means to something else, but an end in itself. Such action would not be heteronomously determined.

At the same time, we can say that for Kant moral obligation is based not upon seeking the good but upon freedom. We obey the categorical imperative because only by doing so are we rationally self-determined and thus free. Here, too, we do not act to realize an external end; our act itself, freedom, is the end. For Marx, too, moral obligation is based upon freedom in this way. Free species activity is itself the end. But this also means that the end is the realization of the essence of the species, its good, and only through the realization of the essence of the species can we realize our powers, capacities, and freedom—our own good.

In this way Marx links Aristotle and Kant. Realizing our essence is identical with acting on a categorical imperative. This identification is possible because Marx understands our essence as a species essence. To realize our essence, we must act consciously and purposefully for the benefit of the species. But to act for the benefit of the species is to act for the universal—it is to act on the categorical imperative. Such species activity is an end in itself. At the same time, to act for the universal is to realize the species and thus to realize one's own essence, and to realize one's own essence is to be free.

Marx does not accept the Kantian notion of a noumenal realm. This is necessary for Kant because without it we would be entirely situated in the phenomenal realm and all of our actions would be determined causally and heteronomously. Instead of a concept of noumena, Marx employs a concept of essence. In the absence of alienation, neither the object nor need for the object indicates heteronomy, because the needed object is not, in itself, heteronomous; it is part of our essence.[28] As we have seen, both the subject and the object are parts of nature and the object is ontologically absorbed into the subject in the sense that

28 *CM*, *MECW* III. 218, 228, and *MEW*, suppl. I. 452, 462-3. Also *Dissertation*, *MECW* I. 52, and *MEW*, suppl. I. 284. See also M. Hess, 'The Philosophy of the Act', in *Socialist Thought*, ed. A. Fried and R. Sanders (Garden City, NY: Doubleday, 1964), 271-3, and for the German, *Moses Hess: Philosophische und Sozialistische Schriften*, ed. A. Cornu and W. Mönke (Berlin: Academie, 1961), 223-5.

the human species constitutes and comes to control collectively the objective world. It finds itself reflected in that world, and finds the world to be one with itself in essence.

Kantian autonomy does not satisfy Marx because only the intentions and volitions of the individual are free. In abstracting so radically from results, consequences, and goods, the individual, for Kant, is free even if the external world frustrates the realization of subjectively free activity.[29] Not so for Hegel and Marx. The external world, the object, must have been transformed to fit our essence. It must be a reflection of oneself which reinforces and confirms the individual. The free action of the subject must be realized in the world for full freedom to be possible. Thus our relation to the object is not only a free relation but it is one that realizes our essence and thus must be universalizable.

To clarify Marx's position, we might notice that contemporary philosophers distinguish between a theory of value, which is concerned with identifying what is good, and a theory of obligation, which is a moral assessment of actions and identifies what is right or what our duty is. They also distinguish between deontological and teleological theories. A teleological theory identifies the good as a specific end to be sought, a consequence to be realized, and defines obligation as the duty to realize these good consequences in the world. Aristotle, in large part, holds a teleological theory of this sort. A deontological theorist, on the other hand, holds that factors besides the realization of good consequences determine our obligation. Kant was a very strict deontologist. He held that ends or goods play no role whatsoever in determining our duty. Interests and inclinations are equally irrelevant. But to hold a deontological theory of obligation, one need not go this far. One must simply hold that there are some elements besides goods or ends which are necessary to determine our obligation. For Marx, just as for Kant, the principle of universalizability, the categorical imperative, not interest, determines our moral obligation. But, unlike Kant, the realization of one's essence, which is an end or good, is also necessary.

Marx does, I think, have a theory of moral obligation, even though he does not put any emphasis on fulfilling burdensome obligations. This, I think, is because morality for Marx, at least in one respect, is not understood as it is for Christian morality or as for Kant, but much more as it was for Aristotle. Marx does not accept the Christian notion that the human essence involves a tension and opposition between a

[29] *F* 10, 44, 53-4, 60-1, and *KGS* IV. 394, 426, 435, 442. *CPrR*, 28, 31, and *KGS* V. 28-9, 31.

physical-natural and a spiritual-supernatural principle, where, to fulfil our spiritual obligations, we must oppose our natural-physical desires. For Marx, as for Aristotle, the human being is exclusively natural and morality is the perfection of our nature. Virtue—the realization of our nature—is something we naturally seek. If our obligations appear as a burden, this is due to an opposition, or alienation, which has arisen within the natural social realm itself. If this opposition were removed, we would naturally seek the moral. The fact that duties do not appear as burdens in opposition to our natural inclinations does not mean that Marx has no theory of obligation. He has a different concept of human nature: obligations need not be burdensome to be obligations.

Moreover, Marx never speaks of duties we must perform; rather he speaks in terms of ideals, goals, or ends—of needs and powers—we ought to realize. We ought to work for the realization of the species in order to realize ourselves. Ideals or ends put a positive emphasis on what should be realized; whereas duties negatively emphasize what is prohibited or burdensome obligations. Nevertheless, ideals or ends involve obligation just as much as duties do.

We have now seen the conceptual core of Marx's synthesis of Aristotle and Kant. There is another less central but just as interesting point that can be made concerning Kant's influence on Marx. Marx's concept of an object allows him to explain how a possessive attitude towards objects might be overcome. In Marx's view, the pervasive relationship in which individuals stand towards objects in an exchange economy is the relation of possession. Things only are securely ours, have real significance for us, can satisfy our needs, if we own them. In an estranged market economy where the objects of our need are not controlled by us and where we are dominated by need, the most obvious way to ensure the satisfaction of need is to seek to possess the object. For the most part, only in this way can we gain control over it. But if objects were not estranged, if they were controlled collectively and distributed in a communal way rather than bought and sold, if the object were recognized as the objectification of our essence, the drive to possess would not be of such importance.[30]

If possession is the main relation of individuals to objects generated by an exchange economy and if it is the case that individuals are formed by their social interaction with others (and Marx claims that consciousness is the theoretical form of social interaction, that individuals repeat

[30] *EPM, MECW* III. 299-301, and *MEW,* suppl. I. 539-41.

their real existence in thought),[31] if this is so, then possessiveness will tend to be an all-pervasive relationship. We will relate to all things and persons as objects to be possessed. This implies that we will relate to them as means rather than as ends. Marx even discusses the fact that the normal relationship of husband to wife has been a relationship of possession. One of the consequences of Marx's argument is that it would be practically impossible for human beings, certainly in a widespread way, to fulfil Kant's categorical imperative never to treat anyone only as a means so long as exchange, private property, and alienation are present.[32] Nor does Marx think that all forms of communism would overcome possessiveness. What he calls 'crude communism' simply generalizes existing relationships; it wants to end the unequal possession of private property by creating equal possessions for all. Here the main aim would still be possession. The relation of individuals to private property simply would be transformed into the relation of the community to its possessions. This sort of communism frequently argues for the community of women. Women, instead of being the possession of individual men become the common possession of the community of men.[33] Rather than being treated as means by individuals, they are treated as means by the community.

The desirable relation to objects—things as well as persons—is to treat them as ends in themselves. In *Schiller, Hegel, and Marx*, I argued that the ideal relationship to the object, for Marx, is to be understood as an aesthetic relationship. For example, Marx says, 'The care burdened, poverty stricken man has no sense of the finest play, the dealer in minerals sees only the commercial value but not the beauty and specific character of the mineral'.[34]

Kant in his *Critique of Judgment* argued that the aesthetic relationship is disinterested in the sense that to experience beauty we must not be

[31] *EPM, MECW* III. 297-9, and *MEW*, suppl. I. 537-9.

[32] *EPM, MECW* III. 294-6, and *MEW*, suppl. I. 534-5. *CM, MECW* III. 224-8, and *MEW*, suppl. I. 459-63. Moreover, this is at least suggested by Aristotle. If in a developed exchange economy, individuals tend to treat virtue as a means to gain wealth (*Politics*, 1258ª), and if individuals are formed by habit, custom, upbringing, and imitation in their society (*NE* 1179ᵇ-1180ᵇ; *Politics*, 1337ª), then in an exchange economy where wealth-getting becomes an end it is not a very big step to say that other individuals would be treated as means to this end. Certainly, slaves are treated in this way for Aristotle (*Politics*, 1253ᵇ-1254ª).

[33] *EPM, MECW* III. 294-6, and *MEW*, suppl. I. 534-5. It is possible that in writing this passage on crude communism Marx was in part reflecting on Aristotle's discussion of Plato's community of women (*Politics*, 1261ª-1263ª), though Marx, unlike Aristotle, totally rejects private property and possession.

[34] See my *Schiller, Hegel, and Marx*, ch. 3. *EPM, MECW* III. 302, and *MEW*, suppl. I. 542.

interested in the object—we must not be drawn to it and dominated by our needs, interests, or inclinations. The aesthetic relationship, Kant argues, involves the *freest* form of satisfaction. The aesthetic experience involves an even freer relationship than does our relation to the good because in the former we are exclusively determined neither by reason nor sense. Moral freedom means being determined by reason and, at least in the *Foundations*, this usually meant an opposition between inclination and duty.[35] We are morally free in the sense that we overcome the determination of our inclinations and obey our reason. The aesthetic condition is understood as one in which we are determined exclusively neither by inclination nor reason. Feeling and intellect, sense and reason, spontaneously and harmoniously agree. Neither dominates the other. In the *Critique of Practical Reason*, Kant shifts away from the suggestion made in the *Foundations* that duty and inclination should be at odds in a moral act. In the *Critique of Practical Reason* he admits that duty and inclination can agree and he takes such agreement to be an ideal of perfection ever to be striven for but never completely reached.[36] Thus in the *Critique of Judgment* he can speak of beauty, which involves the harmony of feeling and reason, as a symbol of the morally good.[37]

Post-Kantian German philosophy tried to develop this connection even further. In *Schiller, Hegel, and Marx*, I argued that Schiller tried to draw Kant's aesthetics, ethics, and philosophy of history much closer together by seeking to make the harmony of duty and inclination, or reason and feeling, not a symbol, but an actual reality, one achieved in the ancient Greek *polis*, which then had been lost, and which history, understood much as in Kant's 'Idea for a Universal History', was on the way to realizing again in the modern world.

Schiller argued that an aesthetic education could synthesize aesthetics and morality. Sense and reason, duty and inclination, could come into harmony not as a far off ideal of perfection, but actually in the individual. Feeling in accordance with duty would produce a higher morality, an aesthetic morality.[38]

---

[35] Kant, *CJ* 38-44, and *KGS* V. 204-10. *F* 13-17, 22-4, and *KGS* IV. 397-401, 406-8.

[36] *CPrR* 33, 86-8, 126 ff., and *KGS* V. 32, 83-5, 122 ff.

[37] *CJ* 72, 198-200, and *KGS* V. 235-6, 352-4.

[38] F. Schiller, 'The Moral Utility of Aesthetic Manners', in *Essays Aesthetical and Philosophical* (*EAP*) (London: Bell, 1879), 126-32, and for the German see *Schillers Werke: Nationalausgabe* (*SWN*), ed. J. Petersen and G. Fricke, (Weimar: Böhlaus, 1934-), XXI. 28-34. 'On Grace and Dignity', *EAP* 209, and *SWN* XX. 287. Schiller's view that morality ought to involve an aesthetic balance between reason and feeling seems to echo Aristotle's doctrine of the mean. Aristotle says that virtue, like a work of

Schiller also tried to connect the aesthetic condition to labour. He argued that if we are able to satisfy our needs through labour, if we are not need-driven, then we can distance ourselves from the object and begin to contemplate it as an end in itself.[39] Labour could well become an aesthetic activity since it involves our sensuous faculties (in our needs and activities) as well as our rational faculties (in our planning and purposes). If both sides could be brought into harmony and balance an aesthetic condition would result. For Schiller an aesthetic education would develop and harmonize the faculties of the individual which then would transform the individual's activity and world. Marx does not think that an aesthetic education will transform the world. But he does hold that if the social world and labour were transformed, then an aesthetic condition could result.

All of the elements necessary for the aesthetic condition discussed by Kant and Schiller are present in Marx. Just as for Schiller, human beings must be in control of their activity and their product; they must not be dominated by need or interest; and they must not be slaves to the object. They must be able to stand back from the product, make it an object of their will and consciousness, and contemplate it freely as an end in itself. Labour ought to be an end enjoyable in itself. The worker's attitude must not be grasping, need-driven, and possessive. It should be disinterested or contemplative. The specific character of the object should be appreciated for its own sake as an end in itself. This would be an aesthetic attitude because sensuous physical activity (labour) as well as conscious intellectual activity (in the form of direction and contemplation) would be in harmony. Then, as Marx says, we would 'form things in accordance with the laws of beauty'.[40]

Furthermore, Kant argued that for the aesthetic experience to be possible a harmony between the object and the faculties of the individual must occur. The natural object must spontaneously appear

---

art, requires a mean where feeling or passion and rational principle accord (*NE* 1106b–1107a, see also 1099a; compare *NE* 1138b to Schiller, *On the Aesthetic Education of Man* (*AE*), trans. E. M. Wilkinson and L. A. Willoughby (Oxford: OUP, 1967), 116-21, and *SWN* XX. 363-5). It might well be argued that Schiller too was trying to reconcile Kant and Aristotle.

[39] *AE* 35, 167 n., 185, and *SWN* XX. 323, 386, 395. Schiller also develops a model for overcoming the opposition between classes (*Naive and Sentimental Poetry*, trans. J. A. Elias (New York: Ungar, 1966), 169-74, and *SWN* XX. 489-90) and between the citizen and the state (*AE* 17-21, and *SWN* XX. 316-18). For a fuller discussion see my *Schiller, Hegel, and Marx*, ch. 1.

[40] *EPM, MECW* III. 276-7, 300-2, and *MEW*, suppl. I. 516-17, 540-2. *CM, MECW* III. 228, and *MEW*, suppl. I. 462-3.

as if it were purposively designed for our faculties.[41] For Marx, existence must be transformed to suit our essence. In the object, the objectification of the human essence, individuals would be able to contemplate their essence. Thus, the objective world would appear to be designed purposively to harmonize with and confirm the human being. Our relationship to such an unalienated world would be an aesthetic relationship. If the objective world can be transformed to confirm the human being, it would no longer frustrate the individual's activity. The needs and feelings of the individual would not be at odds with such a world or with the purposive aim of working for the species. The activity of objectification would be the highest form of human activity and development—a free activity in which rational and purposive aims would be in harmony with needs and feeling. Such activity would be appreciated as an end in itself and the objects produced by such activity would be appreciated for their own sakes.[42]

The aesthetic condition, or aesthetic morality, implies a world in which all objects—not just persons but things—would be ends in themselves appreciated for their own sakes. All objects in so far as they mirror the species and are the expression of the activity of the species would be ends.[43] This is important because it would seem that for Marx it is unlikely that we can treat people as ends while treating things as possessions or means.[44] If things are the objectification of the powers and capacities of human beings and are necessary to satisfy their needs and make possible their development, then to treat objects as means or possessions almost inevitably will be to treat persons as means, if not directly and intentionally, at least indirectly and unintentionally. To treat persons as ends we must treat things as ends.

---

41 *CJ* 58, 64-5, 77-8, 83, and *KGS* V. 222, 228-9, 240-1, 245.

42 For further discussion of these matters see *Schiller, Hegel, and Marx*, ch. 3.

43 Let me be clearer about the status of objects. I have argued that free species activity is for Marx our highest end, not objects as objects of particular interest. I now claim that objects are ends in themselves to be appreciated for their own sakes. In a society dominated by the possessive attitude, objects will be perceived as means to satisfy particular interest. They will not be our highest ends. In a society which has overcome the possessive attitude, objects will no longer be perceived as means to satisfy particular interests, but, since they are the outcome of free activity—the objectification, i.e. the expression and realization, of the essence of the species—they will be appreciated for their own sakes, and, as part of the process of species activity, will be part of our highest end. Our relation to such objects will not be heteronomous because taking such objects as ends is to make our essence the end, and to treat the object as an end in itself is not to see it as an object of particular interest.

44 Here Marx opposes Hegel's views on property; see Hegel, *PR* 41 ff., 66, and *GPR* 57 ff., 90.

If I am correct here, then Marx is holding a very radical position. Certainly, private property, exchange, and the possessive attitude that arises from them must be overcome.[45] In so far as capitalism leads to treating things and persons as means, capitalism is morally objectionable. But Marx is going much further than this. Even in a non-capitalist society without private property, it would still be possible to use things as means to our own ends (as managers might use their factories as means to their own status). It would follow from what has just been said above that even this would involve at least indirectly and unintentionally treating persons (the factory workers) as means to our own ends and would also be objectionable.

Kant argues that human beings must be treated as ends in themselves, never as means only, though they can be treated as means if they are at the same time treated as ends in themselves (workers may be treated as means to increase production only if they are also treated with respect as ends in themselves). Marx's view of things is as strong as Kant's view of persons. Things should not be treated merely as means (factories should not be treated merely as means to production or personal gain or the workers will also be treated as means). Things can be treated as means only if they are also treated as ends in themselves (factories can be used to produce only as long as they are treated as expressions of human activity and thus valued as ends in themselves). On the other hand, Marx's view of persons is much stronger than Kant's view of persons. Marx seems to oppose all conditions which lead to treating persons as means. They should always and only be treated as ends in themselves.

My contention that Marx tries to link Aristotle and Kant can be reinforced by considering another issue. Marx implies in several places that species activity ought to lead to happiness or that it ought to be enjoyable and satisfying.[46] We have discussed already the relation of species activity to morality and freedom; we now must see how it is connected to happiness.

Moral theorists view the relation of virtue to happiness in different ways. Some theorists tend towards identifying the two, others deny such a connection. For example, Plato in the *Republic*, it seems to me, changes the normal meaning of happiness and redefines it so that it is identical with, or at least necessarily accompanies, virtue. The contemplation of the form of the highest good, grasping true being,

---

[45] *CM*, *MECW* III. 224–8, and *MEW*, suppl. I. 459–63.

[46] *EPM*, *MECW* III. 239, 278, 298–301, and *MEW*, suppl. I. 475, 518, 537–41. *CM*, *MECW* III. 227–8, and *MEW*, suppl. I. 462–3.

necessarily involves *true* happiness.[47] There is no suggestion of this in Marx. Classical utilitarians, on the other hand, define virtue so as to make it identical with happiness or at least hold that it follows necessarily from happiness. Virtue consists in acting so as to produce the greatest happiness. I will try to show that this is not Marx's view. Other theorists like Kant and Aristotle reject the tendency to identify virtue with happiness.[48] One can be virtuous without necessarily being happy, though one cannot be happy, at least in the highest sense, without being virtuous. To link virtue and happiness, further conditions are necessary. To use Kant's language, the connection between virtue and happiness is synthetic, not analytic.[49]

Though Marx does not discuss these matters explicitly, he seems to be closer to Aristotle and Kant than to the utilitarians. For example, in disagreeing with Proudhon he says that higher wages for workers would only produce better paid slaves.[50] In other words, higher wages and thus (certainly for utilitarians) greater enjoyment or happiness would be possible without affecting the fact that workers are alienated and unfree. But since, as we have seen, moral good requires freedom and the realization of essence,[51] we can say that happiness without freedom is not a morally acceptable goal. It certainly would not realize the human essence. Again, in the *German Ideology*, Marx argues that the semi-artistic work of the medieval craftsperson was engaging and enjoyable but that this made the work even more slavish.[52] In other words, to make alienated and unfree work enjoyable would be to tie the worker closer to such work and thus to increase the worker's slavishness. Marx also tells us in the *Holy Family* that capitalists are alienated in a market economy, just as anyone else, but may still be happy and satisfied.[53] Again happiness without freedom is morally unacceptable. Morality cannot be identified with producing greater happiness.[54]

[47] *Republic*, 585 A-586 B.
[48] *F* 10-12, 15, 35-6, and *KGS* IV. 395-6, 399, 417-18. *CPrR* 96, and *KGS* V. 93.
[49] *CPrR* 115, 117, and *KGS* V. 111, 112-13. Aristotle does, in effect, define happiness as activity of the soul in conformity with virtue (*NE* 1097b-1098a, 1177a), and thus it might seem that the link between virtue and happiness is analytic for him. But elsewhere in the text we see that virtue is not quite a sufficient condition for happiness; a virtuous person who e.g. lacks a certain amount of wealth, who suffers, or who lacks good health, will not be happy (*NE* 1153b, 1178b-1179a).
[50] *EPM, MECW* III. 280, and *MEW*, suppl. I. 520-1.
[51] 'Free Press', *MECW* I. 158-9, and *MEW* I. 54.
[52] *GI, MECW* V. 66, and *MEW* III. 52.
[53] *HF, MECW* IV. 36, and *MEW* II. 37.
[54] These examples suggest an interesting point, namely, that alienation is not a psychological category for Marx. To be alienated does not mean necessarily that we will

How then does Marx link freedom and morality with happiness in the ideal case? To answer this we first must notice that happiness can be understood in at least two ways. Happiness can mean pleasure, the satisfaction of natural desires or needs, as it does for Kant and at times for Aristotle.[55] Or it can refer to the satisfaction that accompanies a well performed activity, as it does, in other places, for Aristotle. The higher this activity, the more it accords with our essence, the higher the satisfaction or happiness.[56]

Using the first definition of happiness, it is not easy to get morality and happiness to accord. For Aristotle it is largely a contingent matter. The virtuous individual simply may suffer disappointment or pain. For Kant, the agreement of virtue with happiness is called the highest good. To realize this highest good, moral actions in accordance with universal rational principles and the feelings or inclinations which produce happiness would have to agree. For this to be possible, it would mean that the natural world would have to be regulated so that objects which determine feelings and inclination and thus happiness would always determine them in accordance with the demands of morality. For Kant, the highest good thus requires a postulate of practical reason—the existence of a God who would align nature and inclination with

---

be aware of being alienated or feel miserable, alone, or unhappy. Moreover, to overcome alienation it certainly is not sufficient simply to end misery or unhappiness. Workers content with their jobs are not necessarily unalienated. Alienation, most basically, means being unfree, and we can easily be unfree without being aware of it, just as we can be either happy or unhappy in our unfreedom. On the other hand, to overcome alienation does require that we become aware of it and understand its causes.

[55] *F* 35-6, and *KGS* IV. 417-18. *CPrR* 35, 129, and *KGS* V. 34, 124. *NE* 1153b, 1178b-1179a.

[56] Hegel, too, seems to hold both views; see *PS* 375, and *PG* 435. Also *PR* 83, and *GPR* 127. It is true that 'satisfaction that accompanies a well performed activity' is Aristotle's definition of pleasure (*NE* 1174b-1175b), which is not to be simply identified with happiness. But pleasure is certainly linked with happiness (*NE* 1153b), and it is a necessary ingredient of it (*NE* 1177a). In trying to define happiness, Aristotle identifies the proper function of the human being as activity in conformity with a rational principle or with virtue. Happiness then arises out of the performance of these activities, especially when they are performed with excellence (*NE* 1097b-1098a, also 1076a-1077a). When discussing pleasure as the satisfaction that accompanies a well-performed activity, Aristotle is discussing a broader sort of satisfaction that arises from activities which need not in the strictest or highest sense be rational and virtuous. But if they are, then pleasure coincides with happiness. Indeed, there is nothing objectionable about this. Aristotle says we can choose pleasure partly for itself and partly as a means to happiness, though we never choose happiness as a means to pleasure (*NE* 1097b). Happiness arises out of the highest sorts of activities—activities which are ends in themselves and which accord with virtue and rationality (*NE* 1176b). And this happiness involves the highest form of pleasure (*NE* 1177a).

morality so that happiness could accompany virtue.[57] For Marx, we might say, the human species replaces Kant's God. The species itself remakes the natural world in accordance with its essence such that natural objects and thus the feelings determined by these objects would agree with the universal and conscious moral purpose of the species. The species, we might say, realizes the highest good.

At this point we can see that the two forms of happiness can coincide. The satisfaction of need, interest, and feeling would occur as the species transforms its world to suit its essence. But, for Marx, our *highest* end is not the satisfaction of needs or interests; it is free species activity itself. Thus, the satisfaction or happiness which accompanies a well-performed activity—a satisfaction or happiness which is higher when the activity is higher or more essential—would also be present.[58]

Kant also discussed happiness in his 'Idea for a Universal History'. He argued that human beings had to create their own happiness and perfection. In so far as the course of history brings particular interest into accord with morality and institutionalizes this accord in a league of nations and in just civil constitutions, happiness is promoted. Thus an idea for a universal history bears a resemblance not just to regulative ideas but to postulates of practical reason,[59] and in so far as this idea for a universal history gives us a concrete mechanism for realizing happiness and perfection without relying on a God, Kant's views come even closer to Marx's.[60]

A moral theorist who holds a deontological theory of obligation need not reject a theory of the good. In fact, the theory of the highest good plays an important role in Kant's ethics. The highest good involves happiness as well as morality. Happiness is certainly an end or a good to be sought. A life without happiness would not be the highest good; thus

---

[57] *NE* 1153b. *CPrR* 119, 123, 128-30, 133, and *KGS* V. 114-15, 124-5, 128-9.

[58] *CM, MECW* III. 227-8, and *MEW*, suppl. I. 462-3. The aesthetic condition also involves happiness. Feeling which is in harmony with reason gives rise to enjoyment in any activity in which this harmony occurs.

We might also say that the species, for Marx, replaces Aristotle's final cause, that highest being for whose good all action is done. It causes by being loved. Activity done for the final cause involves pleasure or happiness (*Metaphysics*, 1072b). Much the same could be said of the species.

[59] *IUH, On History*, pp. 13-14, and *KGS* VIII. 19-20. Also see Y. Yovel, *Kant and the Philosophy of History* (Princeton University Press, 1980), 29 ff.

[60] We do not find a similar emphasis on happiness in Hegel's *Philosophy of History*. There are golden ages, but, in general, periods of happiness are blank pages in history and history is the slaughter bench on which the happiness of peoples is sacrificed; *PH* 20-1, 24, 26-7, and *SW* XI. 48-9, 53, 56.

to achieve the highest good we must seek happiness. But our moral obligation demands that the desire for happiness not determine our moral action; the categorical imperative alone must do that. The highest good is thus attainable only if God or history manipulates nature such that happiness accompanies morality. So also, for Marx, the realization of the species' essence can be called the highest good. But this good alone does not determine our obligation. The principle of universalization is a necessary component in determining our moral obligation and allowing us to be free.

III

We must now examine some of the problems involved in Marx's ethical views. Up until 1843, Marx employs, accepts, and endorses a concept of rights,[61] and he continues to speak of rights even in the *Critique of Hegel's Philosophy of Law*.[62] However, in his essay, 'On the Jewish Question' (1843), Marx rejects rights and in certain respects he seems to continue to do so as late as the 'Critique of the Gotha Program' (1875).[63]

In his discussion of the 'Declaration of the Rights of Man and the Citizen' (in 'On the Jewish Question'), Marx categorically rejects the concept of the rights of a citizen; this was just after the writing of the *Critique of Hegel's Philosophy of Law* in which he rejected Hegel's concept of a political state standing over and dominating civil society. On the surface it is rather easy to see why the rejection of rights follows from the rejection of the separation of state from society. A civil right would at least in part be a right against the political state—a right to freedom of speech, press, and so forth, which the political state may not infringe upon or allow anyone else to violate. Moreover, it would be a right which would be guaranteed and enforced by the state. If you reject the separation and alienation of state from society, the existence of rights would be objectionable for three reasons. First, rights in fact would presuppose the separation of state from society. A political state would have to exist for you to have a right against it and the state, it

---

[61] e.g. 'Free Press', *MECW* I. 147-8, 155, and *MEW* I. 43, 51. 'Leading Article', *MECW* I. 199, and *MEW* I. 102. 'Wood Theft', *MECW* I. 232-3, 236, and *MEW* I. 117-18, 121.

[62] *CHPL*, *MECW* III. 57, 120 (however, he seems to question rights on pp. 108-12), and *MEW* I. 260, 326, 313-17.

[63] *JQ*, *MECW* III. 160 ff., and *MEW* I. 362 ff. 'Critique of the Gotha Program' in *The Marx-Engels Reader*, 2nd edn., ed. R. C. Tucker (New York: Norton, 1978), 530-1, and *MEW* XIX. 20-2.

would seem, would have to exist in order to guarantee and enforce the right. Second, we have already seen that while Marx rejects the political state, he nevertheless thinks it represents the essence of the species, the community, the realm of the universal, though in a distant, alienated, and illusory way. Thus to demand rights against the state or the community would seem to be to insist upon the isolation of individuals from their essence and from their community with others. Marx argues, for example, that civil liberty, whose main application, he thinks, is the right to private property, is a right of particular interest against the universal. Third, to have the state guarantee and enforce such rights is to turn the community, the universal, into a means to promote particular and individual interests. It is to invert the proper relation of ends to means and of universal to particular.[64] Marx even goes so far as to suggest that when the revolutionary government of France violated in practice the very rights it upheld in theory, it was their violation of rights in practice that was correct.[65]

It is true that Marx accepts what he calls political rights—the rights of the citizen as opposed to the rights of man—which can be exercised only in community with others. Thus he advocates the right to participate in the community.[66] We can safely say that Marx rejects the minimal definition of a citizen as a bearer of rights. He demands the maximal definition of a citizen found in Aristotle and Rousseau. The citizen is one who actually participates in the political sphere—one who takes part in governing.[67]

It is quite clear that Marx rejects a right to private property, but he also seems to reject a wider range of rights. When he discusses and approves the violation of rights by the revolutionary French government, he mentions the right to privacy of correspondence and the right to a free press.[68]

This rejection of rights is odd for several reasons. It would seem that an ideal and free society even without a political state would want to guarantee rights against violation by other individuals.[69] It would seem that there ought to be recognized and established procedures for

---

[64] *JQ, MECW* III. 153, 161-5, and *MEW* I. 354, 362-7. Also *HF, MECW* IV. 113, and *MEW* II. 120.

[65] *JQ, MECW* III. 164-5, and *MEW* I. 367.

[66] *JQ, MECW* III. 160-1, and *MEW* I. 362.

[67] *Politics*, 1275ᵃ-1276ᵇ. Rousseau, *SCn* 15, and *OC* III. 362.

[68] *JQ, MECW* III. 165, and *MEW* I. 367.

[69] Hess argued that to be allowed rights by others was a form of heteronomy ('The Philosophy of the Act', p. 269, and *Moses Hess*, p. 222). Perhaps Marx was influenced by this (see *JQ, MECW* III. 164, and *MEW* I. 366).

redressing such violations. This alone would not seem to presuppose a separation of state from society nor would a political state be necessary to guarantee and enforce these rights. Marx himself, in his writings on the Paris Commune (1871), argues that while there should be no standing army attached to a political state, there should be a citizen militia. Moreover, in one of the drafts to the *Civil War in France*, Marx argues that this militia would be used to see to it that the commune, the governing body, could not seek to become a political state standing over society.[70] If an armed militia would not presuppose, if in fact it would prevent, the reinstatement of a state standing over society, and if it would not isolate individuals from the universal, the community, why would rights do so? Why couldn't rights, especially a right to a free press, even be an added means to ensure the non-existence of a state standing over society?

Perhaps Marx's answer, which one senses rather than finds stated explicitly, would be that if the proletariat does not hold power, rights are an illusion. If it does hold power, rights are unnecessary. Rights for Marx are expressions of class interest. If another class is in power, your interests will be respected only so far as, and not much further than, they agree with the interests of the class in power. But then why not realize these illusory rights rather than reject them? Marx seems to think that if the proletariat comes to power, since it is a universal class, that is, a class whose particular interests coincide with the universal, it will not need rights.

We might explain this a bit further by examining the concept of sovereignty. For Hobbes, the sovereign is an absolute power and authority.[71] This concept is both an empirical concept, which locates where the greatest power in fact is crystallized, and a theoretical concept, which indicates the apex of legitimate authority. It follows from this that rights against the sovereign are an impossibility because the sovereign cannot be limited, either theoretically or in fact, from above or outside itself. Nothing can limit the sovereign's power or legitimate authority; if something can, the sovereign simply would not be the sovereign—it would not be the *highest* power and authority. If the sovereign is the government, the people can have no rights against it. If the sovereign is the people, then there can be rights against the

[70] *Civil War in France* in *Writings on the Paris Commune*, pp. 73-4, 152, 199, and *MEW* XVII. 338-40, 543, 595-6.
[71] T. Hobbes, *Leviathan* in *English Works of Thomas Hobbes* (*EW*), ed. W. Molesworth (n.c.: Scientia Aalen, 1962), III. 179, 312-13. *De Cive, EW* II. 88, 153-4. *Elements of Law, EW* IV. 137, 170-1.

government but individuals can have no rights against the people. Rousseau clearly understood this. He held that the sovereign cannot be bound even by its own past decisions.[72] He realized that the only limits that might be placed upon the sovereign would have to arise from the sovereign itself—from its nature or constitution. Since we cannot defend ourselves against the sovereign once it exists, we must see to it that in creating the sovereign we create something that will not harm us. Thus we must create a sovereign that can only act according to principles of right. If the sovereign never fails to act in accordance with right we cannot object to its absolute power. This is what led Rousseau to his concept of the general will, which is understood as sovereign power in accordance with principles of right.[73] Rousseau argues that the general will will manifest itself given four conditions: (1) all citizens must vote as individuals in the sovereign assembly; (2) they only vote on general or universal questions; (3) they always are asked to decide the general will or the common good rather than vote for their own particular interests; and (4) they realize that the outcome will be enforced equally and vigorously for all.[74] Given these conditions, right will emerge. In fact, these conditions would produce laws in accordance with the categorical imperative. To demand rights against the laws of such a sovereign, besides being impossible in practice, would be to demand an exception from what is right, for one's particular interests.

In rejecting the alienation of the political state from civil society, Marx is denying that the government is the legitimate sovereign. If we can use the concept of sovereignty at all for Marx, we would say that the species or the community is sovereign.[75] If we accept this, then it follows that there is no principle above or outside the essence of the species which can or should limit the species. Rights against the species would not only be impossible but would be morally wrong. The only limits that can be placed upon the species must arise from its own nature. Only what is universalizable accords with the essence of the species. Particular interests in opposition to the universal have no place and will be eliminated as the species develops historically.

Thus, I think that Marx's rejection of rights flows from his concept of essence and, as we shall see, from its consequences for consciousness and community. To explain this we might contrast Marx with Hegel.

[72] *SCn*, pp. 16-17, and *OC* III. 362-3.

[73] *SCn*, pp. 17-18, 23, 26, 36, and *OC* III. 363-4, 368, 371, 379-80.

[74] *SCn*, pp. 16, 29-30, 103-4, 106, and *OC* III. 362, 373-4, 438, 440-1.

[75] e.g. see *CHPL*, *MECW* III. 28-9, and *MEW* I. 229-31. *JQ*, *MECW* III. 168, and *MEW* I. 370.

Hegel accepted rights while denying that the state ought to be a means to protect particular interests, especially interests in private property. The state was supposed to be an end in itself.[76] For Hegel the state embodies the citizen's essence and civil society is the realm of particular interests and rights. But the relation of the individual in civil society to the state is quite different for Hegel than for Marx. Individuals in civil society, for Hegel, work *unconsciously* for the universal. Each seeks only their own particular interests, but through an invisible hand they produce the universal, the common good.[77] This implicit and unrecognized universal is made explicit and is recognized consciously as public law only at the level of the state.[78] The individual's consciousness of this universal, the citizen's own essence, may range from vague patriotism to full rational awareness.[79] One can be absorbed in one's particular interests and wish to have them guaranteed by rights if one's relation to the state need not be explicit in civil society and if one's social activity need not be conscious, communal, and purposively directed toward the universal. For Marx, on the other hand, to realize one's essence, one must do so consciously and this requires communal interaction. One must work consciously within and for the community, for the species, the universal. Rights, then, would be rights against others, against the community, and against one's essence, the universal. One's relation to the object would become heteronomous.[80] Emphasis on rights guaranteeing particular interests would turn the individual away from the community. Widespread concern for individual rights and particular interests would lead towards a society where individuals would work only unconsciously for the community. They would concern themselves consciously with particular interests and rights against others as well as against the community. As for Rousseau, absorption in particular interest is the greatest threat to civic virtue.[81] One of Marx's main objections to rights is that the form of liberty they involve is the liberty of the isolated and egoistic individual in opposition to others. Each sees in others the limits to liberty instead of finding freedom in co-operation and community with others. In rejecting rights Marx is not accepting less but demanding more than rights would give us. He wants

[76] *PR* 156, and *GPR* 208.
[77] *PR* 124-5, 127, 129-30, and *GPR* 167-8, 170, 173-5.
[78] *PR* 134-5, 139, 160-1, and *GPR* 180-1, 187, 214-15.
[79] *PR* 163-4, and *GPR* 218-19.
[80] See 'The Philosophy of the Act', p. 269, and *Moses Hess*, p. 222.
[81] *SCn*, pp. 93-4, and *OC* III. 429.

a community like the one Aristotle has in mind when he says that justice is unnecessary between friends.[82]

Marx identifies rights with particular interests. In so far as particular interests oppose the universal, they have no legitimate place. In so far as they agree with the universal, the insistence on rights is unnecessary. Ordinary laws would be adequate. Marx also assumes that the species' essence in fact will realize the universal. So far this seems acceptable. Trouble would arise only if the community failed to establish the universal. Indeed, rights would seem to be necessary precisely to guarantee against this possibility. But this option is not open to Marx, given his concept of essence. To establish rights in order to protect against failure to establish the universal would prohibit one from realizing the universal. Hegel's concept of essence allowed him to accept rights. For Hegel, the essence is the Idea, which manifests itself in the state and its institutions—the family, civil society, the constitution, and so forth. For Marx, essence is located in each individual thing or person. For this essence to be realized, it must be recognized consciously and community actually be produced. Rights, and the form of consciousness and activity that would accompany them, would frustrate the objectification of such an essence. They would deflect consciousness from the universal which must remain one's purposive end if essence is to be realized. This would not be the case for Hegel because the state already is one's essence whether one fully recognizes it and acts on it in day-to-day activity or not. For Marx, to defend against the failure to achieve the universal would frustrate the drive to produce the universal.

This is particularly ironic. Most Marx scholars, whether they approve of Marx's humanism or not, think, that his humanism is most evident in the early writings and that this humanism is based upon Marx's concept of essence or species-being. If this concept of essence precludes the possibility of rights, then we must begin to wonder whether this humanistic concept of essence is not in certain ways anti-humanistic.

Moreover, if we further reflect upon these matters, we will see that Marx's concept of essence and its consequences for a theory of revolution involve potentially anti-democratic elements. We have seen that Marx's concept of the proletariat as a universal class, that is, a class whose particular interests agree with the universal, allows him to argue that an uprising of workers, no matter how small, contains within it a movement towards the universal—towards the human essence and com-

---

[82] *JQ*, *MECW* III. 162-4, and *MEW* I. 363-6. *NE* 1155ᵃ.

munity. In the *German Ideology* and the *Communist Manifesto*, Marx begins to talk about a majority revolution, but in the earlier writings he does not. His main concern is with revolution in Germany, and he makes it quite clear that in Germany the proletariat does not form a majority. In fact, in the 'Introduction to the Critique of Hegel's Philosophy of Law', he admits that a proletariat hardly exists in Germany.[83] Yet he is advocating a proletarian revolution in Germany, which could be only a minority revolution, and if the proletariat came to power as a minority they could hardly expect to rule democratically. Earlier, in the *Critique of Hegel's Philosophy of Law*, Marx had not yet identified the proletariat as the universal class. There his model for overcoming the opposition between state and society was unlimited voting.[84] In the later 'Introduction to the Critique of Hegel's Philosophy of Law' and in his subsequent early writings, the moral justification of a proletarian revolution and of the early stages of communist society is not that the interests of the proletariat are universal interests in the sense that their interests are the interests of the majority or that the majority interest will rule democratically. Rather the justification is that the interests of the proletariat are universal in the sense that they agree with the categorical imperative or the essence of the species, no matter how small the proletariat might be. Kant's goal, in his political writings, was an autocrat who ruled in a republican way—an autocrat who would issue laws in accordance with the categorical imperative. Marx's views, in their own way, come very close to Kant's on this matter.

Thus, Marx's early humanism is a two-edged sword. It contains humanistic as well as anti-humanistic elements—elements which work to realize the full and free development of individuals as ends in themselves and elements which work against this goal. This raises an interesting possibility. If the later Marx, who, as we shall see, abandons his early concept of essence, still can be shown to be a humanist—thus if Althusser's view that the later Marx is an anti-humanist and that of the essential unity theorists that Marx's humanism continues relatively unchanged throughout his writings are both wrong—then it might be the case, at least in this one respect, that the later rather than the earlier Marx is the real humanist. Such a case might be made out if it could be shown that the later Marx was able to shed the negative aspects of his

---

[83] *CHPLI, MECW* III. 186, and *MEW* I. 390. For further discussion of these matters see my 'Estrangement and the Dictatorship of the Proletariat', *Political Theory*, 7 (1979), 509-20.

[84] *CHPL, MECW* III. 120-1, and *MEW* I. 326.

earlier concept of essence while preserving and transforming the positive aspects of his early humanism. This is a possibility we might well keep in mind as we proceed.

3

The Abolition of Morality (1845–1856)

In the *German Ideology*, Marx's views on ethics begin to turn in a different direction. He abandons his earlier concept of essence and develops a doctrine of historical materialism. He rejects Kantian ethics as well as the notion that freedom can be understood as self-determination. His historical materialism, I hope to show, leaves no room for moral responsibility or moral obligation. Morality becomes ideology and it will disappear in communist society.

I

In the *Holy Family*, written in 1844 and published in 1845, Marx continues to employ a concept of human essence much as he did earlier.[1] He still holds that existence must be measured by essence and that moral good is the result of their accord, whereas a contradiction between them gives rise to moral evil.[2]

In one section of the *Holy Family*, 'The Mystery of Speculative Construction', Marx may seem to be abandoning his earlier concept of essence, but at this point, I suggest, he is rejecting only Hegel's concept of essence. In this section itself, as well as elsewhere in the *Holy Family*, Marx continues to employ his own concept of essence. Marx objects to those who abstract a single general idea from existing empirical phenomena, treat that idea as an entity existing outside these phenomena, and then hold that the empirically existing phenomena are manifestations produced by the one abstract essence existing apart from them. Marx's objection is to treating essence as an absolute Hegelian subject which produces existing phenomena from outside those phenomena. Marx says,

---

[1] *HF, MECW* IV. 21, 39, 41, 42, 114-15, 174, 194, and *MEW* II. 21, 41, 43, 44, 121-2, 185, 206.

[2] *HF, MECW* IV. 36, 169-70, and *MEW* II. 37, 180.

If from real apples, pears, strawberries and almonds I form the general idea 'Fruit', if I go further and imagine that my abstract idea 'Fruit', derived from real fruit, is an entity existing outside me, is indeed the true essence of the pear, the apple, etc., then—in the language of speculative philosophy—I am declaring that 'Fruit' is the 'Substance' of the pear, the apple, the almond, etc. I am saying, therefore, that to be a pear is not essential to the pear, that to be an apple is not essential to the apple; that what is essential to these things is not their real existence, perceptible to the senses, but the essence that I have abstracted from them and foisted on them, the essence of my idea—'Fruit'. I therefore declare apples, pears, almonds, etc., to be mere forms of existence, modi of 'Fruit'.[3]

Here, much as in the *Critique of Hegel's Philosophy of Law*,[4] Marx is contrasting two concepts of essence—Hegel's, which makes the existing entity in its real existence unessential, and his own, which does not strip the existing entity of its essential empirical reality.

In the 'Theses on Feuerbach' (written in 1845), Marx says, 'Feuerbach resolves the essence of religion into the essence of man. But the essence of man is no abstraction inherent in each single individual. In its reality it is the ensemble of the social relations.'[5] Here, it is difficult to decide whether (as in the *Holy Family*) Marx is rejecting simply one concept of essence, in this case, Feuerbach's, and asserting his own, or whether he is rejecting all concepts of essence completely. When he says that the human essence 'is the ensemble of the social relations', he clearly is rejecting Feuerbach's concept of essence, but what is his position? Is he holding that the human essence actually exists and is to be understood as the ensemble of social relations—as Fromm, for example, argues—or is Marx instead simply abandoning the concept of essence and *replacing* it with a different concept—the concept of the ensemble of social relations?[6] The 'Theses on Feuerbach' are not perfectly clear.

In the *German Ideology* (written in 1845-6), Marx's position is a bit clearer. He says, 'This sum of productive forces, capital funds and social forms of intercourse, which every individual and every generation finds in existence as something given, is the real basis of what the philosophers have conceived as 'substance' and 'essence of man', and what they have deified and attacked . . .'.[7] Here, he does not say that

---

[3] *HF, MECW* IV. 57-8, also pp. 59-61, and *MEW* II. 60, 61-3.

[4] *CHPL, MECW* III. 8-9, 11, 23, 39, and *MEW* I. 206-7, 209, 224, 241.

[5] 'Theses on Feuerbach' (*TF*), *MECW* V. 4, and *MEW* III. 6.

[6] E. Fromm, *Marx's Conception of Man* (New York: Ungar, 1973), 78. Also see J. McMurtry, *The Structure of Marx's World-View* (Princeton University Press, 1978), 30 n.

[7] *GI, MECW* V. 54, and *MEW* III. 38.

these social relations *are* the human essence; he says that they are the basis of what philosophers have conceived as the human essence, and elsewhere he makes it clear that these conceptions have been *misconceptions*. He tells us that essences are illusions or fantasies derived from a real basis,[8] and in many places he clearly rejects the concept of essence.[9]

In the *Economic and Philosophic Manuscripts* of 1844, one of the functions that the concept of essence was intended to perform was to distinguish between humans and animals. Marx thought that it was a certain form of consciousness which uniquely distinguished humans from animals and thus constituted the human essence. In the *German Ideology*, he says, 'Men can be distinguished from animals by consciousness, by religion or anything else you like. They themselves begin to distinguish themselves from animals as soon as they begin to produce their means of subsistence, a step which is conditioned by their physical organization.'[10] Here, Marx is *not* denying that a certain form of consciousness distinguishes humans from animals. In fact, in the final draft of the *German Ideology* he crossed out such a claim, namely, that 'the first historical act of these individuals distingushing them from animals is not that they think, but that they begin to produce their means of subsistence'.[11] Thus, humans can be distinguished from animals by consciousness, but the point of the *German Ideology* is that this is not especially relevant and that this difference is not to be taken as a metaphysical difference in essence. Instead, what significantly distinguishes humans from animals is simply a certain form of social activity which is conditioned not by an essence but by physical organization, namely, that humans begin to produce their own means of subsistence.

Social activity replaces the concept of essence. Marx says, 'what individuals are depends on the material conditions of their production', and for Marx what it means to be human 'corresponds to the definite relations predominant at a certain stage of production and to the way of satisfying needs determined by them'. Elsewhere, he even ridicules the notion of using a concept of essence to distinguish humans from animals,

---

[8] *GI, MECW* V. 394-5, 395 n., 430, 517-18, and *MEW* III. 379, 379 n., 415, 506. *Communist Manifesto, MECW* VI. 511, and *MEW* IV. 486.

[9] *GI, MECW* V. 160, 183-4, 236, 429-30, 512, and *MEW* III. 143, 167, 217-18, 415, 500. Marx also ridicules the concept of essence in many places: *GI, MECW* V. 58, 61, 215, 462, 486, 490, and *MEW* III. 42, 48, 196-7, 449-50, 475, 477.

[10] *EPM, MECW* III. 275-6, and *MEW*, suppl. I. 515-16. *GI, MECW* V. 31, and *MEW* III. 21.

[11] *GI, MECW* V. 31 n. and *MEW* III. 20 n.

It is obvious too that this 'whole man', 'contained' in a single attribute of a real individual and interpreted by the philosopher in terms of that attribute, is a complete chimera. Anyway, what sort of man is this, 'man' who is not seen in his real historical activity and existence, but can be deduced from the lobe of his own ear, or from some other feature which distinguishes him from the animals? Such a man 'is contained' in himself, like his own pimple.[12]

It is true that in a few places Marx does speak of 'human nature',[13] but the context usually makes clear that this does not reflect the concept he held in 1844. The term 'human nature' in everyday speech often is used in a loose, non-metaphysical, non-normative, and non-technical sense simply to refer to the forms of behaviour, capacities, and qualities generally characteristic of human beings. This is the way in which Marx uses the term, except that he thinks such capacities, qualities, and behaviour are historically developed and socially conditioned. The difference between the concept he is rejecting and a non-metaphysical, non-normative notion of human nature emerges in the following passage,

Instead of tracing this peculiar nature in the activity and enjoyment of the men who surround him—in which case he would very soon have found how far the products external to us have a voice in the matter, too—he makes activity and enjoyment 'coincide in the peculiar nature of man.' Instead of visualising the peculiar nature of men in their activity and manner of enjoyment, which is conditioned by their activity, he explains both by invoking 'the peculiar nature of man,' which cuts short any further discussion. He abandons the real behavior of the individual and again takes refuge in his indescribable, inaccessible, peculiar nature.[14]

What are the consequences of abandoning the earlier concept of essence? First, it follows that Marx's concept of species essence or species-being also must be abandoned, and, indeed, Marx himself rejects this concept. He tells us that Kriege's ideal communist

'determines his own goals according to the goals of the species' (as if the species were a person who could have goals) 'and seeks to be completely his own, solely in order to dedicate himself to the species with everything that he is and is

12 *GI, MECW* V. 32, 432, 512, and *MEW* III. 21, 417-18, 500.

13 *GI, MECW* V. 289, and *MEW* III. 270-1. *Poverty of Philosophy*, VI. 192, and *MEW* IV. 160. *Capital*, I. 609 n., and *MEW* XXIII. 636-7 n.

14 *GI, MECW* V. 465, and *MEW* III. 452. The German word which has been translated here as 'peculiar nature' is 'Eigentümlichkeit' not 'Wesen', but the point, I think, remains clear.

15 'Circular against Kriege', *MECW* VI. 45, and *MEW* IV. 11. See also *GI, MECW* V. 77, 236, and *MEW* III. 75, 217-18.

capable of becoming' (total self-sacrifice and self-abasement before a vaporous fantasy-concept).[15]

It also follows that Marx's concept of alienation from the species—the central concept of alienation in the *Economic and Philosophic Manuscripts*—must go. This does not mean that other forms of alienation—alienation from the product, in the process of production, from the state, and in exchange—are eliminated. Marx continues in the *German Ideology* and in later writings to use the concept of alienation, but stripped of the notion of alienation from the species or from the human essence.[16] Thus, the human essence or species-being is no longer a goal or a norm which human activity ought to seek to realize. 'Communism is for us not a state of affairs which is to be established, an ideal to which reality will have to adjust itself. We call communism the real movement which abolishes the present state of things.' And Marx also says, 'With "Stirner", "communism" begins with searchings for "essence" . . . That communism is a highly practical movement, pursuing practical aims by practical means, and that only perhaps in Germany, in opposing the German philosophers, can it spare a moment for the problem of "essence"—this, of course, is of no concern to our saint.'[17]

Marx's theory of social development no longer employs an Aristotelian concept of essence. History can no longer be conceived as the realization and manifestation of a true, inner, universal form. Nor can social criticism any longer proceed by measuring existence against such a form or by identifying those elements which frustrate the realization of such a potential.

If we look back at the writings of 1843-4, we now can begin to see that Marx's arguments for communism and revolution were more arguments for the moral necessity of communism and revolution than empirical studies of how they might actually occur. It was the proletariat's alienation from the human essence that would drive it towards revolution. But in what sense would the proletariat be 'driven'? In what sense was the revolution 'necessary'? Very little was said of the actual mechanics of the process, and what there was was wrapped up with moral arguments concerning the necessity of realizing an essence.[18]

[16] e.g. *GI*, *MECW* V. 281-2, and *MEW* III. 262-3. *Capital*, I. 432, 608, 645, and *MEW* XXIII. 455, 635, 674. Instead of 'alienation', Marx at times uses the term 'fetishism'; see *Capital*, I. 71 ff., and *MEW* XXIII. 85 ff. For a more thorough discussion of these matters and of shifts in Marx's concept of alienation, see my *Schiller, Hegel, and Marx*, chs. 3-4.

[17] *GI*, *MECW* V. 49, 50, 215, and *MEW* III. 35, 45, 196-7.

[18] *CHPLI*, *MECW* III. 175-6, 182-7, and *MEW* I. 378-9, 385-91. 'King of Prussia', *MECW* III. 204-5, and *MEW* I. 407-8.

It might be argued that any social or political theory is weakened in so far as it bases its arguments on a concept of human essence, as it loses its force if that particular concept is not accepted. Furthermore, how does one argue convincingly for a concept of human essence? In a passage quoted above, Marx himself suggests that such a concept is 'indescribable' and 'inaccessible'.[19] In reading the social contract tradition, for example, one often feels that in order to justify certain institutions in which the theorist believes—an absolute sovereign for Hobbes, private property for Locke, or political equality for Rousseau— the theorist merely packs into the concept of a state of nature that picture of human nature which when fully examined will require and justify the particular institutions that the theorist sought to justify in the first place. In fact, Marx's arguments in 1843-4 are also susceptible to this sort of criticism. In order to justify communism, he argued that the human essence was such that it could only be realized in a communist society. Certainly his concepts of species-being and community functioned in this way.

In the *German Ideology*, Marx came to think that any discussion of history, society, or the achievement of communism must be completely scientific in the sense that all stages of the theory be verifiable empirically.[20] Theory must eschew metaphysical assumptions, philosophical ideals, and moral values. Thus, in the *German Ideology*, Marx's discussion of communism, as he himself points out, shuns any discussion of 'man' or the human essence. Instead, it proceeds in a wholly empirical and materialist way. Marx first argues that the existing forces of production are destructive and that individuals will have to control these forces if they are to safeguard their existence. Next he argues that the nature of this control will be determined by the character of the forces of production themselves. Since the forces of production are too complex to be controlled by individuals or small groups, individuals will have to organize themselves collectively in order to achieve and maintain control.[21] I will return to this later. At this point, I only want to point out that this argument for the necessity of communism never once appeals to ideals, moral principles, or essences; it simply examines the nature and development of the forces of production in order to discover the necessity they give rise to. All arguments now proceed in this empirical, historical materialist way. It

19 *GI, MECW* V. 465, and *MEW* III. 452.
20 *GI, MECW* V. 31, 35-7, and *MEW* III. 20, 25-7.
21 *GI, MECW* V. 87-9, and *MEW* III. 67-9.

is now historical materialism which explains the necessity of social transformation, not a concept of essence.

II

The historical materialist method starts by studying the mode of production of a given society, the form of intercourse (or the relations of production) created by and connected with this mode of production, and the reciprocal interaction that occurs between the forces and relations of production. Only after it has understood these material conditions does it try to explain how ideas or forms of consciousness arise. It traces the formation of ideas from these material conditions and claims that the process is verifiable empirically. It does not explain practice from ideas but explains the formation of ideas from material practice.[22] For Marx, it is material conditions that determine ideas. In early history, ideas—including the mental production of laws, morality, and religion—are directly interwoven with the material activity and intercourse of human beings; they are a direct efflux of their material behaviour. This is not to reduce ideas to processes of matter. Consciousness is different from matter and humans produce their own ideas, but these are conditioned by the development of productive forces and the intercourse corresponding to them. Morality and other forms of consciousness are not independent of these conditions. For example, they have no history of their own. To understand their historical development it is necessary to understand the historical development of material conditions and to trace the rise of ideas from those conditions. Consciousness does not determine life, but life determines consciousness.[23]

Consciousness develops due to the development of the forces of production, due to more complex division of labour, and more extensive intercourse. At a certain point a division between material and mental labour appears. Then consciousness can seem to be something other than consciousness of existing practice,

from now on consciousness is in a position to emancipate itself from the world and to proceed to the formation of 'pure' theory, theology, philosophy, morality, etc. But even if this theory, theology, philosophy, morality, etc., come

---

[22] *GI, MECW* V. 36, 53-4, and *MEW* III. 26-7, 37-8.
[23] *GI, MECW* V. 36-7, 44, and *MEW* III. 26-7, 30-2. *HF, MECW* IV. 119, and *MEW* II. 126.

into contradiction with the existing relations, this *can only occur because existing social relations have come into contradiction with existing productive forces.*[24]

The part of this passage that I have italicized directly contradicts those who would argue that for Marx in the *German Ideology* ideas and material conditions reciprocally and equally determine each other. Ideas, including moral ideas, cannot lead to action in opposition to material conditions—they cannot contradict them—unless there already exists a contradiction within material conditions themselves. As Marx tells us elsewhere, even the alteration of consciousness divorced from material conditions is an illusion which is the product of existing relations.[25] Ideas are not independent of material conditions. They cannot play even a reciprocal and equal role in transforming material conditions. They can only be a part of the process of transformation which material conditions undergo and in which material conditions are the determining element.[26] I do not think that Marx is saying that ideas cannot arise or be formulated except as determined by material conditions, but that the ideas that do arise will not be taken to be significant or alter the consciousness of others in any widespread way, unless they are reinforced by material conditions.

Engels gives a good example of the way in which morality is related to material conditions. Suppose the leaders of a radical party were forced to assume power before the movement they represent is ready and before the material conditions necessary for that movement to carry out its social programme have developed. The leaders would feel bound by the principles and demands hitherto propounded by their party. That, we might say, is what they feel they ought to do. But what they can do will be determined by the level of development of the material conditions of production, by commerce, and by their own abilities and insights. These leaders may well find that they cannot do what they ought to do. They may even be compelled to represent not their own party but the party for whose domination the moment is ripe.[27]

---

[24] *GI, MECW* V. 44-5 (my emphasis), and *MEW* III. 30-2.

[25] *GI, MECW* V. 379, and *MEW* III. 363.

[26] Marx even argues that suicides and crime are caused by social conditions: 'Peuchet: On Suicide', *MECW* IV. 598-604, 610, and for the German see *Marx Engels historisch-kritische Gesamtausgabe*, ed. D. Rjazanov (Berlin: Marx-Engels Verlag, 1927-), sect. i, III. 392-5, 403-4. 'Capital Punishment', *MECW* XI. 497, and *MEW* VIII. 508. He also holds that individual development and personality are socially determined: *GI, MECW* V. 51, 255, 262-4, and *MEW* III. 37, 237, 245-7.

[27] F. Engels, *The Peasant War in Germany, MECW* X. 470, and *MEW* VII. 400-1. This passage might seem to suggest that moral obligations actually exist. As we shall see, this is not Marx's view in this period.

We must say a bit more about the relationship of ideas—especially moral ideas—to material conditions. We have seen that for Marx ideas can appear to be independent of material conditions, but in fact cannot contradict those conditions unless the material conditions themselves embody the contradiction. We must discover what degree of independence ideas might have. This is most important for ethics. Without a certain degree of independence we could not speak of moral obligation or an 'ought' at all. We would have only social conditioning, not morality. On the other hand, if we grant too much independence to moral ideas, the historical materialist claim to be able to trace these ideas in an empirical way from material conditions would not be tenable.

Marx's discussion of ruling ideas is important in this context. The ideas of the ruling class of any epoch express the dominant material relations of a given society. Since the ruling class controls the means of production, including the means of intellectual production—the media, educational institutions, and so forth—their ideas naturally will predominate. Thus, the ruling class will be the ruling intellectual force and the ideas of other classes will be subordinate.[28] This makes it quite clear that ideas are not determined exclusively or immediately, by material conditions. Ideas can also be determined by other ideas, especially ruling ideas.

In other places, Marx argues that ideologists can develop and elaborate existing ideas and that contradictions can emerge between the ideas of different classes or between sections of a single class due to contradictions within material conditions.[29] Thus, all ideas are the expression of material conditions, but conflicts can occur, ideas can be elaborated, and they can influence other ideas, though ideas can never contradict material conditions without a contradiction existing within the material conditions themselves.

Marx also admits that during a revolutionary period a small section of the ruling class can go over to the side of the revolutionary class. From this, however, it does not follow that they are able to make decisions independently of the influence of material conditions. They are able to reach such decisions, Marx says, because they have been able to comprehend theoretically the historical movement as a whole. Their decision has been conditioned by a clear and correct understanding of the development of material conditions. In Marx's discussion of the communist party we see much the same thing. The party does not

[28] *GI, MECW* V. 59, and *MEW* III. 46.
[29] *GI, MECW* V. 59-60, 363, and *MEW* III. 46-7, 347.

preach its own independent interests or principles (let alone ideals). It does not try to shape and mould the proletarian movement from outside. It merely studies, in a relatively passive and empirical way, the actual historical movement. The party understands this movement and communicates that understanding to other sectors of the proletariat.[30]

Marx's method for the study of material conditions and for the study of their transformation does not depend on moral ideas; in fact, even the method's dependence on theoretical ideas is mimimal. Marx says, 'Where speculation ends, where real life starts, there consequently begins real positive science'. For Marx, this involves

a summing-up of the most general results, abstractions which are derived from the observation of the historical development of men. These abstractions in themselves, divorced from real history, have no value whatsoever. They can only serve to facilitate the arrangement of historical material, to indicate the sequence of separate strata. But they by no means afford a recipe or schema, as does philosophy, for neatly trimming the epochs of history.[31]

Just as ideas have no independent effect on historical transformation, so, for Marx, in the science that studies this transformation, ideas have a similarly passive role. Scientific abstractions, categories, or theoretical concepts are generated by empirical study much as ordinary ideas are generated in history. These ideas arise from, express, and sum up the arrangement of the scientific material. Besides this, Marx says, they have no value whatsoever. They do not affect the material and they are not necessary in the way that some contemporary philosophers of science, like Kuhn, think that a paradigm is necessary for empirical study. Many contemporary philosophers of science argue that there are no ready-made facts. All observation interprets or constructs objects or facts and must rely on a theoretical paradigm to do so. Something of this view can be found in Marx's early writings and it is quite clear in the *Grundrisse*,[32] but it is rejected in the *German Ideology*.

Nevertheless, we have seen that ideas appear to be independent of or to determine material conditions. This is due to the development of division of labour—especially the separation of physical and mental labour—and due to the complexity of society—the possibility of conflict between classes and between sections of a single class. Marx's notion of ideology is a very complex one, but we can at least say that the term is used in two ways. First, it is used to designate the realm of ideas as

---

30 *Manifesto*, *MECW* VI. 494, 497-8, and *MEW* IV. 471-2, 474-5.
31 *GI*, *MECW* V. 37, and *MEW* III. 27.
32 *Marx' Method, Epistemology, and Humanism*, ch. 3.

opposed to the realm of material conditions. Second, and more narrowly, it is used often to designate the illusion that ideas are independent of and appear to determine material conditions when in fact only the reverse is so.[33] In the second case, when we attempt to trace ideas from material conditions, we do find that we can explain how their significance arises from these conditions. But there is at least one sense in which they are not accurate reflections of those conditions and thus not scientifically valid. They are false or distorted in so far as they appear independent and able to determine material conditions. In this, their function often is to assist domination. Thus, just to suggest that morality is ideology, as Marx does, is to suggest that morality is illusion, that is, that it is an illusion to think that moral principles can independently determine us or influence material conditions. If morality is ideology, it would seem that moral obligation is illusion. Marx says,

the conditions of existence of the ruling class (as determined by the preceding development of production), ideally expressed in law, morality, etc., to which [conditions] the ideologists of that class more or less consciously give a sort of theoretical independence; they can be conceived by separate individuals of that class as vocation, etc., and are held up as a standard of life to the individuals of the oppressed class, partly as an embellishment or recognition of domination, partly as a moral means for this domination. It is to be noted here, as in general with ideologists, that they inevitably put the thing upside-down and regard their ideology both as the creative force and as the aim of all social relations, whereas it is only an expression and symptom of these relations.[34]

We must recognize that Marx is concerned with morality in two ways. First, he must give a sociological or historical treatment of what morality actually has been for specific societies, what its content was, and how it arose and developed—morality must be traced from material conditions. But secondly, he also must analyse and come to a decision about moral obligation—does it actually exist and can it be justified or is it an ideological illusion? In the above passage the latter alternative is at least suggested—moral obligation has no independent effect and is merely a masked and distorted form of the interests of the ruling class

[33] *GI, MECW* V. 36, 379, and *MEW* III. 26, 363.
[34] *GI, MECW* V. 419-20, and *MEW* III. 405. See R. G. Peffer, 'Morality and the Marxist Concept of Ideology', *Marx and Morality*, ed. K. Nielsen and S. C. Patten, *Canadian Journal of Philosophy*, suppl. vol. 7 (1981), 67-91. Peffer lists and analyses eleven different defining characteristics of ideology and argues that morality is not ideological illusion for Marx. But Peffer does not discuss the crucial sense of ideology in which to hold that consciousness can determine material conditions is an ideological illusion.

determined by material conditions. This suggestion is even stronger in the following passage,

The more the normal form of intercourse of society, and with it the conditions of the ruling class, develop their contradiction to the advanced productive forces, and the greater the consequent discord within the ruling class itself as well as between it and the class ruled by it, the more fictitious, of course, becomes the consciousness which originally corresponded to this form of intercourse (i.e., it ceases to be the consciousness corresponding to this form of intercourse), and the more do the old traditional ideas of these relations of intercourse, in which actual private interests, etc., etc., are expressed as universal interests, descend to the level of mere idealising phrases, conscious illusion, deliberate hypocrisy. But the more their falsity is exposed by life, and the less meaning they have for consciousness itself, the more resolutely are they asserted, the more hypocritical, moral and holy becomes the language of this normal society.[35]

At least under the conditions described here, namely a contradiction between the traditional interests and the changing material conditions of the ruling class, moral obligation, for Marx, is illusion. In fact, the passage suggests that a strong sense of moral obligation is produced only when material conditions fail to determine behaviour in accordance with the interests of the ruling class. It also seems to be suggested that in periods where this contradiction is absent, a strong sense of moral obligation would not arise. In either case, moral obligation is illusion—it is not to be distinguished from the interests of the ruling class. In the *Communist Manifesto*, Marx explicitly says that, 'Law, morality, religion, are . . . so many bourgeois prejudices, behind which lurk in ambush just as many bourgeois interests.'[36]

Is Marx claiming that moral obligation is an illusion in certain cases or is he denying the existence of moral obligation altogether? If morality reduces to class prejudice and interest, if all consciousness is determined by material conditions, is there any room for moral obligation? In the *Holy Family*, Marx seemed to think so. In discussing the moral views of Helvétius, he said,

If man draws all his knowledge, sensation, etc., from the world of the senses and the experience gained in it, then what has to be done is to arrange the empirical world in such a way that man experiences and becomes accustomed to what is truly human in it and that he becomes aware of himself as man. If correctly understood interest is the principle of all morality, man's private interest must

---

[35] *GI, MECW* V. 293, and *MEW* III. 274.
[36] *Manifesto, MECW* VI. 494-5, and *MEW* IV. 472.

be made to coincide with the interest of humanity . . . . If man is shaped by environment, his environment must be made human.[37]

When Marx says that the empirical world must be made human, is he assuming that this humanizing will be determined by the same sort of causality as that through which the ordinary empirical world shapes and determines us, or rather that we can act independently of the empirical world and only thus transform the effect that it has on us? MacIntyre points out that the latter view is rejected in the 'Theses on Feuerbach'. Marx says, 'The materialist doctrine concerning the changing of circumstances and upbringing forgets that circumstances are changed by men and that the educator must himself be educated. This doctrine must, therefore, divide society into two parts, one of which is superior to society.'[38] Here, Marx is pointing out that the activity of educating the educator (or of humanizing the empirical world) presupposes a part of society which is superior to the ordinary materialistically determined processes of society, and he rejects such a view.

The question, then, is whether Marx continues to reject this view in the *German Ideology*. Is it even possible for new moral ideas to arise which will influence the transformation of society, when, as Marx says, changes in consciousness will only 'be affected by altered circumstances, not by theoretical deductions'?[39] Can moral principles arise which are capable of contradicting existing conditions enough to be able to transform those conditions when put into practice? The question here is not whether material interests contradictory to society can arise. Marx admits and explains this possibility. It is even the case for Marx that the material interests of the proletariat, generated and supported by material conditions, will lead to the overthrow of existing society. Our problem is whether or not there is room for a *moral* dimension in this process. Is this historical process exclusively a process of material conditions (and interests which arise from and express those conditions) that can be studied as empirical fact, or can values and moral obligations somehow arise from or be derived from this empirical process? Will moral obligation even arise after communism is achieved? Since Marx has abandoned a concept of essence, that particular approach to linking facts and values is no longer open to him. Does he have another way to do this or does he simply abandon morality? After all, he even

---

[37] *HF, MECW* IV. 130-1, and *MEW* II. 137-8.
[38] *TF, MECW* V. 4, and *MEW* III. 5-6. A. MacIntyre, *After Virtue* (University of Notre Dame Press, 1981), 81.
[39] *GI, MECW* V. 56, and *MEW* III. 40.

denies that his own science can or should appeal to any theoretical concepts other than those which reflect sheer empirical observation. We must search carefully for the possibility of moral obligation as we proceed, but I do not think we shall find it.

In the *German Ideology*, Marx again discusses the reconciliation of particular interests with the common interest, but unlike his earlier treatment of Helvétius in the *Holy Family* he no longer sees it as a moral goal and he does not mention education or reform. For Marx, the development of the division of labour and private property implies a contradiction between the interests of individuals and the common interests of those who interact with one another. Marx uses the term 'common interest' to refer to those interests actually shared by individuals and determined by the material conditions of society. The term 'general interest', on the other hand, refers to shared interests which are imaginary or illusory. There is a real contradiction between particular interests and common interests, and the latter come to be represented by state power divorced from individual interests in society. At the level of the state, struggles take place over issues like democracy, aristocracy, monarchy, and the franchise. These struggles are concerned with the 'general interest', which is merely the illusory form of the common interest. By this Marx seems to mean that struggle over abstract general interests at the political level will never succeed in actually reconciling particular interests with the common interest—that would require reconciliation at the socio-economic level. The task is not to achieve reforms at the political level but rather to reconcile particular interests with the common interest in society, and this requires a radical transformation of the material conditions of society. Private property, specialization in the division of labour, classes, and state power must be overcome.[40]

Marx still agrees with Helvétius that particular interests and the common interest must agree, but thinks this will require an actual revolutionary transformation of society, not mere reform or education (which might however be enough to reconcile particular interests with an illusory general interest at the political level). Nor does Marx's programme seem to have much to do with morality. In another passage, he argues that the specific sort of conflict that actually occurs between particular interests and the common interest will determine in an empirical way whether an individual appears more as an egoist or more selfless. Then, in criticizing Stirner, Marx says,

[40] *GI, MECW* V. 46-7, 61, and *MEW* III. 32-3, 48.

Communism is quite incomprehensible to our saint because the communists do not oppose egoism to selflessness or selflessness to egoism, nor do they express this contradiction theoretically either in its sentimental or in its highflown ideological form; they rather demonstrate its material source, with which it disappears of itself. The communists do not preach *morality* at all, as Stirner does so extensively. They do not put to people the moral demand: love one another, do not be egoists, etc.; on the contrary, they are very well aware that egoism, just as much as selflessness, *is* in definite circumstances a necessary form of the self-assertion of individuals.[41]

This passage makes it clear that for Marx communists do not appeal to moral obligation, but this alone does not tell us whether or not moral obligation exists. However, Marx goes further. He argues that if the material source of the ideological contradiction between egoism and selflessness is revealed, 'it disappears of itself'. What disappears? Certainly it cannot be the material conditions which generate egoism or selflessness, nor even the egoism or selflessness generated by these conditions. To hold either of these positions would be to hold that a demonstration of the material source of this contradiction—a mere theoretical demonstration or conceptual deduction—could change the world. Such a view is repeatedly ruled out by Marx's historical materialism. What disappears then can be only our tendency to understand and express the conflict between egoism and selflessness in an ideological form—as a *moral* issue. The moral or ideological issue is reduced to a practical matter of material conditions. As Marx says elsewhere, the task is to reduce philosophical problems to problems of empirical fact.[42] This seems to suggest that the reason why communists do not appeal to moral obligation is because historical materialism allows us to see through it. Marx also denies that moral demands are capable of altering our consciousness.[43] Thus moral obligation certainly seems to be ideological illusion.

Marx holds similar views with regard to laws, rights, crime, and punishment. He tells us that communists are opposed to laws and to the rights of man. Laws are the expression of the interests and prejudices of the class in power which are determined by the economic conditions of existence of that class.[44] He also says,

[41] *GI, MECW* V. 245-7, also see pp. 250, 262-3, and *MEW* III. 227-9, 232, 245-6.

[42] *GI, MECW* V. 39, and *MEW* III. 43. In a passage crossed out in the final MS, Marx says, 'The communists are the only people through whose historical activity the liquefaction of fixed desires and ideas is in fact brought about and ceases to be an impotent moral injunction' (*GI, MECW* V. 255 n., and *MEW* III. 238 n.).

[43] *GI, MECW* V. 250, and *MEW* III. 232.

[44] *GI, MECW* V. 209, and *MEW* III. 190. *Manifesto, MECW* VI. 494-5, 501, and *MEW* III. 472, 477.

But society is not founded upon the law; that is a legal fiction. On the contrary, the law must be founded upon society, it must express the common interests and needs of society—as distinct from the caprice of the individuals—which arise from the material mode of production prevailing at the given time. This *Code Napoléon*, which I am holding in my hand, has not created modern bourgeois society. On the contrary, bourgeois society . . . merely finds its legal expression in this Code. As soon as it ceases to fit the social relations, it becomes simply a bundle of paper.[45]

Marx tells us that ideologists try to give laws the appearance of theoretical independence from material conditions as if they were a creative force in society, but this is to turn things upside down.[46] Laws arise from material conditions and are used as a means of domination; they are the expression of the will of a class which is given a universal expression as the will of the state. The state as a separate dominating force is an organizational form necessary to the bourgeoisie as a means of guaranteeing its property and as the form through which the individuals of the ruling class assert their common interest. The notion that law is based upon free will—a will which is independent of its basis in material conditions and interests—is an illusion. For Marx, justice is reduced to statute law and law is the expression of interests.[47] Thus laws seem to have nothing to do with right or moral obligation. They are the expression of class interest determined by material conditions.

Marx treats rights much as he does laws and rejects them for the same reasons.[48] However, he does say, 'But in reality the proletarians arrive at this unity only through a long process of development in which the appeal to their right also plays a part. Incidentally, this appeal to their right is *only* a means of making them take shape as 'they', as a revolutionary united mass.'[49] Marx does not hold that rights are morally grounded. Rights, like laws, are merely the expression of material conditions at a particular stage of their development. The appeal to rights may help to unite the proletariat as a class but rights have no moral significance.

Marx tells us that crime is also determined by material conditions. He says that crime is due to the 'the fundamental conditions of modern

[45] 'The Trial of the Rhenish Committee of Democrats', *MECW* VIII. 327-8, and *MEW* VI. 245. See also *GI, MECW* V. 329, and *MEW* III. 311.

[46] *GI, MECW* V. 419-20, and *MEW* III. 405.

[47] *GI, MECW* V. 90-1, 329, and *MEW* III. 62-3, 311. *Manifesto, MECW* VI. 501, and *MEW* IV. 477.

[48] *GI, MECW* V. 209-10, 327, and *MEW* III. 190-1, 309. See also *HF, MECW* IV. 113-14, and *MEW* II. 120.

[49] *GI, MECW* V. 323 (my emphasis), and *MEW* III. 305.

bourgeois society in general, which produce an average amount of crime in a given national fraction of society'.[50] For this reason, Marx had opposed punishment in the *Holy Family*: 'crime must not be punished in the individual, but the anti-social sources of crime must be destroyed'.[51] In reviewing an article on capital punishment in 1853, Marx says,

It is astonishing that the article in question does not even produce a single argument or pretext for indulging in the savage theory therein propounded; and it would be very difficult, if not altogether impossible, to establish any principle upon which the justice or expediency of capital punishment could be founded, in a society glorying in its civilization. Punishment in general has been defended as a means either of ameliorating or of intimidating. Now what right have you to punish me for the amelioration or intimidation of others?[52]

This passage raises two important issues which might appear to contradict the interpretation of Marx's views on morality that I have been arguing for. When Marx says that it would be difficult if not impossible to establish a moral principle or a principle of expediency which could justify capital punishment (perhaps even punishment in general), is he actually leaving open the possibility of morally justifying punishment? Second, it might even seem that Marx's own argument against punishment is a moral argument. It is possible that here Marx has started to become dissatisfied with his rejection of morality. Later in this chapter we will see that such a claim might also be made with regard to other articles he wrote in 1853. Nevertheless, let us see if his views here are compatible with those of the *German Ideology*. Let us examine the review of 1853. Marx first rejects arguments from expediency. He denies that punishment actually improves, ameliorates, or intimidates the criminal.[53] Even if it did, he argues, it cannot give you a right to punish me. Is this a moral argument? In the *Holy Family*, Marx did seem to object to punishment on moral grounds. No one had a right to punish an individual because the individual was not responsible—society was the real source of crime.[54] In the *German Ideology*, we have found no appeal to moral principles and that such appeals are frequently rejected. Has Marx in 1853 returned to the view of the *Holy Family*?

[50] 'Capital Punishment', *MECW* XI. 497, and *MEW* VIII. 509; see also *GI, MECW* V. 530, and *MEW* III. 312.
[51] *HF, MECW* IV. 131, and *MEW* II. 138.
[52] 'Capital Punishment', *MECW* XI. 496, and *MEW* VIII. 507.
[53] Ibid. See also *HF, MECW* IV. 177, and *MEW* II. 188.
[54] *HF, MECW* IV. 131, 179, and *MEW* II. 138, 190.

One possible reason why there might be no right to punish could be because such a right cannot be derived from or would contradict actual principles of right—principles which Marx might be holding do exist. Or it may be instead that Marx is holding that there can be no right to punish simply because there are no principles of right at all and thus nothing to derive a right to punish from (nor even any plausible pretext in a civilized society). Marx's position is simply not clear in the passage which has been quoted.

In the following passage of the review of 1853 (and there is a parallel text in the *Holy Family*). Marx goes on to suggest that the best theory of punishment is that of Kant and Hegel,

From the point of view of abstract right, there is only one theory of punishment which recognizes human dignity in the abstract, and that is the theory of Kant, especially in the more rigid formula given to it by Hegel. Hegel says: 'Punishment is the *right* of the criminal. It is an act of his own will. The violation of right has been proclaimed by the criminal as his own right. His crime is the negation of right. Punishment is the negation of the negation, and consequently an affirmation of right, solicited and forced upon the criminal by himself.'[55]

In the immediately following passage of the 1853 review, Marx goes on to reject this theory of punishment,

There is no doubt something specious in this formula, inasmuch as Hegel, instead of looking upon the criminal as the mere object, the slave of justice, elevates him to the position of a free and self-determined being. Looking, however, more closely into the matter, we discover that German idealism here, as in most other instances, has but given a transcendental sanction to the rules of existing society. Is it not a delusion to substitute for the individual with his real motives, with multifarious social circumstances pressing upon him, the abstraction of 'free-will'—one among many qualities of man for man himself! This theory, considering punishment as the result of the criminal's own will, is only a metaphysical expression for the old 'jus talionis': eye against eye, tooth against tooth, blood against blood. Plainly speaking, and dispensing with all paraphrases, punishment is nothing but a means of society to defend itself against the infraction of its vital conditions, whatever may be their character.[56]

[55] 'Capital Punishment', *MECW* XI. 496, and *MEW* VIII. 507. See also *HF, MECW* IV. 179, and *MEW* II. 190. 'Wood Theft', *MECW* I. 229, and *MEW* I. 114. *PR* 70-3, and *GPR* 95-9.

[56] 'Capital Punishment', *MECW* XI. 496-7, and *MEW* VIII. 508.

This rejection of punishment is not based upon an appeal to moral principles nor does it assume the existence of such principles. Attempts at the moral justification of punishment merely reflect material conditions; they attempt to give those conditions a transcendental moral sanction; and this attempt is specious. Marx does suggest that Hegel's moral justification of punishment fails because it relies on a concept of free will and free will is an illusion. This reminds us of the argument in the *Holy Family* to the effect that we must not punish the individual who cannot be held responsible, because society is the real source of crime. In the *Holy Family*, Marx still believed in morality and this seemed to be a moral argument. But in 1853, Marx's argument is only a negative one. It points out that, in order to give a moral justification of punishment, Hegel assumed the existence of free will. Since free will is an illusion, Hegel has not established a right to punish. Marx does not argue that we have a moral obligation *not* to punish or even that punishment conflicts with moral principles we do or should hold. Perhaps it is the exclusively negative character of his argument that causes Marx to leave open the possibility of justifying punishment. After all, he has merely ruled out existing arguments for it. Or perhaps he is just employing a rhetorical device to avoid the appearance of dogmatism. Or perhaps here in 1853 he is taking the first hesitant step towards considering the possibility of morality—something we will notice again in other articles of 1853 and will consider later in this chapter. But, if so, he has not moved very far towards morality. In these passages he bases nothing on moral arguments and he clearly rejects free will.

In the *Holy Family*, Marx suggests that in communist society punishment will not exist,

under human conditions punishment will really be nothing but the sentence passed by the culprit on himself. No one will want to convince him that violence from without, done to him by others, is violence which he had done to himself. On the contrary, he will see in other men his natural saviours from the punishment which he has imposed on himself; in other words, the relation will be reversed.[57]

This passage is not perfectly clear, but it seems to suggest that in a society attempting to root out the social causes of crime, the individual will feel that others are working to save him or her from the possibility of punishment.

[57] *HF, MECW* IV. 179, and *MEW* II. 190.

III

How can we characterize Marx's views on ethics? They have been called a form of utilitarianism. In the *German Ideology*, Marx traces the development of utilitarianism from Hobbes and Locke, Helvétius and Holbach, to Bentham and James Mill, and he rejects it:

The apparent absurdity of merging all the manifold relationships of people in the one relation of usefulness, this apparently metaphysical abstraction arises from the fact that in modern bourgeois society all relations are subordinated in practice to the one abstract monetary-commercial relation. . . . Now these relations are supposed not to have the meaning peculiar to them but to be the expression and manifestation of some third relation attributed to them, the relation of utility or utilisation . . . the utility relation has a quite definite meaning, namely, that I derive benefit for myself by doing harm to someone else (exploitation of man by man) . . . for him [the bourgeois] only one relation is valid on its own account—the relation of exploitation; all other relations have validity for him only insofar as he can include them under this one relation; and even where he encounters relations which cannot be directly subordinated to the relation of exploitation, he subordinates them to it at least in his imagination . . . Incidentally, one sees at a glance that the category of 'utilisation' is first abstracted from the actual relations of intercourse which I have with other people (but by no means from reflection and mere will) and then these relations are made out to be the reality of the category that has been abstracted from them themselves, a wholly metaphysical method of procedure. . . . Hence Holbach's theory is the historically justified philosophical illusion about the bourgeoisie just then developing in France, whose thirst for exploitation could still be regarded as a thirst for the full development of individuals in conditions of intercourse freed from the old feudal fetters.[58]

If Marx is assuming that all utilitarians hold that individuals should seek to benefit themselves at the expense of others, he is mistaken. Nevertheless, his main point is still a good one. His argument against utilitarianism is very similar to one of his arguments against the concept of essence. He objects to abstracting or singling out one characteristic of human activity, a single relationship to things, and taking that as the essence of all other characteristics and relations.[59]

[58] *GI, MECW* V. 409-10, also pp. 411-14, and *MEW* III. 394-5, 395-9.

[59] See *GI, MECW* V. 512, and *MEW* III. 500. Also 'Capital Punishment', *MECW* XI. 496-7, and *MEW* VIII. 508. It has been argued that, despite Marx's rejection of utilitarianism, he mischaracterizes that theory and is in fact himself a utilitarian. I do not think that is the case. I hope to show that Marx rejects the notion that we have any moral obligations and thus cannot hold a utilitarian theory of ethics. See D. Allen, 'The Utilitarianism of Marx and Engels', *American Philosophical Quarterly*, 10 (1973), 189-99. Allen's article has provoked some debate. See also G. G. Brenkert, 'Marx and

Utilitarian theorists usually approach ethics by engaging in a sociology of morals and by developing a theory of moral obligation. In other words, they claim both that the principle of utility describes the way in which people actually do behave and that it prescribes how they ought to behave.[60] We can see from the passage just quoted, and the passages immediately following it in that work, that Marx in a limited way is willing to accept utilitarianism as a sociology of morals. He admits that it is capable of describing with some accuracy a limited range of human behaviour, characteristic of certain classes in specific historical periods, though he denies that it is an accurate description of all behaviour at all times. Historical materialism is a broader and subtler theory than utilitarianism which it undercuts. It traces utilitarianism's development and claims that it is conditioned by and is the expression of existing material conditions, but denies that all relations can be characterized as relations of utility or all behaviour as determined by considerations of utility. On the other hand, in the *German Ideology* Marx completely rejects utilitarianism as a theory of moral obligation. As we saw earlier, and as I hope to show further, historical materialism denies the existence of moral obligation.

It may seem even more likely that Marx's views on ethics could be characterized as a form of egoism. In the *Holy Family*, he said, in discussing Helvétius, that 'correctly understood interest is the principle of all morality', and in the *German Ideology* he talks of reconciling particular interests with the common interest.[61] He even seems to come close to holding a principle of psychological egoism when he says that 'no one can do anything without at the same time doing it for the sake of one or other of his needs'.[62] However, in several places, Marx makes his opposition to egoism quite clear. He denies that individuals are or should be determined exclusively by egoistic motives and he claims that under communism the individual's consciousness of social relations will be changed such that the principle which motivates the individual 'will no more be the "principle of love" or devotion than it will be egoism'. He holds that whether an individual appears more an egoist or more selfless depends upon material conditions and he claims that the

Utilitarianism', *Canadian Journal of Philosophy*, 5 (1975), 421-34; D. Allen, 'Reply to Brenkert's "Marx and Utilitarianism"', *Canadian Journal of Philosophy*, 6 (1976), 517-34; G. G. Brenkert, 'Marx's Critique of Utilitarianism', *Marx and Morality*, pp. 193-220.

[60] e.g. J. S. Mill, *Utilitarianism* (Indianapolis: Bobbs-Merrill, 1957), 44-8.

[61] HF, *MECW* IV. 130, and *MEW* II. 137. GI, *MECW* V. 46-8, 60-1, and *MEW* III. 32-4, 47-8.

[62] GI, *MECW* V. 255, and *MEW* III. 238.

ideological issue of a moral conflict between egoism and selflessness is dissolved as soon as it is traced to its source in material conditions.[63]

Marx not only denies that we can speak of egoistic motives apart from the determination of material conditions but he holds that we cannot even speak of an ego apart from such conditions, 'If for a moment Sancho abstracts from all his thoughts ... there remains his real ego, but his real ego within the framework of the actual relations of the world that exist for it.'[64] After thinking away all our thoughts, we are left with an ego conditioned by its social relations. Somehow, an ego that is not given to us in the content of any thought remains and this ego, it seems to be suggested, will have a certain character due to its actual relations, relations which, it appears, structure the ego despite the fact that we have abstracted away all thoughts including thoughts of these relations. Whatever problems might be involved here, it is clear that for Marx the ego is determined by material conditions and thus an ethical theory which holds that egoistic motives determine our behaviour independently of material conditions would be rejected.

Marx also discusses and rejects hedonism. He argues that the forms of enjoyment characteristic of any period arise and must be traced from material conditions.[65] We are determined by material conditions, not by a desire for enjoyments or pleasures independent of those conditions.

Historical materialism undercuts all of these ethical theories by showing that material conditions can give rise to motives and behaviour other than what the theories would indicate and by denying that the ethical principles which they propose can be established independently of material conditions. In general, Marx is opposed to reducing all motives or behaviour to a single type. However, he is willing to admit that each of these theories is able to describe and explain a range of behaviour in certain historical periods. These ethical theories have a limited value as sociology of morals, but none at all as theories of moral obligation. In fact, if we cannot establish the existence of moral obligation, we must conclude that historical materialism reduces all ethical theory to the sociology of morals.

We have already seen that in the *German Ideology* Marx rejects the concept of essence he had held earlier. We must now see that he also rejects Kantian ethics. Marx tells us that Kant's *Critique of Practical Reason* arose from and reflected the state of affairs existing in Germany

---

[63] *GI, MECW* V. 246-7, 248, 255, 329, 439, and *MEW* III. 228-9, 230, 237-8, 311-12, 425.

[64] *GI, MECW* V. 434, also p. 289, and *MEW* III. 419, 270.

[65] *GI, MECW* V. 417-19, 465, and *MEW* III. 402-3, 452.

at the end of the eighteenth century. Economically, Germany was backward by comparison with other European countries. The conflicting interests of its petty bourgeoisie had not developed into the common national interest of a class. Germany was also backward in its agricultural methods, industrial technology, and commerce. It was fragmented into numerous small principalities and free imperial cities. It lacked the economic conditions for political concentration and thus, during the period of absolute monarchy, the state bureaucracy in Germany acquired an abnormal independence; this explains the apparent independence of German theoreticians in relation to middle-class interests,

The characteristic form which French liberalism, based on real class interests, assumed in Germany we find again in Kant. Neither he, nor the German middle class, whose whitewashing spokesman he was, noticed that these theoretical ideas of the bourgeoisie had as their basis material interests and a will that was conditioned and determined by the material relations of production. Kant, therefore, separated this theoretical expression from the interests which it expressed; he made the materially motivated determinations of the will of the French bourgeois into pure self-determinations of 'free-will', of the will in and for itself, of the human will, and so converted it into purely ideological conceptual determinations and moral postulates.[66]

This passage suggests that moral obligation and a free will taken to be undetermined by material conditions are pure ideological illusions.

While the French Revolution was actually conquering Europe and while the British were revolutionizing industry and subjugating India, the impotent German, Marx says, 'did not get any further than "good will". Kant was satisfied with "good will" alone, even if it remained entirely without result, and he transferred the realisation of this good will, the harmony between it and the needs and impulses of individuals, to the world beyond.'[67] What occurred in Germany was that,

the political forms corresponding to a developed bourgeoisie were passed on to the Germans from outside by the July revolution . . . Since German economic relations had by no means reached the stage of development to which these political forms corresponded, the middle class accepted them merely as abstract ideas, principles valid in and for themselves, pious wishes and phrases, Kantian self-determinations of the will and of human beings as they ought to be. Consequently their attitude to these forms was far more moral and disinterested

---

[66] *GI, MECW* V. 193-5, and *MEW* III. 176-8.
[67] *GI, MECW* V. 193, and *MEW* III. 176-7. See also *Class Struggles in France, MECW* X. 114, and *MEW* VII. 76.

than that of other nations, i.e., they exhibited a highly peculiar narrowmindedness and remained unsuccessful in all their endeavours.[68]

Both here and in the 'Introduction to the Critique of Hegel's Philosophy of Law' of 1843, Marx agrees that Kantian morality reflected the state of affairs in Germany after the French Revolution. But in 1843, Marx thought that Kantian ethics would explain, morally justify, and help produce a proletarian revolution in Germany. The needs of the proletariat accorded with the categorical imperative to eliminate all relations in which 'man [was not] the highest being for man'.[69] In the *German Ideology*, Kantian morality reflects the material interests of the rising bourgeoisie in France and England. These interests, determined by material conditions, were real forces of social transformation. The principles of Kantian ethics, on the other hand, were ideological ideas or pious wishes which were separated from material conditions and thus had no effect on historical development.

There is another difference between the 'Introduction to the Critique of Hegel's Philosophy of Law' and the *German Ideology*. In both texts Marx recognizes Germany's social, economic, and political backwardness. Despite this, he held in the 'Introduction' of 1843 that, philosophically, Germany was the most advanced of nations. Marx was concerned with this sort of gap in 1843, in the *German Ideology*, and again in the *Grundrisse*, where he tries to explain how Greek art could be in advance of its material conditions.[70] In the 'Introduction' of 1843, Marx argues that this gap would not hinder but actually would help produce a proletarian revolution in Germany. Advanced philosophical ideals, ideals of freedom, would fit the needs of the proletariat. Philosophy would be the head and the proletariat the heart of this revolution.[71] In the *German Ideology*, Marx gives a much more sophisticated historical explanation of Germany's backwardness and, if we still can call it that, of Germany's 'advanced' philosophy. At the same time he rejects the notion that philosophical ideas have any power to transform material conditions. In fact, it is at least suggested in the passages quoted above

---

[68] *GI, MECW* V. 196, and *MEW* III. 179.

[69] *CHPLI, MECW* III. 180-2, and *MEW* I. 383-5.

[70] *CHPLI, MECW* III. 176-87, and *MEW* I. 379-91. *GI, MECW* V. 193-7, and *MEW* III. 176-80. *G* 110-11, and *GKPO* 30-1. In the *Grundrisse*, Marx thinks that Greek art was in advance of its material conditions. It constitutes a norm and an unattainable model, yet it occurred at an undeveloped stage of social organization. This lack of development allowed the imagination a great deal of scope and thus allowed for high art (also see below, Ch. 4, sect. i). In the *German Ideology*, Marx resists this sort of conclusion.

[71] *CHPLI, MECW* III. 182-7, and *MEW* I. 385-91.

that Marx no longer thinks that German philosophy (at least Kant's) is to be considered advanced. In abstracting so radically from material conditions, it is impotent ideology which, rather than being in advance of German backwardness, actually reflects it. In the *German Ideology*, it is not philosophy but science which is the advanced form of consciousness; Marx says, 'Philosophy and the study of the actual world have the same relation to one another as onanism and sexual love.'[72]

IV

Marx also changes his mind about what it means to call the proletariat a universal class. In the 'Introduction to the Critique of Hegel's Philosophy of Law', he argued that for any class to make a revolution it had to appear as the general representative of society. Any class, the bourgeoisie included, seeks domination in order to assert its own particular class interest, but to achieve this, its particular interests for a time must coincide with the interests of other classes. After this class assumes power, its interests then would diverge from those of other lower classes. The proletariat, however, was different. It was so oppressed, and thus its needs were so basic, that its needs were truly universalizable—the sorts of needs which the categorical imperative would demand be satisfied in order to realize 'man [as] the highest being for man'. In freeing itself, the proletariat would free all human beings and its actions would accord with universal principles of morality. Universal philosophical ideals would be the head of this revolution and the particular needs of the proletariat would be its heart.[73] Thus, the proletariat would be truly a universal class. In the *German Ideology*, Marx ridicules a similar view put forth by Stirner. He rejects the notion that freedom is achieved by forming a concept of the 'ideal man' and then setting about the task of realizing it in society: 'In reality, of course, what happened was that people won freedom for themselves each time to the extent that it was dictated and permitted not by their ideal of man, but by the existing productive forces.' Since the productive forces, hitherto in history, have not been sufficient to provide for all of society, only some persons were able to satisfy their needs at the expense of others.[74]

In the *German Ideology*, Marx continues to argue that the proletariat

[72] *GI*, *MECW* V. 236, and *MEW* III. 218.
[73] *CHPLI*, *MECW* III. 182-7, and *MEW* I. 385-91. See also *HF*, *MECW* IV. 36-7, and *MEW* II. 38.
[74] *GI*, *MECW* V. 431-2, and *MEW* III. 417.

is a universal class but in doing so he carefully avoids any discussion of morality, ideals, or the categorical imperative. Instead, he refashions his argument along historical materialist lines and makes it considerably more complex. The productive forces of society, which at first are supported by the relations of production, eventually develop to the point where they come into conflict with these relations of production and thus become destructive. The conditions under which the productive forces can be applied and which are the conditions for the rule of a certain class thus are undermined. This gives rise to a polarization between classes and increasingly intolerable poverty for the lower class. A revolution then is set in motion. Only in the practical process of a revolution can the consciousness of the revolutionary class be transformed and developed. In this way—in a proletarian revolution—a communist consciousness arises.[75] But in any revolution, since

the conditions of life of an individual always coincided with the conditions of life of a class, when, therefore, the practical task of each newly emerging class was bound to appear to each of its members as a universal task, and when each class could actually overthrow its predecessor only by liberating the individuals of all classes from certain chains which had hitherto fettered them—under these circumstances it was essential that the task of the individual members of a class striving for domination should be described as a universal human task.[76]

Moreover, since the class coming to power would not be fully developed yet, 'its interest really is as yet mostly connected with the common interest of all other non-ruling classes, because under the pressure of hitherto existing conditions its interest has not yet been able to develop as the particular interest of a particular class'. The emerging ruling class thus can serve as the general representative of society and thus at least appear as a universal class, 'Every new class, therefore, achieves domination only on a broader basis than that of the class ruling previously; on the other hand the opposition of the non-ruling class to the new ruling class then develops all the more sharply and profoundly.'[77] The interests of the ruling class, which are based upon the conditions under which it can rule, are then thought of as having an independent existence as general interests and are conceived of as ideal interests. They are given a universal form in law and are enforced against conflicting particular interests. This must be the case if the ruling class

[75] *GI, MECW* V. 48-9, 52-3, and *MEW* III. 34-5, 69-70. *Manifesto, MECW* VI. 489–90, and *MEW* IV. 467–8. Also *Critique of Political Economy* (*CPE*), trans. S. W. Ryazanskaya (London: Lawrence & Wishart, 1971), 20-2, and *MEW* XIII. 8-10.

[76] *GI, MECW* V. 290, and *MEW* III. 271.

[77] *GI, MECW* V. 61, and *MEW* III. 48.

is to preserve the material conditions necessary for its rule—conditions which are common to many individuals.[78]

On the other hand, the proletariat will become a truly universal class—but not immediately. In any society with private property, division of labour, and classes, particular interests will diverge from the common interest and the state will have to enforce the common interest in the form of an illusory general interest opposed to particular interests. Even the proletariat, Marx thinks, when it first comes to power, will be forced into this position. At this stage, the proletariat's universality as a class resembles the quasi-universality of the bourgeoisie. This will be the case until private property, specialization in the division of labour, and classes are eliminated.[79]

Thus, as the conflict between the forces and relations of production produces a polarization of classes and the pauperization of the proletariat, the proletariat will be forced towards revolution—towards an appropriation of the productive forces—if they are to safeguard their existence. The proletariat then will be transformed into a truly universal class, not by ideals, philosophy, or a categorical imperative, but due to their class interest and due to the nature of the existing forces of production,

This appropriation is first determined by the object to be appropriated, the productive forces, which have been developed to a totality and which only exist within a universal intercourse. Even from this aspect alone, therefore, this appropriation must have a universal character corresponding to the productive forces and the intercourse. The appropriation of these forces is itself nothing more than the development of the individual capacities corresponding to the material instruments of production. The appropriation of a totality of instruments of production is, for this very reason, the development of a totality of capacities in the individuals themselves ... in the appropriation by the proletarians, a mass of instruments of production must be made subject to each individual, and property to all. Modern universal intercourse cannot be controlled by individuals, unless it is controlled by all.

This appropriation is further determined by the manner in which it must be effected. It can only be effected through a union, which by the character of the proletariat itself can only be a universal one . . .[80]

To control a complex totality of productive forces, the controllers will have to develop in themselves the capacities necessary to do this

[78] *GI*, *MECW* V. 329, and *MEW* III. 311-312.
[79] *GI*, *MECW* V. 46-8, 51-2, 61, 245-7, and *MEW* III. 32-4, 37, 48, 327-9.
[80] *GI*, *MECW* V. 87-8, and *MEW* III. 67-8.

controlling, and the more complex the productive forces, the more complex individual development will have to be. Thus the proletariat will be forced to educate itself and unfold its powers and capacities simply in order to safeguard its existence. It is not immediately clear, however, why this control must take the form of a co-operative union. This can be explained by examining Marx's concept of alienation in exchange. If production is carried out privately—if there is a division of labour at this level—and if products are brought to a market where they are exchanged, then market laws will set in and will come to control the process of exchange independently of the will of any of the individuals involved. These laws will also come to control production, which, after all, depends upon the market. Eventually the forces of production will come into contradiction with the relations of production and crises will occur. For individuals to end this estrangement, Marx thinks, they must end private production (thus private ownership and division of labour at this level) and they must do away with private, unregulated commodity exchange. They must consciously and co-operatively control production and distribution.[81] Thus, they will be forced by material circumstances toward this communist solution and toward a communist consciousness.

The proletariat is not a universal class because its universalizable needs fit an ideal or accord with a categorical imperative, but for two basic reasons. First, Marx says that any class achieves domination on a broader basis than earlier classes in the sense that its class interests represent more universally the interests of other classes. For the proletariat, this universality eventually will be complete. In the *German Ideology*, Marx expects the proletariat to come to power as a majority,[82] and he expects it eventually to reconcile the particular interests of individuals with the common interest by ending private property, specialization in the division of labour, and eventually even by ending classes themselves. The particular interests of the proletariat will drive it to bring about the common interest of all in a classless, collective, and co-operative society. All of this will be determined by material conditions, not moral ideals. It is true that both here and in 1843 the interests of the proletariat are taken to be universalizable, but in the *German Ideology* this is understood only as the outcome of material conditions. Universalizability does not function as a moral justification

[81] *CM, MECW* III. 216-27, and *MEW*, suppl. I. 451-61. *GI, MECW* V. 47-8, and *MEW* III. 33-4. *Capital*, I. 71-6, and *MEW* XXIII. 85-90.
[82] *GI, MECW* V. 48-9, and *MEW* III. 34-5.

nor is it intended to assert the pull of a moral ideal. Second, the proletariat is a universal class because it will come to control the totality of productive forces which exist within a universal intercourse and, to do so, individuals will have to develop their capacities universally. This does not mean that at the point when the proletariat comes to power, or any time soon thereafter, the forces of production or the capacities of individuals will have reached their universal—their fullest—development. The forces of production under capitalism have become a very complex, world-wide, interconnected, and interdependent totality, which along with the capacities necessary to control them, of course, can continue to develop under the proletariat. The proletariat is a universal class not because its forces of production are universally developed but because for the first time in history it will finally be able to bring this totality of productive forces completely—universally—under the control of human beings who develop the capacities to do this. It asserts its control universally and thus achieves real freedom.

It is true that such universality is necessary for freedom, but it is no longer the case that freedom is understood as it was in 1843-4 or as it was for Kant. In the *German Ideology*, Marx makes a shift which is rarely noticed by commentators. He changes his mind about what freedom means. In a passage which was crossed out in the final draft of the *German Ideology* but the point of which is made elsewhere in that text, Marx says,

Up to now freedom has been defined by philosophers in two ways; on the one hand, as power, as domination over the circumstances and conditions in which an individual lives—by all materialists; on the other hand, as self-determination, riddance of the real world, as merely imaginary freedom of the spirit—this definition was given by all idealists, especially the German idealists.

Marx is claiming that philosophers have defined freedom in two different ways—as control and as self-determination. Marx accepts the former definition but not the latter. He also rejects self-determination in a passage already quoted above, 'There is no doubt something specious in this formula, inasmuch as Hegel, instead of looking upon the criminal as the mere object, the slave of justice, elevates him to the position of a free and self-determined being.' In another passage quoted above, Marx rejects Kantian self-determination as a purely ideological conception. Moreover, in many places Marx rejects the notion of a free will. If free will is impossible, so then is self-determination.[83] It is clear that Marx now rejects the Kantian concept of freedom as self-determination (which was a part of his concept of freedom in the early writings). He accepts only the concept of freedom as control (which he had also seemed to include in his earlier concept of freedom).[84] Marx now says, 'All-round dependence, this primary natural form of the world-historical co-operation of individuals, will be transformed by this communist revolution into the control and conscious mastery of these powers, which born of the action of men on one another, have till now overawed and ruled men as powers completely alien to them.'[85]

Thus, these two forms of freedom can help us to understand what Marx means when he says that under capitalism individuals appear freer than before but are in fact to a greater extent determined by material conditions.[86] Due to competition, division of labour, and the seemingly accidental nature of intercourse in a market economy, the individual's will seems to be able to act arbitrarily within a wide field of choice, self-determination seems present and significant, yet individuals do not control the increasingly more powerful forces and relations of production which determine them. Until they do, they will be free in an imaginary, not a real, way.

We can also see why Marx claims that it is only in a community that individuals can become free. Marx has argued that, given the complex nature of the forces of production in modern society, they can be controlled only if individuals organize themselves collectively.[87] Thus, Marx's argument is no longer a moral argument as it was in 1844; community is no longer necessary because it realizes the human essence and freedom. Community is necessary to control the forces and relations of production. The proletariat will be forced to control them to safeguard its existence, and control means freedom.

We must notice that Marx also rejects the notion of a split between spirit and nature,

The only reason why Christianity wanted to free us from the domination of the flesh . . . was because it regarded our flesh, our desires as something foreign to

---

[83] *GI, MECW* V. 301 n., see also pp. 90, 195, 291-2, 306, 329, and *MEW* III. 282 n. and pp. 62, 178, 272-3, 287, 311. See also 'Capital Punishment', *MECW* XI. 496, and *MEW* VIII. 508. E. Kamenka e.g. denies that there are any shifts in Marx's thought and also claims that, for Marx, freedom means self-determination: *The Ethical Foundations of Marxism*, pp. vii, 27-30. Also see G. G. Brenkert, *Marx's Ethics of Freedom*, pp. 128-9.

[84] *EPM, MECW* III. 275-6, and *MEW*, suppl. I. 515-17.

[85] *GI, MECW* VI. 51-2, and *MEW* III. 37.

[86] *GI, MECW* V. 78-9, and *MEW* III. 76.

[87] *GI, MECW* V. 78-9, 87-8, 291-2, 438-9, and *MEW* III. 74, 67-8, 272-3, 424-35.

us; it wanted to free us from determination by nature only because it regarded our own nature as not belonging to us. For if I myself am not nature, if my natural desires, my whole natural character, do not belong to myself—and this is the doctrine of Christianity—then all determination by nature—whether due to my own natural character or to what is known as external nature—seems to be a determination by something foreign, a fetter, compulsion used against me, heteronomy as opposed to autonomy of the spirit.[88]

Marx's view is that the human being is completely natural. Does this mean that our inclinations, desires, and interests (since we have ruled out a realm of spirit or noumena) become heteronomous? This issue is rather complex. In 1844, as we have seen, Marx also rejected Kant's phenomena-noumena distinction, and for freedom to be possible an object was taken to be the objectification of the human essence. The individual's relation to the object was an essential relationship. The object was part of the individual's essence and thus was not heteronomous. Marx ontologically absorbed the natural world into the human essence. The object was socially constituted by the human being and the two were in unity. One question that now arises is: why did Marx object to particular interests in 1844? Why did particular interests involve heteronomy?

In 1843, the particular class interest of the proletariat accorded with the categorical imperative and led to revolution, but it did not seem that acting on particular interests itself was moral. We also saw that when the ideal society was achieved, humans would not seek an object because it satisfied a particular interest or need, but because it satisfied the human essence—the needs of all, needs which were universalizable and thus in accord with the categorical imperative. But why did Marx reject particular interests if there was no phenomena-noumena or nature-spirit split and needed objects were part of our essence? It is true that if particular interests were to conflict with the interests of others, this conflict would reduce our freedom. But what about the case where particular interests agreed with the categorical imperative or the common interest? Why hold that it is objectionable to act on particular interest in that case? It is true that we cannot be need-driven or dominated by need if we are going to be free, but if we are in control and are able to satisfy our needs smoothly, why not act on particular interests?

I suggest that the answer in 1843-4 was that at least in part freedom

[88] *GI, MECW* V. 254, and *MEW* III. 237. *HF, MECW* IV. 171-3, 177-8, and *MEW* II. 181-4, 188-9.

meant self-determination. An act had to be initiated consciously by the individual. If the individual was determined by external forces or by interests determined by external objects, the individual was not free. It is true that both the individual and the object were parts of a single natural realm—there was no split between phenomena and noumena or spirit and nature. Nevertheless, within this single realm Marx insisted that natural objects were external to and independent of the individual,[89] even though they were part of the individual's essence, and were needed by the individual. To be determined by external objects, or by needs and interests determined by those objects, was not to be self-determined autonomously. To be free meant to be determined by one's own consciousness and purposively directed toward the realization of oneself through the satisfaction of universal species needs. To be self-determined, one had to act in accordance with one's essence, and since one's essence was a species essence, one thus had to act to realize the species. Since the human being was a species-being—a being created and defined by society or the community—the realization of the individual could occur only through the realization of the species. The individual only developed through the development of the species. Thus, to be self-determined—determined by one's own essence and directed toward the realization of oneself—one had to be determined by the species. It thus followed that one had to be determined by the universal, not by particular interests. To be self-determined, a species-being had to be determined in accordance with the universal, essential species needs of humankind. Objects had to be universal objects which accorded with the essence of the species or the categorical imperative. Only universal objects were the objectification of the human essence and thus were not heteronomous.

In the *German Ideology*, Marx drops the concept of species-being as well as the notion that freedom requires self-determination. It is not necessary to act for the universal or to be self-determined in order to be free; we need only be in control. It is still the case that all is natural—both the human being and external objects—and now Marx even denies that we should identify ourselves with our will any more than with our breathing or blood circulation as if the former were any more ourselves than the latter.[90] Thus, as long as particular interests do not conflict with the common interest to the extent of interfering with collective control of the forces and relations of production, then we are

[89] See above, Ch. 2, sect. ii. Also *EPM, MECW* III. 336-7, and *MEW,* suppl. I. 577-9.

[90] *GI, MECW* V. 291, and *MEW* III. 272.

free to act on our particular interests. Nowhere in the *German Ideology* does Marx suggest that humans ever act except for particular interests or needs. In fact, he denies this and seems to think it ideology to suggest anything else.[91] So is it Marx's view that human action is always heteronomous or that heteronomy has been overcome? I think he holds that heteronomy is objectionable only if we think we need self-determination. It is objectionable to be determined from without or by particular interests only if we think freedom requires autonomous self-determination, and Marx rejects this notion. Self-determination does not exist. The self initiates nothing autonomously. For historical materialism, we are parts of a social, historical, and natural process and we are determined by that process, as is our will.[92] We must come to control this process in accordance with our interests—interests which agree with the common interest. Control, unlike self-determination, is quite compatible with heteronomy, as we shall see shortly.

In the *Holy Family*, Marx argued that correctly understood self-interest was the basis of all morality and also that our interests were shaped by our environment. If we humanized our environment, our interests would be moral. As we saw in the 'Theses on Feuerbach', this might imply that a section of society was taken to be superior to the ordinary determination of society—a form of independence or self-determination—and this assumption was rejected. In the *German Ideology*, Marx holds that our interests and the ability eventually to control the forces and relations of production in accordance with them are determined, as all else is, by those very forces and relations of production. He does not appeal to a superior section of society; nor to self-determination. Nevertheless, if we come to be in control, no matter how we achieve this, then we are free. And if control is compatible with heteronomy, then freedom is compatible with heteronomy.

For Marx, freedom and determinism can be perfectly compatible. Engels comments on this in *Anti-Dühring*,

Hegel was the first to state correctly the relation between freedom and necessity. To him, freedom is the appreciation of necessity. 'Necessity is blind only in so far as it is not understood.' Freedom does not consist in the dream of independence of natural laws, but in the knowledge of these laws, and in the possibility this gives of systematically making them work toward definite ends.

---

[91] *GI, MECW* V. 195-6, 246-7, 255, and *MEW* III. 178-9, 228-9, 238.
[92] *GI, MECW* V. 90-1, 195, 329, 465, and *MEW* III. 62-3, 178, 311, 452-3. 'Capital Punishment', *MECW* XI. 496-7, and *MEW* VIII. 507.

This holds good in relation both to the laws of external nature and to those which govern the bodily and mental existence of men themselves . . .[93]

Despite the fact that we are determined by these laws, we need not be controlled or dominated by them. We can say even that determinism increases the possibility of freedom. If social processes were not determined, it would be near impossible to understand and control them. If social processes are determined and if we can come to understand these processes through science, then we can become free. Scientific study would tell us what conditions must obtain for us to produce certain ends. If material conditions will allow these to be produced and if we have the scientific knowledge and techniques to do this, we can realize our ends. If material conditions or the state of science will not allow this, then we need not waste time but can use science to look for alternate ways to satisfy our needs or interests. If we are determined by these laws we cannot be self-determined, but we can come to control our situation, make use of these laws, and become free.

We must give a final answer to the question that we have been wrestling with throughout this chapter. If freedom as self-determination is ruled out, is morality possible? I think that for Marx it is not. For Kant (as well as for many other moral theorists) we cannot be held responsible unless we are free in the sense of being self-determined, and we cannot be held to have moral obligations if we are not responsible. To eliminate self-determination is to eliminate moral obligation. I think Marx agrees with this. We have already seen that, without free will, Marx thinks that Hegel's moral justification of punishment becomes specious, and in discussing Kantian ethics he claimed that our will was determined by material conditions.[94]

[93] F. Engels, *Anti-Dühring*, trans. E. Burns (New York: International, 1939), 125, and *MEW* XX. 106.

[94] 'Capital Punishment', *MECW* XI. 496-7, and *MEW* VIII. 507. *GI, MECW* V. 195, see also pp. 90-1, 329, 465, and *MEW* III. 178, 62-3, 311, 452-3. This also seems to be suggested at *HF, MECW* IV. 130-1, and *MEW* II. 137-8. In discussing a similar issue, Engels seems to contradict himself. At one point he claims that the bourgeoisie are responsible for social murder and at another point that communists do not hold individuals responsible (*The Condition of the Working Class in England, MECW* IV. 393-4, 407, 582, and *MEW* II. 324-5, 338, 505). Later, in *Capital*, Marx says, 'My standpoint, from which the evolution of the economic formation of society is viewed as a process of natural history, can less than any other make the individual responsible for relations whose creature he socially remains, however much he may subjectively raise himself above them' (*Capital*, I. 10, and *MEW* XXIII. 16). While Marx does rule out responsibility here, we shall see that in the later writings this is not incompatible with morality.

In the *German Ideology*, Marx says, starting with Machiavelli, Hobbes, Spinoza, Bodinus and others of modern times, not to mention earlier ones, might has been represented as the basis of right. Thereby the theoretical view of politics was freed from morality . . . Later in the eighteenth century in France and in the nineteenth century in England, all right was reduced to civil law . . . and the latter to a quite definite power, the power of the owners of private property.

That this is also Marx's own view is made clear elsewhere.[95] There is no right and no morality, but simply power—and Marx does not suggest that right can be derived from power. Marx, I think, takes the distinction between facts and values seriously and accepts that moral values cannot be deduced from facts. The attempt to do so is ideological illusion. His goal is to cut through such ideology in order to reach the facts. He says of his method, 'when things are seen in this way, as they really are and happened, every profound philosophical problem is resolved . . . quite simply into an empirical fact'.[96]

Moreover, in the *Communist Manifesto*, Marx admits that communism abolishes all morality. He characterizes a hypothetical bourgeois objection to communism as follows:

'Undoubtedly,' it will be said, 'religious, moral, philosophical and juridical ideas have been modified in the course of historical development. But religion, morality, philosophy, political science, and law, constantly survived this change.

There are, besides, eternal truths, such as Freedom, Justice, etc., that are common to all states of society. But Communism abolishes eternal truths, it abolishes all religion and all morality, instead of constituting them on a new basis; it therefore acts in contradiction to all past historical experience.'[97]

How does Marx respond to this objection? He does not argue against it. He accepts it and tries to explain why morality will be abolished and why it is reasonable to contradict all past historical experience,

What does this accusation reduce itself to? The history of all past society has consisted in the development of class antagonisms, antagonisms that assumed different forms at different epochs.

But whatever form they may have taken, one fact is common to all past ages, viz., the exploitation of one part of society by the other. No wonder, then, that

---

[95] *GI, MECW* V. 90, 322, and *MEW* III. 62, 304. Also 'The Crisis in Berlin', *MECW* VIII. 3-4, and *MEW* IV. 5-6. Also 'The Trial of the Rhenish District Committee of Democrats', *MECW* VIII. 325-8, and *MEW* VI. 242-6.

[96] *GI, MECW* V. 39, and *MEW* III. 43.

[97] *Manifesto, MECW* VI. 504, and *MEW* IV. 480.

the social consciousness of past ages, despite all the multiplicity and variety it displays, moves within certain common forms, or general ideas, which cannot completely vanish except with the total disappearance of class antagonisms.

The Communist revolution is the most radical rupture with traditional property relations; no wonder that its development involves the most radical rupture with traditional ideas.[98]

In a similar context in the *German Ideology*, Marx argues that communism and socialism 'shattered the basis of all morality'.[99]

An objection might be raised to Marx's claim in the *Communist Manifesto* that communism abolishes all morality. Stanley Moore points out that Marx's argument is faulty. It rests upon the false view that all previous societies in history have been class societies.[100] At a later point in his intellectual development, Marx realized that this had not been the case. Engels added a footnote to the 1890 edition of the *Manifesto*, pointing out that many primitive societies had been classless.[101] If all societies have not been class societies (and, of course, if morality could be found in these classless societies), then morality is not merely a phenomenon of class society and will not necessarily be abolished when the latter is overcome. Nevertheless, we must notice that for Marx to assert that morality will disappear, he must do more than claim that morality is a form of consciousness peculiar to class society—he must do more than give an analysis of morality from the perspective of a sociology of morals. He must also hold that moral obligation does not exist and cannot be established. Suppose for a moment that morality *has* existed only in class societies. It would not follow that the basis of morality would be shattered or that there would be no moral obligation under communism unless moral obligation is, in fact, an illusion—one which communist society comes to see through. For morality to be abolished it must be the case that all ideology disappears *and* that morality is nothing but ideology. Now, that is precisely what has been argued in the *German Ideology*. In the *German Ideology*, as we have seen, consciousness is not independent of material conditions and it cannot contradict such conditions unless the contradiction exists within those conditions themselves; all action is determined by interests arising from

[98] *Manifesto*, *MECW* VI. 504, and *MEW* IV. 480-1. Kamenka argues that Marx rejects the possibility of ethics in class society but thinks that communist society will produce a truly human ethic; the *Communist Manifesto* denies this. (See Kamenka, *Marxism and Ethics*, pp. 20-1.)

[99] *GI*, *MECW* V. 419, and *MEW* III. 404.

[100] *Manifesto*, *MECW* VI. 482, 504, and *MEW* IV. 462, 480. S. Moore, 'Marx and Lenin as Historical Materialists', *MJH* 214-17.

[101] *Manifesto*, *MECW* VI. 482 n., and *MEW* IV. 462 n.

material conditions, and moral principles that are separate from or transcend such conditions are ideology; there is no right, but only power; and there is no free will or self-determination. It is not merely his theory of classes and historical development which causes Marx to conclude that morality will be abolished; he does not think that there can be moral obligation at all.

Contemporary moral philosophers distinguish between hard and soft forms of determinism. Marx is definitely a determinist, but at first sight it is difficult to decide which category he falls under. Hard determinists deny that freedom is compatible with determinism, while soft determinists think that these are compatible. In this respect, Marx seems to agree with the soft determinists. On the other hand, soft determinists hold that, though determined, we still can be held morally responsible. Hard determinists deny that we can be held morally responsible or that we can have moral obligations. In this respect, Marx agrees with the hard determinists. But how can Marx hold that freedom is compatible with determinism yet deny that we are morally responsible? His concept of freedom is actually quite different from that held by soft determinists, who see freedom as the absence of external constraint. They reject indeterminism and hold that none of our actions, choices, or inner states occur without being determined, but we call ourselves free when we meet with no external compulsion. For Marx, this is unacceptable. We *are* externally constrained. We are determined by the forces and relations of production, coerced by the laws of the market, and dominated by ruling ideas. This external constraint need not always contradict our will and desires, but that is only because our will and desires are also determined by these factors. For Marx, freedom can only mean controlling these external constraints, not eliminating them entirely. Soft determinists can also hold that freedom means self-determination. This means that our actions and inner states are subject to determinism by external causal factors, but that the decisive element in determining any action cannot be traced back to these causal factors. It stems from us, from our self-determination. As we have seen, Marx also rejects this concept of freedom. Thus, we can say that Marx only appears to be a soft determinist. When he says that freedom is compatible with determinism, he only means that control is possible, not self-determination or the absence of external constraint. This position is quite compatible with the denial of moral obligation and thus Marx seems at least closer to being a hard determinist.

V

So far, I have argued that Marx rejects the possibility of moral obligation. But in certain of his writings in 1853 we find that he is quite willing to make moral judgements. Let us look at some passages from 'The British Rule in India' (1853). Marx claims that

England has broken down the entire framework of Indian society, without any symptoms of reconstitution yet appearing. This loss of his old world, with no gain of a new one, imparts a particular kind of melancholy to the present misery of the Hindoo, and separates Hindostan, ruled by Britain, from all its ancient traditions, and from the whole of its past history.

From time immemorial, Marx tells us, the Indian government had been in charge of public works—it established and maintained the artificial irrigation canals which were the basis of agriculture. The British, on the other hand, had entirely neglected the department of public works and all agriculture not capable of being conducted on capitalist lines had deteriorated. Moreover, the British had uprooted domestic industry and thus destroyed the village system. Nevertheless, Marx says,

Now, sickening as it must be to human feeling to witness those myriads of industrious patriarchal and inoffensive social organizations disorganized and dissolved into their units ... we must not forget that these idyllic village-communities, inoffensive though they may appear, had always been the solid foundation of Oriental despotism, that they restrained the human mind within the smallest possible compass, making it the unresisting tool of superstition, enslaving it beneath traditional rules, depriving it of all grandeur and historical energies.... We must not forget that these little communities were contaminated by distinctions of caste and by slavery, that they subjugated man to external circumstances instead of elevating man the sovereign of circumstances, that they transformed a self-developing social state into never changing natural destiny, and thus brought about a brutalizing worship of nature, exhibiting its degradation in the fact that man, the sovereign of nature, fell down on his knees in adoration of Kanuman, the monkey, and Sabbala, the cow.

England, it is true, in causing a social revolution in Hindostan, was actuated only by the vilest interests, and was stupid in her manner of enforcing them. But that is not the question. The question is, can mankind fulfil its destiny without a fundamental revolution in the social state of Asia? If not, whatever may have been the crimes of England she was the unconscious tool of history in bringing about that revolution.[102]

---

[102] 'British Rule in India', *MECW* XII. 126-32, and *MEW* IX. 129-33. See also F. Engels, 'Democratic Pan-Slavism', *MECW* VIII. 365-6, 370, and *MEW* VI. 273-4, 278.

This passage is obviously shot through with value judgements. It is very difficult to decide how to treat such passages. One way would be to see them as a transition stage between the *German Ideology* and *Capital*. As we shall see in Chapter 4, in Marx's later writings he changes his mind about ethics. For example, in *Capital*, he says, 'The justice of the transactions between agents of production rests on the fact that these arise as natural consequences out of the production relationships. . . . The content is just whenever it corresponds, is appropriate, to the mode of production. It is unjust whenever it contradicts that mode.'[103] As we shall see, Marx also accepts and employs moral concepts elsewhere in the later writings. What is moral in a specific society is determined by whether or not it corresponds to the prevailing mode of production. Nowhere in the period from the *German Ideology* to 1856, that I can find, do we hear Marx saying this sort of thing; valid moral principles do not arise as natural consequences out of production relationships and principles do not morally oblige us because they correspond to the mode of production. For Marx to make this change, he will have to loosen up his notion that consciousness is determined by material conditions. As far as I can see, he has not made this shift in 'The British Rule in India'. In the passage from that text cited above, Marx is saying that England's behaviour in India does correspond to the prevailing mode of production—it is bringing India into the modern capitalist world. But far from such action being moral because it corresponds to the prevailing mode of production, as is suggested in the passage from *Capital*, Marx holds that England's behaviour is immoral. Thus, it would be most difficult to treat these passages from 'The British Rule in India' as compatible with Marx's ethical views in *Capital*. It is true that in *Capital* Marx will also denounce, as immoral, behaviour that corresponds to the prevailing mode of production, but that, as we shall see in Chapter 4, is made possible by the development of a rather complex new method which Marx had not developed in 1853. Perhaps, however, it is possible to see in these passages of 1853 a dissatisfaction with his earlier rejection of morality and the first tentative and wavering steps away from it.

It is also possible to interpret these passages as a refinement upon but not a rejection of the ethical views of the *German Ideology*. I cannot conclusively argue that this *is* the way to interpret these passages. I can only suggest it as a possible way.

In the passage from 'The British Rule in India' Marx is certainly

---

[103] *Capital*, III. 339-40, and *MEW* XXV. 351-2. Though the passage is not clear, this view might be anticipated at *GI*, *MECW* V. 318, and *MEW* III. 300.

making moral judgements. But this fact alone does not require us to hold that Marx has a moral theory which justifies such judgements. Modern emotivism, for example, sees moral judgements as expressions of opinion or attitudes which may well serve to influence others, but denies that they are or ever can be morally justified. It is worth noticing that, for Marx, ideology or ruling ideas express moral judgements which certainly influence others, but at the same time cannot be morally justified—the moral obligations implied or claimed in such ideologies cannot be derived from material conditions. Furthermore, Marx himself said in a passage quoted above that an appeal to rights can be influential in helping to unify the proletariat at certain stages of its development, but denied that rights could be justified.[104] The way in which Marx treats rights and ruling ideas in these cases is certainly parallel to the outlook of modern emotivism.

For emotivism, and also for Marx in the *German Ideology*, only science can be justified, not morality. Moral judgements cannot be empirically verified and therefore are not true or false. Nevertheless, for emotivists, even within the realm of ordinary disapproval not justified by a moral theory, one can distinguish between mere opinions and those which follow upon careful scientific study, and one can do so without claiming that the latter have a justified basis. Even emotivists like C. L. Stevenson admit that reasons and scientific investigation can be relevant in discussing moral issues and in influencing others.[105] Changing a person's view of the facts can change their attitude about what is desirable under such conditions. Attitudes cannot be derived from or justified by the scientific facts, but can be influenced by them. Thus, we might say that Marx's moral disapproval is ideological. It will not independently affect historical development and, while it may influence others, it will not do so independently of reinforcement by material conditions and the interests that arise from those conditions.

In a second article on British rule in India, written a month after the first, Marx says, 'The question, therefore, is not whether the English

[104] *GI, MECW* V. 323, see also pp. 209-10, and *MEW* III. 305, 190-1.

[105] C. L. Stevenson, *Ethics and Language* (New Haven: Yale University Press, 1944), 27 ff., 113. Also see K. Nielsen, 'Marxism, Ideology, and Moral Philosophy', *Social Theory and Praxis*, 6 (1980), 53-68. And also, though he comes to a different conclusion than I do, see Peffer, 'Morality and the Marxist Concept of Ideology'. Hare objects to Stevenson's view that ethical statements are intended to influence others, 'the distinction is important for moral philosophy; for in fact the suggestion, that the function of moral judgements was to persuade, led to a difficulty in distinguishing their function from that of propaganda' (R. M. Hare, *The Language of Morals* (New York: OUP, 1964), 13-14). In this respect, Marx seems closer to Stevenson. He would probably accept the view that morality is a form of propaganda.

had a *right* to conquer India, but whether we are to *prefer* India
conquered by the Turk, by the Persian, by the Russian, to India
conquered by the Briton.' The question is not one of right but one of
preference. What then determines this preference? Marx declares:

England has to fulfil a double mission in India; one destructive, the other
regenerating—the annihilation of old Asiatic society, and laying the material
foundations of Western society in Asia. . . .

The bourgeois period of history has to create the material basis of the new world
. . . When a great social revolution shall have mastered the results of the
bourgeois epoch . . . and subjected them to the common control of the most
advanced peoples, then only will human progress cease to resemble that
hideous, pagan idol, who would not drink the nectar but from the skulls of the
slain.[106]

Marx's moral judgements here—above and beyond the historical
materialist views embedded in these passages—have nothing to do with
questions of right but with preferences that stem from his interest
in historical materialist development and his attitude towards the
realization of control or freedom. The social revolution in India is a step
towards the realization of this end, the replacement of subjugation by
sovereign control. This, at least, is a possible reading of these passages.
Moreover, it is a reading which fits with what we have said of Marx's
moral views in the *German Ideology*.

On the other hand, Isaiah Berlin defends a view which might seem to
fit here:

it has often been asked, how can a moral precept, a command to do this or that,
be deduced from the truth of a theory of history? Historical materialism may

---

[106] 'The Future Results of British Rule in India', *MECW* XII. 217-18 (my emphasis),
222, and *MEW* IX. 221, 226. When Marx argues that bourgeois values are contradictory,
hypocritical, and so forth, one might want to claim that this is a moral criticism on
Marx's part (e.g. *GI*, *MECW* V. 293, and *MEW* III. 274, quoted above in sect. ii). It
would not be a moral criticism that appeals to some higher moral standard apart from
bourgeois moral standards, but an immanent critique which condemns bourgeois society
by using that society's moral standards or at least by using standards which arise from an
analysis of bourgeois morality. This would certainly be a criticism of morality, but would
it be a *moral* criticism? Marx would call it a scientific criticism, not a moral one, and I
think he would be right. Marx rejects morality not just because it is inconsistent or
hypocritical but because it is ideological illusion—it is delusion to think that morality can
have effect in the real world or that it rests on some ground which can determine us
above and beyond determination by material conditions. We would cause Marx to
contradict himself if we were to hold that his criticism of bourgeois morality was based
on some authority above and beyond material conditions. However, we can call his
criticism of morality moral criticism as long as we are clear that these criticisms are not
justified by a moral theory. Marx's views are like those of contemporary emotivism.

account for what does in fact occur, but cannot, precisely because it is concerned solely with what is, provide the answer to moral questions, that is, tell us what ought to be. Marx, like Hegel, flatly rejected this distinction. Judgments of fact cannot be sharply distinguished from those of value: all one's judgments are conditioned by practical activity in a given social milieu which, in its turn, are functions of the stage reached by one's class in its historical evolution: one's views as to what one believes to exist and what one wishes to do with it, modify each other. If ethical judgments claim objective validity—and unless they do so, they cannot, according to Marx, be either true or false—they must be definable in terms of empirical activities and be verifiable by reference to them. He rejected any notion of a non-empirical, purely contemplative or specifically moral intuition or moral reason. The only sense in which it is possible to show that something is good or bad, right or wrong, is by demonstrating that it accords or discords with the historical process i.e. the collective activity of men, that it assists it or thwarts it, will survive or will inevitably perish. All causes permanently lost or doomed to fail, are, by that very fact, made bad and wrong, and indeed this is what constitutes the meaning of these terms.[107]

This view, at least as far as Marx's writings between the *German Ideology* and 'The British Rule in India' are concerned, is mistaken. In the *German Ideology*, Marx does not suggest that moral judgements are empirically verifiable. He dismisses them as ideological illusion. Nor will saying that actions are moral or immoral to the extent that they assist or thwart history make sense of what Marx is claiming in 'The British Rule in India'. What the British are doing in India is clearly assisting history—bringing about a desirable social revolution there. Nevertheless, Marx morally condemns the British.

Thus, if Marx's moral judgements here are taken as emotivist expressions, then the views expressed in 'The British Rule in India' can be seen as compatible with Marx's ethical views in the *German Ideology*. The Indian Revolution which will lay the foundation of future sovereignty is an empirically determined process. It will lead towards the replacement of subjugation by control. It is not being produced by self-determination and even the motives behind this revolution cannot be called moral, certainly not in the sense that the revolution is being consciously sought. An invisible hand is at work here. In the 'Introduction to the Critique of Hegel's Philosophy of Law', Marx used an invisible hand argument to justify proletarian revolution in Germany. There the motives of the proletariat were not moral either—they were particular

---

[107] I. Berlin, *Karl Marx: His Life and Environment*, 3rd edn. (Oxford: OUP, 1963), 154-5. For a similar view, see K. R. Popper, *The Open Society and its Enemies*, 4th edn. (Princeton University Press, 1963), II. 204-6.

interests. But the end was moral—it accorded with the categorical imperative and self-determination would finally occur. Here in 1853, however, the revolution in India, though motivated by particular interests, is not motivated by the particular interests of the Indians. It is not being carried out by the Indians at all, but heteronomously, from outside, by the British. Nor does Marx argue that the results will accord with the categorical imperative or that self-determination will finally occur. Western society is being imposed upon India by Britain. The revolutionary process does not arise from nor satisfy the short-term interest of the Indians and the British certainly do not seek sovereignty for the Indians. The point is rather that sovereign control will result even if brought about unintentionally and from outside. In the *Holy Family*, Marx said of the proletariat, 'It is not a question of what this or that proletarian, or even the whole proletariat, at the moment regards as its aim. It is a question of what the proletariat is, and what, in accordance with this being, it will historically be compelled to do.'[108] In 1853, Marx holds a similar position in the context of world history. The same facts hold in both East and West; there is no self-determination anywhere—all is heteronomy. There is only control or lack of control. The rest, sickening as it may be, is a matter of attitudes.

What about after the revolution is complete—when humans have become sovereign? What about after the establishment of communism? Will we then become self-determined? Will our motives become moral? Will we be able to establish moral obligations? Marx's views are not perfectly clear, but one possible interpretation of them is that even under communism we will be forced to be free—forced to be sovereign and in control. If we fail to gain control, we will fall back into subjugation. We have seen in the *German Ideology* that the proletariat will be forced to control the forces and relations of production due to the nature of those forces and relations of production and to avoid crises. In communist society we will control consciously the material conditions which hitherto have controlled us,[109] but we will not be self-determined or autonomous. If morality means autonomy, free choice, and self-determination—and that is what it means for the German Idealist tradition and, as far as I can see, for Marx—then morality never occurs and the illusion of morality will disappear under communism. It is true that in being forced to control our material conditions we will not be forced against our consciousness, inclinations, or will, but that is

108 *HF, MECW* IV. 37, and *MEW* II. 38.
109 *GI, MECW* V. 51-2, and *MEW* III. 37.

because these too have been moulded by material conditions. We can only study this social development empirically and come to control it accordingly. Marx seems to take the fact-value distinction seriously. There is no room for moral values established independently of material conditions and we cannot derive moral values from facts. Morality will be replaced by empirical science and technical control. Marx does not try to create a scientific morality which confuses facts and values and distorts the meaning of morality. Morality, for Marx, means what it traditionally meant and Marx rejects it as impossible.

There is, however, one sense in which ideas can be independent of material conditions. Ideological illusions are obviously independent of material conditions in a certain way—or at least apparently so. For example, Kantian ethics abstracted from the material interests of French liberalism. However, Marx says that even this appearance of independence is determined by material conditions and the interests arising from them. For example, Kantian abstraction was the outcome of German backwardness. Thus, in one sense, these apparently independent ideas reflect the aspirations of the rising bourgeoisie under conditions which make it impossible for them to be realized. But, in another sense, these ideas cannot be traced from material conditions. Kant took his moral principles to be imperatives, abstract self-determinations of the will, divorced from real material interests. The scientific tracing of ideas from material conditions will not be able to derive an 'ought' from material conditions or justify it, though science will be able to explain why an abstract 'ought' came to replace real material interests. The only form of justification that Marx allows in the *German Ideology* is that of empirical science, understood in a very positivistic sense[110] such that moral values cannot be derived from facts. Even in the case where evaluative judgements are not hypocritical, not distorted by interest in domination, even where they follow upon accurate scientific study (as Marx, no doubt, would consider the evaluations he made in the articles on British rule in India), these are mere attitudes or opinions.

In one sense it is true for Marx that values cannot be sharply distinguished from facts. Since our consciousness is determined by material conditions, our values will be also. And since our practical activity will be the outcome of our interests, these interests or values will be involved in the ongoing process of transforming material conditions. Facts and values thus cannot be neatly separated. Nevertheless, our ideas, values, or interests never determine material conditions independently. They are a part of the process of historical transformation, but

[110] *GI, MECW* V. 36-7, and *MEW* III. 26-7.

material conditions predominate in that process and determine our ideas, values, and interests. Thus, we could say only that *non*-moral values derive from facts. In other words, odd as it may sound, precisely because values are inseparable from facts, *moral* values cannot be derived from facts. To derive moral values from facts would mean that moral values would oblige us to act independently of material conditions in that we would have an obligation above and beyond what material conditions determine us to do. It would mean that our values could have a practical effect on the world either independently of material conditions or at least that material conditions and moral values would determine each other mutually and equally. Since this is not the case for Marx—for whom ideas and values are always determined by material conditions—we cannot derive *moral* values from material conditions.

If moral ideas can have no independent effect, then we must abandon the notion of moral obligation. In accordance with Kant's well-known dictum,[111] to hold that we ought to do something, we must be able to hold that we can do it. If we are unable to hold that we can do it, then we cannot hold that we ought to do it. On the other hand, if we can only do it when our doing it is determined—if we can do it only when we cannot but do it—it is meaningless to hold that we ought to do it.

There are different ways to overcome an 'ought'. One way is fully to realize morality and thus to go beyond it. Kant held that for a divine will it was impossible to speak of an 'ought'.[112] If a being always, unfailingly, necessarily, does what it ought, if it can do nothing else, then an 'ought' and morality would be irrelevant for this being. This is very much like Hegel's concept of *Sittlichkeit* in which customary moral behaviour transcends an 'ought' and simply 'is'. In 1843-4, Marx wanted a society of this sort, which, unlike Hegel, he did not think had been realized in the modern world. I can see no evidence for this ideal in the period from 1845 to 1856. Here, all is fact; all is determined by material conditions. The appeal to an 'ought' is ideology. Autonomous self-determination is impossible. Like God, the human being does act in a necessary way, but does not do so as self-determined. It is not as if we have an all-powerful will that never fails to self-determine itself the way it ought. For Marx, 'ought' disappears not because it never fails, but because it never occurs.

I cannot say that I agree with Marx's views in this period, but I think I have accurately described what they are.

111 *CPrR* 30, and *KGS* V. 30. *CPR* A 555-B 583, A 807-B 853, and *KGS* III.
112 *F* 31, and *KGS* IV. 414.

4

Morality and
the Dialectic Method (1857–1883)

I

Marx's doctrine of historical materialism, as developed in the *German Ideology*, led to the implication that morality was ideological illusion, an implication that at least before 1853 Marx fully accepted and even embraced. I hope to make it clear in this and the following chapter that Marx does not continue to embrace this implication. Perhaps, as we have already seen, he began to struggle against it as early as 1853 in his discussion of British rule in India, though the views expressed there were by no means as developed as the views we will find in *Capital*, and it could be argued that those views were compatible with the views of the *German Ideology*. At any rate, in grappling with the complexities of his doctrine of historical materialism and in qualifying it, Marx transforms his moral views.

There is a good deal of evidence in Marx's later writings (1857 to 1883) to suggest that he no longer thinks of morality as ideological illusion destined to disappear in communist society. He tells us in the 'Inaugural Address of the International Working Men's Association' that the working class must 'vindicate the simple laws of morals and justice, which ought to govern the relations of private individuals'. It is true that in a letter of 1864 Marx says that he was obliged by others to insert such passages in the text. There he seems to reject this passage or at least to be ambiguous about it. But in the *Civil War in France*, Marx repeats this passage on his own and thus finally seems to approve it.[1]

Marx also says that communist society, as it first emerges from capitalist society, is 'in every respect, economically, *morally*, and

---

[1] 'Inaugural Address of the Working Men's Association', in *The Marx-Engels Reader*, 2nd edn., ed. R. C. Tucker, p. 519, and *MEW* XVI. 13. In a letter of 1864 Marx seems to repudiate his comments on morality and justice in the 'Inaugural Address'; see 'Marx to Engels on 4 Nov. 1864', *Marx Engels Selected Correspondence* (*SC*), ed. S. Ryazanskaya (Moscow: Progress, 1965), 148, and *MEW* XXXI. 15. But Marx repeats the same passage in *CWF* 35, and *MEW* XVII. 3.

intellectually, still stamped with the birth marks of the old society from whose womb it emerges.' In the *Civil War in France*, he says that 'every social form of property has "morals" of its own'. Furthermore, he says that communism, 'the form of social property which makes property the attribute of labour, far from creating individual "moral constraints," will emancipate the "morals" of the individual from its class constraints'.[2]

Marx also seems to revive certain of the moral views he held in 1844. He again agrees with Aristotle's criticism of money and exchange. Marx tells us that the development of money in the ancient world made greed possible: individual desires no longer were limited, kept in bounds, and regulated by specific needs for particular products. Instead, money became an end in itself and the individual's Sisyphus-like desires became boundless. Money caused the dissolution of the ancient community, and for the ancients money was the 'source of all evil'. Money was 'subversive of the economic and moral order of things'. Moreover, much as in his 'Comments on Mill', Marx again, like Aristotle, thinks that exchange perverts human virtue. It turns 'conscience, honor, etc.' into commodities 'capable of being offered for sale by their holders'.[3] It thus turns ends into means.

In the *German Ideology*, morality was ruled out because consciousness was thought to be so strictly determined by material conditions that it could not be said to influence those conditions independently. Marx also rejected the notion of freedom as self-determination and thus there was no room for moral values or moral obligations above and beyond determination by material conditions. Morality was ideological illusion.

In the later writings, I would like to suggest, Marx begins to qualify and to resist drawing the conclusions he drew from his doctrine of historical materialism in the *German Ideology*. He begins to loosen up, to move in a new direction, and to develop a view of morality compatible with his historical materialism. In the first place, the quotations we have just considered suggest that morality is no longer seen as ideolo-

---

[2] 'Critique of the Gotha Program', in *Marx-Engels Reader*, p. 529 (my emphasis), and *MEW* XIX. 20; *CWF* 168 n., 169, and *MEW* XVII. 563. For other examples, see 'History of the Opium Trade', *MECW* XVI. 16-17, and *MEW* XII. 552-3. *Capital* (*C*), I. 408, and *MEW* XXIII. 430. *C* III. 545, and *MEW* XXV. 561. *Theories of Surplus Value* (*TSV*), ed. S. Ryazanskaya (Moscow: Progress, 1969), I. 387, and *MEW* XXVI. part i. 363. *Value, Price and Profit* (*VPP*), ed. E. M. Aveling (New York: International, 1935), 9, and *MEW* XVI. 103.

[3] *G* 221-6, 270, 540, and *GKPO* 133-7, 181, 438. *CPE* 27 n., 50, and *MEW* XIII. 15 n., 36. *C* I. 102, 132-3, 151, 152 n., 153, and *MEW* XXIII. 117, 146-7, 166, 167 n., 168. Aristotle, *Politics*, 1257^{b}-1258^{a}.

gical illusion. Morality, both now and in the communist society of the future, has a positive role to play and will not wither away.

Moreover, Marx begins to shift away from the view that consciousness is as strictly determined as he had claimed in the *German Ideology*. There, all ideas were to be traced from material conditions in a strictly empirical and verifiable way. In the Preface to the *Critique of Political Economy*, on the other hand, Marx says,

> In studying such transformations it is always necessary to distinguish between the material transformation of the economic conditions of production, which can be determined with the precision of natural science, and the legal, political, religious, artistic or philosophical—in short, ideological forms in which men become conscious of this conflict and fight it out.

While it is still the case, Marx tells us in another passage, that ideology corresponds to material conditions and that consciousness must be explained by the contradictions that occur between forces and relations of production,[4] nevertheless, as the quoted passage suggests, forms of consciousness are not determined strictly enough for us to be able to trace them with the same precision as in the area of material production. This is a distinction that Marx did not make in the *German Ideology*.

However, one might want to deny that this passage implies that consciousness is not determined strictly and interpret it as holding that, while consciousness *is* determined very strictly by material conditions, it would be very difficult *in practice* actually to trace consciousness from these conditions with precision. I do not think that this is Marx's view. In *Capital*, he says,

> Labour is, in the first place, a process in which both man and Nature participate, and in which man of his own accord starts, regulates, and controls the material re-actions between himself and Nature . . . A spider conducts operations that resemble those of a weaver, and a bee puts to shame many an architect in the construction of her cells. But what distinguishes the worst architect from the best of bees is this, that the architect raises his structure in imagination before he erects it in reality. At the end of every labour-process, we get a result that already existed in the imagination of the labourer at its commencement. He not only effects a change in form in the material on which he works, but he also realizes a purpose of his own that gives the law to his modus operandi, and to which he must subordinate his will.[5]

It cannot be the case that the consciousness of the labourer is determined strictly by material conditions if by raising his structure in

---

[4] *GI, MECW* V. 36, 53, and *MEW* III. 26, 37-8; *CPE* 21-2, and *MEW* XIII. 8-9.
[5] *C* I. 177-8 (my emphasis), and *MEW* XXIII. 192-3.

the imagination he is able to realize a 'purpose *of his own*' and '*of his own accord*' is able to regulate and control his relations to the material reactions taking place between himself and nature. Here it is suggested that the ideas of the labourer have a certain independent effect. This is to move away from the *German Ideology* where Marx admitted that ideas were necessarily involved in material practice, but claimed that the proper approach does not 'explain practice from the idea but explains the formation of ideas from material practice'.[6] The passage from *Capital* does not rule out explaining the formation of ideas from practice, but it certainly is claiming, at least in part, that practice is to be explained from the idea.

The same point is made even more clearly in the Introduction to the *Grundrisse* where Marx discusses 'the uneven development of material production relative to e.g. artistic development'. Certain periods of the development of art are 'out of all proportion to the general development of society, hence also to the material foundation . . . of its organization'. Marx argues that the Greek epic—which he counts 'as a norm and as an unattainable model' in the modern world—was possible only at a low level of the development of society. Greek art was based upon a mythology which was able to overcome, dominate, and shape the forces of nature and society in and through the imagination—a domination which became impossible as society and a technological relation to nature developed and became more complex.[7]

Marx is clearly holding that the now unattainable norm of Greek art was not determined by the development of material conditions in the way outlined in the *German Ideology*, where higher levels of consciousness followed upon a higher and more complex development of material conditions:

In the case of an individual, for example, whose life embraces a wide circle of varied activities and practical relations to the world, and who, therefore, lives a many-sided life, thought has the same character of universality as every other manifestation of his life. . . . The extent to which these qualities develop on the universal or local scale, the extent to which they transcend local narrow-mindedness or remain within its confines, depends . . . on the development of world intercourse . . . That under favourable circumstances some individuals are able to rid themselves of their local narrow-mindedness is . . . due to the fact that in their real empirical life individuals, actuated by empirical 'needs', have been able to bring about world intercourse.[8]

---

[6] *GI*, *MECW* V. 54, and *MEW* III. 38.
[7] *G* 109-11, and *GKPO* 29-31.
[8] *GI*, *MECW* V. 263-4, also p. 51, and *MEW* III. 246-7, 37.

But in the *Grundrisse* we find the now unattainable norm of art at a period of low economic development. To explain this, Marx holds that mythological consciousness was able to dominate nature and society in imagination with greater scope and totality than ever would be possible in more highly developed society. Here in the *Grundrisse*, then, this power of consciousness, its independence from material conditions, is no longer being discounted as ideological illusion. We have seen that both in the 'Introduction to the Critique of Hegel's Philosophy of Law' and in the *German Ideology*, Marx examined situations in which consciousness was in advance of material conditions, or at least where there was a gap between the two. In the *German Ideology*, Marx attempted to show that this gap could be explained by material conditions themselves and that the seeming independence of consciousness was ideological illusion which had no effect on material conditions and perhaps was not to be considered even an advanced form of consciousness at all. In the 'Introduction' of 1843, however, advanced consciousness did have effect—it helped produce revolution. While Marx would not go this far in the *Grundrisse*, he *is* holding that consciousness can be in advance of material conditions, that this is not ideological illusion, and that it can have important consequences, if not in transforming material conditions, at least in enriching culture and producing art which is now an unattainable norm.[9]

Furthermore, in the *Grundrisse*, Marx says that the working class's

recognition of the products as its own, and the judgement that its separation from the conditions of its realization is improper (*ungehörigen*)—forcibly imposed—is an enormous advance in awareness, itself the product of the mode of production resting on capital, and as much the knell to its doom as, with the slave's awareness that he cannot be the property of another, with his consciousness of himself as a person, the existence of slavery becomes a merely artificial, vegetative existence, and ceases to be able to prevail as the basis of production.[10]

Here the consciousness of the individual transcends existing conditions and calls the prevailing form of society into question. Far from being ideological illusion, this sounds the knell of that society's doom.

In the later writings, Marx clearly holds that moral consciousness can have a very powerful effect. For example, in his *Ethnological Notebooks*, he speaks of the power that customary morality can have, 'The vast mass of influences, which we may call for shortness moral . . . perpetu-

[9] *G* 111, and *GKPO* 31. See above, Ch. 1, sect. ii, and Ch. 3, sect. iii.
[10] *G* 463, and *GKPO* 366-7.

ally shapes, limits, or forbids the actual direction of society by its Sovereign.' Here and in other texts, Marx makes it clear that customs, traditions, and laws, while they do arise from and express material conditions and are determined by those conditions, nevertheless, themselves have a stabilizing effect on material conditions.[11]

Thus, morality is not ideological illusion. Moral consciousness is not strictly determined as a *mere* expression and outcome of material conditions, and moral consciousness can have an important effect on material conditions. Moreover, Marx seems to change his mind about freedom, coming to accept it as self-determination.

Certainly, labour obtains its measure from the outside, through the aim to be attained and the obstacles to be overcome in attaining it. But Smith has no inkling whatever that this overcoming of obstacles is in itself a liberating activity—and that, further, the external aims become stripped of the semblance of merely external natural urgencies, and become posited as aims which the individual himself posits—hence as self-realization, objectification of the subject, hence real freedom, whose action is, precisely, labour.

What is required for this freedom in labour? Marx says that labour can be free

(1) when its social character is posited, (2) when it is of a scientific and at the same time a general character, not merely human exertion as a specifically harnessed natural force, but exertion as subject, which appears in the production process not in a merely natural, spontaneous form, but as an activity regulating all the forces of nature.[12]

Elsewhere, Marx explains the requirement that labour must have a social character. In *Capital*, he describes a socialist community of free individuals who consciously apply their labour according to a social plan in order to control nature and their social relations.[13] The control necessary to make freedom possible involves communal co-operation according to a conscious plan.

As for the second requirement of human freedom—the scientific aspect of this control—Marx says that the labourer,

inserts the process of nature, transformed into an industrial process, as a means between himself and inorganic nature, mastering it. He steps to the side of the

[11] *The Ethnological Notebooks of Karl Marx*, ed. L. Krader (Assen: Van Gorcum, 1972), 329, also p. 334; this text is not available in *MEW* but it contains Marx's original MS written in a mixture of English, German, and other languages. *C* III. 793, and *MEW* XXV. 801. *G* 98, and *GKPO* 19.

[12] *G* 611-12, and *GKPO* 505.

[13] *C* I. 78-81, and *MEW* XXIII. 92-5.

production process instead of being its chief actor ... Nature builds no machines, no locomotives, railways, electric telegraphs, self-acting mules etc. These are products of human industry; natural material transformed into the organs of the human will over nature ... They are organs of the human brain, created by the human hand; the power of knowledge objectified. The development of fixed capital indicates to what degree general social knowledge has become a direct force of production, and to what degree, hence, the conditions of the process of social life itself have come under the control of the general intellect and been transformed in accord with it.[14]

Just as in the *German Ideology*, both requirements for freedom place a strong emphasis on control. But here there is also a very strong emphasis on the independent role of will, intellect, science, and knowledge—factors which in the *German Ideology* were not emphasized as playing an independent role in determining the control and mastery of social forces. Moreover, as we have seen already, the architect, for Marx, first raises his structure in his imagination in order to realize a purpose of 'his own' and of 'his own accord' to control the relations between himself and nature.[15] Individuals achieve their own aims and in doing so achieve self-realization. It is clear then that humans can be self-determined. Indeed, if consciousness is not determined strictly by material conditions, if it can predominate in controlling nature and society, and can realize its own aims, then it follows that self-determination is possible.

In the third volume of *Capital*, Marx says that within the realm of material production, freedom

can only consist in socialised man, the associated producers, rationally regulating their interchange with Nature, bringing it under their common control, instead of being ruled by the blind forces of Nature; and achieving this with the least expenditure of energy and under conditions most favourable to, and worthy of, their human nature. Beyond it begins that development of human energy which is an end in itself, the true realm of freedom, which, however, can blossom forth only with this realm of necessity as its basis. The shortening of the working-day is its basic prerequisite.[16]

Within material production, freedom is understood as rational control of nature. It is freedom which is achieved by the overcoming of obstacles, but in so far as it is conditioned by these obstacles, it remains

---

[14] *G* 705-6, also pp. 699-700, 712, and *GKPO* 592-4, 587-8, 599-600. For an e.g. of the lack of freedom science can produce in the absence of communal control, see *C* I. 423, and *MEW* XXIII. 445-6.

[15] *C* I. 177-8, and *MEW* XXIII. 192-3.

[16] *C* III. 820, and *MEW* XXV. 828.

a realm of necessity. Beyond this realm, that is, in the realm of leisure time, one overcomes necessity and comes to be related to one's activity as an end in itself. This point is made very clearly in the *Theories of Surplus Value*, 'But free time, disposable time, is wealth itself, partly for the enjoyment of the product, partly for free activity—which unlike labour—is not dominated by the pressure of an extraneous purpose which must be fulfilled, and the fulfilment of which is regarded as a natural necessity or a social duty'.[17]

If individuals are not dominated by an external purpose, if on their own accord they achieve a purpose of their own, and if their activity is an end in itself, then individuals are not determined heteronomously but self-determined.[18]

II

An interesting controversy has recently been provoked by Allen Wood. He argues that capitalism, for Marx, 'cannot be faulted as far as justice is concerned'. For Marx, the concept of justice belonging to any society is rooted in, grows out of, and expresses that particular society's mode of production. Right and justice, Wood says, 'are rationally comprehensible only when seen in their proper connection with other determinations of social life and grasped in terms of their role within the prevailing productive mode'. Justice is not a standard by which human

---

[17] *TSV* III. 257, and *MEW* XXVI. part iii. 253. For a fuller discussion of these matters, see my *Schiller, Hegel, and Marx*, pp. 114-32.

[18] In the Afterword to the 2nd German edn. of *Capital*, Marx does quote a Russian reviewer who says, 'Marx treats the social movement as a process of natural history, governed by laws not only independent of human will, consciousness, and intelligence, but rather, on the contrary, determining that will, consciousness, and intelligence'. Since this is the only place in the later writings where we find a clear claim that the will is determined, I do not think we need accept the reviewer's interpretation as Marx's own view. Marx does not tell us that he accepts everything in the quotation from the reviewer; he merely says that it describes his *method* in a striking and generous way (*C* I. 18-19, and *MEW* XXIII. 26-7). In a letter of 1868, Marx writes that he is 'ever mindful of the fact that every one of us is dependent more on circumstances than his own will'. ('Marx to Schweitzer on 13 Oct. 1868', *SC* 216, and *MEW* XXXII. 571). This does not imply that our will is strictly determined or that we have no free will but that at least to some extent we are dependent upon our will. Furthermore, even to admit that we are determined by circumstances would not rule out the eventual possibility of self-determination. In socialist society where circumstances had been brought under the control of human beings, self-determination would become possible. It seems to me that these passages must be read in this way. If not, then they would contradict the many passages cited above concerning freedom. Even if we were to accept such contradiction, we would still have to say that Marx's predominant view is that we can be self-determined.

reason in the abstract measures actions or institutions—there is no eternal, unchanging norm of justice. Each social epoch gives rise to its own standard; each generally lives up to it; and each must be measured by this standard alone. Thus, in Wood's view, capitalism is perfectly just for Marx.[19]

Nor does Wood think that the capitalist's appropriation of surplus value is taken to be unjust by Marx. In capitalist society, workers generally are paid the full value of their labour power. The value of labour power is determined, like the value of any other commodity, by the amount of labour time required for its production, here, what it takes to keep the labourer alive and working. The exchange between capitalist and worker is assumed to be an exchange of equivalents, and, as Wood says, is, in Marx's opinion, 'no injustice at all' to the worker. It is true that the labourer is not paid the value of the product which is produced—a value which would be higher than the value of the worker's labour power. The difference between these two sums is appropriated by the capitalist and is the source of surplus value. But in capitalist society, according to Wood, the worker is not due this extra sum. The capitalist purchases labour power from the worker, not finished products. The exchange between worker and capitalist is thus an exchange of equivalents, and according to Wood it is a just transaction, both for capitalism and for Marx.[20]

It follows from all of this, for Wood, that one cannot condemn a society as unjust by using the standards of a later or different society. Thus, in Wood's opinion, slavery, for Marx, must be accepted as perfectly just in the context of ancient society despite the fact that it would be unjust in a capitalist or socialist society. So also, capitalism must be accepted as just, despite the fact that socialist society would have a very different standard of justice. Socialist society would not be able to condemn capitalism as unjust because its standards would not be rationally applicable to capitalism.[21] There are no transcultural or transhistorical norms of justice.

Wood's views have been rejected by other writers, including Husami.

[19] A. W. Wood, 'The Marxian Critique of Justice' ('Critique'), *MJH* 3, 13, 15-16. A. W. Wood, 'Marx on Right and Justice: A Reply to Husami' ('Reply') in *MJH* 107-9. For a similar view, see R. C. Tucker, *The Marxian Revolutionary Idea* (New York: Norton, 1970), 37-48, and *Philosophy and Myth in Karl Marx* (Cambridge: CUP, 1964), 18-22, 222.

[20] 'Critique', pp. 19-22. Also see *C* I. 193-4, and *MEW* XXIII. 208.

[21] 'Critique', pp. 18-19. 'Reply', pp. 131-2. G. G. Brenkert also holds this view, at least as far as justice is concerned: 'Freedom and Private Property in Marx', in *MJH* 80-105.

The latter cites many passages where Marx, if he actually does not say that capitalism is unjust, certainly employs the sort of language typically used in moral condemnation. Husami agrees with Wood that the moral standards of any epoch are determined by the given mode of production, but he thinks they are also determined by class structure, that is, by the conditions, consciousness, and interests of particular classes. Thus, while capitalism will be just for the capitalist class by capitalist standards, it will be unjust for the proletariat by proletarian standards. Moreover, it is clear that the proletarian standard of justice is higher. This is so, Husami argues, because the proletarian standard of justice comes closer to Marx's ideal of man, which is the norm by which Husami thinks Marx measures different standards of justice.[22]

It is also the case, for Husami, that from the proletarian perspective the capitalist's appropriation of surplus value is unjust, and he finds no evidence to suggest that it is illegitimate in Marx's view to judge an earlier or a different society by an independent moral standard. In fact, he thinks that we can find Marx doing so.[23]

The disagreement between Wood and Husami appears direct, straightforward, and clear cut. It seems that we must simply decide which view is correct. In reality, however, the matter is not so simple. In some respects both writers are correct; in other respects both are wrong. But, more importantly, each is attacking the issue one-sidedly and peripherally.

In the 'Notes on Adolph Wagner', Marx says,

In fact, in my presentation, profit is not 'merely a deduction or "robbery" on the labourer.' On the contrary, I present the capitalist as the necessary functionary of capitalist production and show very extensively that he does not only 'deduct' or 'rob', but forces the production of surplus value, therefore the deducting only helps to produce; furthermore, I show in detail that even if in the exchange of commodities only equivalents were exchanged, the capitalist—as soon as he pays the labourer the real value of his labour-power—would secure with full rights, i.e. the rights corresponding to that mode of production, surplus value . . . But all of this does not make 'profit' into a 'constitutive' element of value, but only proves that in the value not 'constituted' by the labour of the capitalist, there is a portion which he can appropriate 'legally', i.e. without infringing the rights corresponding to commodity exchange.

---

[22] Z. I. Husami, 'Marx on Distributive Justice', *MJH* 43 ff., 47-50, 60. See also G. Young, 'Doing Marx Justice', *Marx and Morality*, ed. K. Nielsen and S. C. Patten, *Canadian Journal of Philosophy*, suppl. vol. 7 (1981), 251-68.

[23] Husami, 'Marx on Distributive Justice', *MJH* 49-51, 53-4, 59, 66 ff.

When Wood comments on this passage, he makes a great deal out of Marx's claim that the capitalist appropriates surplus value with full rights, and he tries to explain away the parts of the passage in which Marx also claims that it is a robbery. On the other hand, Husami focuses on the claim that this appropriation is robbery, but discounts the claim that it also is in accord with right.[24] I can see no way around this. In this passage Marx says *both* that the capitalist robs and that he acts in accordance with right. The capitalist is acting both justly and unjustly in the same act. It is not legitimate to dismiss one or the other side of this apparent contradiction. To explain it and to unravel the dispute between Wood and Husami, we must understand the method which Marx employs in his later writings for the study of political economy. This method, which is outlined for the first time in the Introduction to the *Grundrisse* and which in *Capital* Marx calls his 'dialectic method',[25] goes quite far beyond the method of the *German Ideology*, which, as far as I can see, Wood and Husami assume Marx to be operating with in the later writings. The one-sidedness of their views seems to stem from this assumption. A correct understanding of Marx's new method will go a long way towards helping us to comprehend the ethical views to be found in his later writings.

III

I have discussed the new method which Marx outlines in the *Grundrisse* in *Marx' Method, Epistemology, and Humanism*, and so I ask the reader's indulgence while I cover some of the same ground again.[26] Marx's method in the *Grundrisse* does not begin, as it did in the *German Ideology*, by tracing the development of production through its different historical stages, nor by selecting a specific epoch which it then studies in a straightforward historical fashion. Instead, it begins by isolating—sifting out by comparison and analysis—certain abstract and general categories common to all epochs of production. It does not begin historically; it begins conceptually or logically. Marx holds that, in each particular epoch, these general characteristics or categories split

[24] 'Notes on Adolph Wagner', in *Texts on Method*, trans. T. Carver (New York: Barnes & Noble, 1975), 186, and *MEW* XIX. 359-60. A. W. Wood, *Karl Marx* (London: Routledge & Kegan Paul, 1981), 137 ff. 'Reply', pp. 115-18. Husami, 'Marx on Distributive Justice', *MJH* 76-7.

[25] *C* I. 19, and *MEW* XXIII. 27. There is a discussion of Marx's new method in Wood's book (*Karl Marx*, pp. 216-34), but it does not seem to have influenced his treatment of Marx's ethics.

[26] See my *Marx' Method, Epistemology, and Humanism*, ch. 3.

into different determinations. The task is not to focus on the common characteristics as eternal laws independent of history, but rather to see how these general characteristics are determined differently in different periods. The general must be distinguished from the specific. For example, Marx says that 'all production is appropriation of nature on the part of an individual within and through a specific form of society'. However, he then goes on to tell us that in one epoch this appropriation can take the form of communal property and in another the form of private property. Moreover, the development of a specific epoch is determined not by those characteristics which are common to all but by those which are specific to that epoch.[27]

Traditional political economy did not begin in this way, but by studying the real and the concrete—the actual historical period. From there it had to move analytically to simple categories or abstract general relations. Only at that point could the scientifically correct method begin. It takes up these simple concepts, works out the relationships that exist between them in modern society, and only then works back towards an understanding of the concrete. It can then grasp the concrete as a 'rich totality of many determinations and relations'. The concrete, for Marx, is the organized and articulated concentration of many determinations and relations—it is not given at the start *for thought*, but is the outcome of a process of comparison, analysis, and investigation. Marx admits that the actual concrete is the starting-point for real historical development as well as for observation, but we can grasp it at the start only as a vague and chaotic conception. For science, the

---

[27] *G* 85-8, and *GKPO* 7-10. Marx also approaches the category of labour in this way; see *C* I. 177-8, 183-4, 508, and *MEW* XXIII. 192-3, 198-9, 531. The same applies to the concept of the commodity. Ch. 1 of *Capital* does not set out to discuss capitalism exclusively, but discusses any form of exchange or commodity-producing society in general; e.g. Marx tells us that we find commodities in pre-capitalist economies (*C* I. 61, 79, and *MEW* XXIII. 76, 93; *C* III. 177, and *MEW* XXV. 182). Marx specifically excludes the discussion of wage labour from ch. 1; he says 'Wages is a category that, as yet, has no existence at the present stage of our investigation.' (*C* I. 44 n. and *MEW* XXIII. 59 n.). A society without wage labour is obviously not capitalist. Marx explicitly states that even fetishism can occur in pre-capitalist societies (*C* I. 82, and *MEW* XXIII. 97). Capitalism proper is not introduced until chs. 3 and 4 where Marx finally distinguishes two forms of exchange characterized by the two formulas: C-M-C and M-C-M´, only the latter of which is the capitalist form of exchange. The commodity then appears as a simple abstraction which can be grasped through analysis in higher stages of social development and which had existed in other earlier and lower stages of society (*C* I. 59-60, and *MEW* XXIII. 73-4). The point is to begin with this simple category, distinguish general characteristics from specific capitalist ones, and discover interconnections with other categories in modern society in order to work towards an understanding of the concrete. For a fuller discussion of this matter see my *Marx' Method, Epistemology, and Humanism*, ch. 3, sect. i.

concrete is a *result*. The concrete for thought must be constructed or reproduced. Only then do we achieve through analysis a clear and scientific understanding of the concrete. Marx is very careful to point out, however, that the method of moving from abstract general categories to the concrete is merely the way in which our thought grasps the concrete. It is by no means the way in which the concrete actually is produced, as Hegel thought. The conceptual method does not produce, nor even transform, the actual concrete. For theoretical knowledge, the object retains its autonomous existence outside the head, unchanged, just as before.[28]

In the *Poverty of Philosophy*, Marx had said of Proudhon's method, 'How, indeed, could the single logical formula of movement, of sequence, of time, explain the structure of society, in which all relations coexist simultaneously and support one another?'[29] This implies a rejection not just of Proudhon's method but also of the straightforward historical method that Marx himself had employed in the *German Ideology*. Only an analysis and reconstruction of relations is now seen as adequate to explain their synchronicity, connectedness, and structure.

As we have said, these general categories common to all epochs of production are determined differently in particular epochs. The categories are transformed historically. In each epoch, Marx says, a particular form of production predominates. It assigns rank and influence to the other elements. It is 'a general illumination which bathes all the other colours and modifies their particularity'. Each category is stamped and moulded by the particular structure of the period because the economic reality which the category expresses has been transformed in each period. The context of interconnected relations is changed by the development which the particular form of production undergoes.[30] These categories develop historically in two important ways, by becoming more abstract or general and increasingly subordinate to a complex economic structure.

In earlier, less developed economies, the main categories stand out in their simplicity and express dominant relations. In more highly developed societies, the categories express subordinate relations of a more developed and complex whole. Compare, for example, money in

[28] *G* 100-2, and *GKPO* 21-2.

[29] *Poverty of Philosophy*, *MECW* VI. 167, and *MEW* IV. 131. This text was written shortly after the *German Ideology*. Nevertheless, Marx did not develop his concept of structure until the *Grundrisse*. To have done so earlier would have involved undermining the historical method of the *German Ideology*, which it seems he was not ready to do.

[30] *G* 107, also p. 776, and *GKPO* 27, 662.

the form of cattle or precious metals in early history to credit or interest in modern society. Again, in early history, Marx says, an individual or clan simply *possess* land or goods. Only in more developed societies do individuals hold *property*, and this involves complex juridical relations determined by and subordinate to a complex economic structure. Thus, a category can stand out, predominate, and express dominant relations of a less developed economy or it can express the subordinate relations of a more developed one.[31] Only in this way does the historical development of the categories parallel the scientific path of abstract thought. Both rise from the simple to the combined. But the scientifically correct method does not take up categories in the same sequence in which they developed historically. The proper sequence, as we shall see, is determined instead by the relationships which categories have to each other in modern society.

Categories also become more abstract as history progresses. The best example of this is labour. The Physiocrats finally identified labour as the creator of all wealth, but only in a particular form, agricultural labour. Later, Adam Smith identified labour in general—all forms of labour—as the creator of wealth. It was only possible for Smith to make this advance, Marx thinks, in a society where no specific form of labour was predominant—in a developed capitalist economy where individuals transfer easily from one form of labour to another and where the individual is relatively indifferent to the specific form of labour involved. The most general abstractions arise only in a complex society 'where one thing appears common to many, to all. Then it ceases to be thinkable in a particular form alone.' Abstract labour is not merely a product of abstract thought. Labour itself has become abstract—labour in general creates wealth and is linked no longer to a specific form.[32]

Again, Marx holds that the development of exchange value to its abstract purity and generality presupposes a mode of production in which the product is not produced directly to satisfy a particular need of the producer. Exchange value develops only in a complex market economy where products are produced for exchange, thus, where the producer becomes increasingly indifferent to what particular sort of thing is produced and is concerned only with the exchange value to be achieved through the sale of the product.[33]

We thus see that abstract categories, with which the scientifically correct method must begin, can achieve their full development, reach

31 *G* 102, and *GKPO* 22-3.
32 *G* 104, and *GKPO* 24-5.
33 *G* 251-2, and *GKPO* 163-4.

full abstraction, only in highly developed and complex societies which only arise relatively late in history.[34] In some cases, it is not even possible to grasp a category earlier in history. For example, Marx points to Aristotle, who argued that exchange '"cannot take place without equality and equality not without commensurability" . . . Here, however, he [Aristotle] comes to a stop, and gives up the analysis of the form of value.' For Aristotle, it was impossible that 'unlike things can be commensurable,—i.e., qualitatively equal. Such an equalisation can only be something foreign to their real nature'. Why was Aristotle unable to grasp the category of value and see that different commodities can be equal to each other in value if they both required equal amounts of labour time for their production? There was

an important fact which prevented Aristotle from seeing that, to attribute value to commodities, is merely a mode of expressing all labour as equal human labour, and consequently as labour of equal quality. Greek society was founded on slavery . . . The secret of the expression of value, namely, that all kinds of labour are equal and equivalent . . . cannot be deciphered until the notion of human equality has already acquired the fixity of a popular prejudice.[35]

Thus, the scientifically correct method must be able to start with highly developed abstract categories in order to work out the interconnections between them and thus to understand modern society, and also, as we see in Marx's discussion of Aristotle's attempt to understand the concept of value, so that the method can come to understand past societies sometimes more clearly than they could understand themselves. For Marx,

Bourgeois society is the most developed and the most complex historic organization of production. The categories which express its relations, the comprehension of its structure, thereby, also allows insights into the structure and relations of production of all vanished social formations out of whose ruins and elements it built itself up, whose partly still unconquered remnants are

---

[34] *G* 103, and *GKPO* 23-4.

[35] *C* I. 59-60, and *MEW* XXIII. 73-4. See also Aristotle, *NE* 1133[b]. Marx also says that the exchange of commodities at their value occurs only at a low stage of economic development. Nevertheless, the study of modern society in *Capital* begins theoretically by assuming that commodities exchange at their values. Only slowly do we come to see in *Capital* that they exchange at their prices of production which diverge from their values. Thus, the concept of value can be grasped theoretically only at a high stage of economic development where categories become abstract and fully developed. We begin with this category theoretically in studying modern society, but, historically, products only exchange at their values in early less developed societies where relations are simple and not subordinate to a complex structure (*C* III. 177, 896, and *MEW* XXV. 186-7, 905-6).

carried along within it, whose mere nuances have developed explicit significance within it, etc. Human anatomy contains a key to the anatomy of the ape. The intimations of higher development among the subordinate animal species, however, can be understood only after the higher development is already known. The bourgeois economy thus supplies the key to the ancient, etc.

Just as Cuvier could reconstruct the entire anatomy of a particular animal from one of its bones, since he knew the higher fully developed structure of the species,[36] or just as 'Relics of bygone instruments of labour possess the same importance for the investigation of extinct economic forms of society, as do fossil bones for the determination of extinct species of animals',[37] so given an understanding of modern categories and their structural interconnections, we can begin to understand past societies.

An understanding of categories and their interconnection in modern society is necessary in the way that for some contemporary philosophers of science a paradigm is necessary before it becomes possible to study empirically the phenomena under consideration. Moreover, this paradigm or articulated structure of categories makes it possible to understand and illuminate the specific determination of categories in earlier societies. One can see what is missing (as in the case of Aristotle or the Physiocrats discussed above), and one can identify elements which have been modified, transformed, or even inverted.

One must start with the fully developed categories of modern society. One cannot begin with the categories that express earlier forms of society and hope to trace their development to modern society. For example, if one studies the feudal period, one will discover that landed property predominates over other forms of production and that they are dependent upon it; it will also appear that only agricultural labour creates wealth. In capitalism, landed property and agriculture become subordinate forms of production. The relationship becomes inverted. Landed property becomes a branch of capital and industry, and, of course, we finally see that labour in general creates wealth. Marx also adds that ground rent, derived from landed property, 'cannot be understood without capital. But capital can certainly be understood without ground rent.' For the scientifically correct method,

it would therefore be unfeasible and wrong to let the economic categories follow one another in the same sequence as that in which they were historically

---

[36] *G* 105, also p. 776, and *GKPO* 25-6, 662. Also *C* I. 8-9, and *MEW* XXIII. 12. For a discussion of Cuvier's method see G. W. F. Hegel, *Hegel's Philosophy of Nature*, trans. J. Petry (London: Allen & Unwin, 1970), III. 178-84, and *SW* IX. 674-84.

[37] *C* I. 179-80, and *MEW* XXIII. 194.

decisive. Their sequence is determined rather by their relation to one another in modern bourgeois society, which is precisely the opposite of that which seems to be their natural order or which corresponds to their historical development.[38]

Again, Marx says that the historically earlier form of merchant's capital

is incapable by itself of promoting and explaining the transition from one mode of production to another. Within capitalist production merchant's capital is reduced from its former independent existence to a special phase in the investment of capital . . . The special social conditions that take shape within the development of merchant's capital are no longer paramount. On the contrary, wherever merchant's capital still predominates we find backward conditions.[39]

In the *German Ideology*, Marx argued that one must begin by empirically studying the concrete historical world, tracing its material development, and then the rise of ideas determined by that development. One did not make use of abstract categories in any significant way—in fact, such an approach was rejected explicitly. Abstract categories appeared only at the end of the study and merely summed things up. They were generated by the study of material conditions, much as ideas in general were generated by the historical development of material conditions, that is, as results which did not affect the process of development.[40] In the *Grundrisse*, Marx has changed his mind. He begins with abstract categories, works them into a paradigm, and only then, he thinks, does it become possible to understand empirically the actual world or its historical development. The working up of this paradigm must *precede* the study of material conditions and the latter can only be understood *through* the paradigm.[41]

Nevertheless, Marx has not abandoned the historical materialist claim that material conditions, the forces and relations of production, at least

---

[38] *G* 107, and *GKPO* 27-8.

[39] *C* III. 327, and *MEW* XXV. 339.

[40] *GI, MECW* V. 37, 53-4, and *MEW* III. 27, 37-8.

[41] I have argued elsewhere that the new method of the *Grundrisse* implies that consciousness could not be determined as strictly by material conditions as Marx held that it was in the *German Ideology*. Since the working up of the paradigm—the scientific thought processes involved—must precede the understanding of material conditions, it cannot be strictly determined by material conditions or at least we could never know how it was because we can understand material conditions, their development, and their effect on consciousness only *after* we have constructed the paradigm and *through* that very paradigm. Thus, as we have seen, in the Preface to the *Critique of Political Economy* of 1859, Marx denies that consciousness can be determined with the same precision that is possible in studying transformations within the realm of material production (see my *Marx' Method, Epistemology, and Humanism*, ch. 3, sects. i-iii. Also *CPE* 20-1, and *MEW* XIII. 9).

predominate in determining society and consciousness. Marx says, 'the conclusion we reach is not that production, distribution, exchange and consumption are identical, but that they all form members of a totality, distinctions within a unity. Production predominates not only over itself . . . but over the other elements as well'. He also says, 'from the specific form of material production arises in the first place the specific structure of society, in the second place a specific relation of men to nature. Their State and their spiritual outlook is determined by both. Therefore also the kind of their spiritual production.'[42]

We must discuss yet another aspect of Marx's method. As we have seen, in the *German Ideology* Marx ceased to employ the concept of essence which had been central to his thought in 1844. In the *Grundrisse* and *Capital*, he again begins to operate with a concept of essence, though, as we shall eventually see, a very different one than in 1844.

In *Capital*, Marx tells us that 'all science would be superfluous if the outward appearance and the essence of things directly coincided'. Surface phenomena are quite different from the concealed essence of things.[43] He says that it is a 'paradox that the earth moves around the sun, and that water consists of two highly inflammable gases. Scientific truth is always paradox judged by everyday experience, which catches only the delusive appearance of things.'[44]

This distinction between essence and appearance enables us to understand the category of value. It is quite clear that value is to be considered an essence behind surface appearance. Marx tells us that 'use-value becomes the form of manifestation, the phenomenal form of its opposite, value'. And also, 'Value . . . does not stalk about with a label describing what it is. It is value, rather, that converts every product into a social hieroglyphic. Later on, we try to decipher the hieroglyphic, to get behind the secret of our own social products'.[45] As we have seen already, Aristotle was unable to discover this hidden essence. That could be accomplished only in a more complex society where categories had reached their highest development. We must see also that the scientifically correct method seeks this inner essence behind phenomenal appearance. The method does not begin with an empirical study of a historical period—the vague and chaotic surface

[42] *G* 99, also pp. 94-5, and *GKPO* 20, 15-16. See also *TSV* I. 285, and *MEW* XXVI. part i. 257; *C* I. 18, and *MEW* XXIII. 26.
[43] *C* III. 209, 817, and *MEW* XXV. 219, 825. See also *CPE* 61, and *MEW* XIII. 46.
[44] *VPP* 37, and *MEW* XVI. 129.
[45] *C* I. 56, 74, and *MEW* XXIII. 70, 88.

appearance of the real and concrete. It begins with abstract categories arrived at by analysis and it works these categories into an inter-connected structure which grasps an essence. Only then does it return to the study of the actual empirical concrete. The first volume of *Capital* begins by studying abstract categories (for example, the commodity, value, labour), and, as Marx tells us in the third volume of *Capital*, slowly works back towards the phenomenal surface of society (to prices, profit, rate of profit).[46] He tells us, in *Capital*, that 'a scientific analysis . . . is not possible, before we have a conception of the inner nature of capital, just as the apparent motions of the heavenly bodies are not intelligible to any but him, who is acquainted with their real motions, motions which are not directly perceptible by the senses'.[47]

We have spent enough time describing Marx's method. To sum up our findings, we can say that it involves four principles: (1) One begins not with an empirical and historical study of society, but with abstract categories reached by analysis. (2) As these categories are transformed through history, they become more abstract and general, and they increasingly become subordinate to a complex economic structure. (3) When one has discovered the interconnection of categories in modern society and worked them into a paradigm, only then does it become possible to gain a clear empirical understanding of modern society and also a clear understanding of past societies. (4) This categorial structure grasps the essence of things behind surface appearance.

So far, we have considered Marx's method solely as a method for the study of political economy. Marx tells us that it also applies in religion, mathematics, anthropology, and he seems to suggest that it applies in natural science and astronomy.[48]

It is also clear that Marx uses this method in the study of aesthetics. As we noticed earlier, at the end of the Introduction to the *Grundrisse*, after he had laid out his method, Marx told us that Greek art constituted a now unattainable norm, despite the fact that it arose in a society with a very low level of economic development. Just as the categories of political economy stand out in their simplicity and express clear predominant relations in less developed economies, so in Greek society

---

[46] *C* I. 8, and *MEW* XXIII. 12. *C* III. 25, and *MEW* XXV. 33.

[47] *C* I. 316, and *MEW* XXIII. 335; see also *C* III. 48, and *MEW* XXV. 57-8.

[48] *G* 106, 460-1, and *GKPO* 26, 364-5. F. Engels, *Origin of the Family, Private Property, and the State* (New York: International, 1942), 27, and *MEW* XXI. 38. *VPP* 37, and *MEW* XVI. 129. *C* III. 817, and *MEW* XXV. 825. *C* I. 316, and *MEW* XXIII. 335.

simple predominant relations stood out and were grasped easily by the imagination of the artist. The simplicity of Greek society allowed for the predominance of consciousness and thus for the power of its art. Nature, society, and the individual could be dominated and shaped into an imaginative unity which made possible the scope and totality of the epic. In more complex societies, we have seen, categories become subordinate to a complex structure, and so the predominance of the imagination vanishes in the face of complex social relations where only the technological mastery of nature remains possible. Achilles is not possible with powder and lead. What chance, Marx says, has Vulcan against Roberts and Company or Jupiter against the lightning rod?[49]

Marx has similar things to say about the individual of the ancient world.

In earlier stages of development the single individual seems to be developed more fully, because he has not yet worked out his relationships in their fullness, or erected them as independent social powers and relations opposite himself.[50]

In bourgeois economics—and in the epoch of production to which it corresponds—the complete working-out of the human content appears as a complete emptying-out, this universal objectification as total alienation and the tearing-down of all limited, one-sided aims as sacrifice of the human end-in-itself to an entirely external end. This is why the childish world of antiquity appears on the one side as loftier. On the other side, it really is loftier in all matters where closed shapes, forms and given limits are sought for.[51]

Again the individual of the ancient world stands out, predominates, whereas in the modern world the individual is subordinate, alienated, and thus less realized as an individual.

However, the main question that concerns us here is whether this method can be said to apply to ethics. Marx writes in the *Theories of Surplus Value* that 'Jones outlines the changes in the development of the productive forces characteristic of [the capitalist] mode of production. How the (economic) relations and consequently the social, moral and political state of nations changes with the change in the material powers of production, is very well explained.'[52] Here, at least the point is made that the historical development of capitalism produces changes in morality. But nothing is said about how these changes, or changes in

---

[49] *G* 110-11, and *GKPO* 30-1.
[50] *G* 162, and *GKPO* 80.
[51] *G* 488, and *GKPO* 387-8.
[52] *TSV* III. 430, and *MEW* XXVI, part iii. 422.

moral categories, are to be understood. In *Capital*, however, Marx writes,

> But original sin is at work everywhere. As capitalist production, accumulation, and wealth become developed, the capitalist ceases to be the mere incarnation of capital. He has a fellow feeling for his own Adam, and his education gradually enables him to smile at the rage for asceticism, as a mere prejudice of the old-fashioned miser. While the capitalist of the classical type brands individual consumption as a sin against his function and as 'abstinence' from accumulating, the modernized capitalist is capable of looking upon accumulation as 'abstinence' from pleasure ... At the historical dawn of capitalist production—and every capitalist upstart has personally to go through this historical stage—avarice, and desire to get rich, are the ruling passions. But the progress of capitalist production not only creates a world of delights; it lays open in speculation and the credit system, a thousand sources of sudden enrichment. When a certain stage of development has been reached, a conventional degree of prodigality, which is also an exhibition of wealth, and consequently a source of credit, becomes a business necessity to the 'unfortunate' capitalist. Moreover, the capitalist gets rich, not like the miser, in proportion to his personal labour and restricted consumption, but at the same rate as he squeezes out of the labour-power of others, and enforces on the labourer abstinence from all life's enjoyments.[53]

If we look closely, we can see at least a hint of Marx's method here. To make this clearer, let us recall something we saw in Chapter 2. In the 'Comments on Mill', Marx claimed that the credit system perverted virtue. For example, trustworthiness, instead of being a moral value and an end in itself, became subordinate to the credit system. It became a means to get credit or a guarantee that loans would be repaid.[54] So also here in *Capital*, the original virtue of abstinence gives way to prodigality as capitalism develops. Moreover, this transformation is produced by the credit system. The display of wealth becomes a business necessity—it ensures good credit. The individual's behaviour increasingly becomes subordinate to and is transformed by complex economic processes. Virtues no longer stand out as accomplishments of the individual. Furthermore, the capitalist's desire for wealth is no longer achieved through his own particular and personal effort, but through a complex and abstract process of squeezing wealth out of the labour power of others.

We might look for a moment to Engels for some guidance on these matters. For him, human beings 'derive their moral ideas in the last

[53] *C* I. 593-4, and *MEW* XXIII. 619-20.
[54] *CM, MECW* III. 214-15, and *MEW*, suppl. I. 448-9.

resort from the practical relations on which their class position is based—from the economic relations in which they carry on production and exchange'. He also notes a progress in morality, a development from Christian-feudal morality, to bourgeois morality, and on to proletarian morality. The latter will be a 'really human morality which transcends class antagonisms and their legacies in thought'.[55]

Proletarian morality is clearly the highest morality, but this claim must be understood in a specific way. For Engels, we must 'reject every attempt to impose on us any moral dogmas whatsoever as an eternal, ultimate and forever immutable moral law on the pretext that the moral world too has its permanent principles which transcend history and the differences between nations'. Proletarian morality is not the highest because it is closest to an objective or absolute moral norm for there are no such norms for Engels. How then do we compare moral systems? Engels asks, 'Which then is the true one? Not one of them, in the sense of having absolute validity; but certainly that morality which contains the maximum of all durable elements is the one which, in the present, represents the overthrow of the present, represents the future, that is, the proletarian.'[56] Basically, Engels thinks, as Brenkert has shown convincingly, that proletarian morality is the highest morality only because it is an outgrowth and expression of a higher stage of *society*.[57] Eventually, we must decide whether or not this is also Marx's view.

If we now look closely at certain categories connected with morality—namely, equality and freedom—we can get a better view of Marx's method at work. These categories are transformed in different periods of production and become more abstract and increasingly subordinate to a complex social structure. Marx says,

Equality and freedom as developed to this extent are exactly the opposite of the freedom and equality in the world of antiquity, where developed exchange value was not their basis, but where, rather, the development of that basis destroyed them. Equality and freedom presuppose relations of production as yet unrealized in the ancient world and in the Middle Ages.

[55] F. Engels, *Anti-Dühring (AD)*, trans. E. Burns (New York: International, 1939), 105, and *MEW* XX. 88.

[56] *AD* 104-5, and *MEW* XX. 87-8.

[57] G. G. Brenkert, 'Marx, Engels, and the Relativity of Morals', *Studies in Soviet Thought*, 17 (1977), 201-24, esp. pp. 212-13, 216-17. I have argued elsewhere that Engels' understanding of method is quite different from Marx's and that Engels misunderstands Marx's method. I have also argued that for Engels our thought processes are strictly determined—a position which Marx does not hold—and that in general he holds to a much stricter form of determinism than Marx (*Marx' Method, Epistemology, and Humanism*, ch. 4). For these reasons, in so far as Marx's ethical views are linked to his views on method, Engels is not a good guide.

Equality and freedom are produced as individuals become subordinate to and determined by the complex economic structure of the market. With the development of capitalist exchange and exchange value, all buyers and sellers meet freely in the market-place as equals. This relationship is abstract in two different senses. It is abstract in the sense of being universal or general—*all* individuals meet as free equals in the market-place. It is also abstract in the sense that capitalism abstracts from all characteristics of individuals except their equality and freedom in the market-place. In other respects they may not be equal and free at all.[58]

Capitalist equality is imperfect. Nor will it explain the higher development of equality to be found in socialist society. For Marx, as we have seen, the categories of one stage neither explain nor promote the development of a subsequent higher stage. Marx criticizes socialists like Proudhon who seek to realize the sort of equality and freedom which exist as ideals in capitalist society but which they think merely have been perverted in practice,

The proper reply to them is: that exchange value or, more precisely, the money system is in fact the system of equality and freedom, and that the disturbances which they encounter in the further development of the system are disturbances inherent in it, are merely the realization of equality and freedom, which prove to be inequality and unfreedom.

For example, Marx rejects the view that it is possible to realize an equality of wages within capitalist society,

[58] *G* 245-6, and *GKPO* 156-7. *C* I. 168 and *MEW* XXIII. 182. These two different notions of abstraction can be made clearer if we look at Hegel. Hegel held that moral categories become increasingly abstract and general as history progresses. Early in history justice took the form of revenge. Were an outsider to murder a member of one's clan, one had an obligation to avenge that murder. This would be perfectly just in so far as it was retribution, but nevertheless it would appear to outsiders as merely the particular act of a subjective will and thus would become a new transgression to be avenged in return. The problem here is that moral principles are not universal. Outsiders are treated differently from one's own clan. The killing of a fellow clan member is considered murder, but the killing of the outsider is legitimate retribution. However, to the outsider this retaliation is not legitimate retribution, but simple murder. One's moral obligations and the moral prohibition against murder do not extend beyond one's own clan. Later in history, certainly by the time of Kantian morality, moral principles have become abstract and general. A moral principle is universal in scope. Indeed, the categorial imperative holds that universality is the test of the morality of an action. At the same time, for Hegel, Kantian morality is also abstract in another sense. It is formal and contentless. It is abstract as opposed to concrete. It isolates a particular feature of reality, abstracts it out of the living whole of concrete ethical life, formulates it as a general principle, and then asks if it can be universalized. See Hegel, *PR* 71, 89-90, and *GPR* 96, 120-1. See also *PS* 256-61, and *PG* 305-11.

Upon the basis of the wages system the value of labouring power is settled like that of every other commodity; and as different kinds of labouring power have different values . . . they must fetch different prices in the labour market. To clamour for equal or even equitable retribution on the basis of the wages system is the same as to clamour for freedom on the basis of the slavery system.[59]

For Marx, we cannot use a capitalist notion of equality to explain or promote a higher form of equality. However, in the first stage of communist society, the principle of equal right is finally achieved without principle and practice being at loggerheads. An equality of wages is achieved in the sense that what individuals draw from the social stock of means of consumption is in equal proportion to the labour time which the individuals contribute.[60]

However, this equal right still will be, Marx thinks, a right of inequality. Given individuals with unequal endowment and unequal productive capacity, inequality will result,

Right by its very nature can consist only in the application of an equal standard; but unequal individuals (and they would not be different individuals if they were not unequal) are measurable only by an equal standard in so far as they are brought under an equal point of view, are taken from one definite side only, for instance, in the present case, are regarded only as workers and nothing more is seen in them, everything else being ignored. Further, one worker is married, another not; one has more children than another, and so on and so forth . . . to avoid all these defects, right instead of being equal would have to be unequal.[61]

Here, equality is still abstract—both in the sense that it is universal and in the sense that we abstract from all the characteristics of the individual except the fact that he or she is a worker contributing a certain amount of labour time. The latter form of abstraction finally is overcome in the second stage of communist society where goods will be distributed in proportion to the concrete needs of the individual. There the individual will be treated as a concrete being, not an abstraction.

However, in the second stage of communist society, it might seem that equality is done away with. This society will operate upon the principle, 'From each according to his ability, to each according to his needs!' Brenkert points out that, as Marx says, 'Right by its very nature can consist only in the application of an equal standard', and since the principle 'to each according to his needs' is not a principle of equality, Marx is abandoning equal right here. Wood also makes a similar

[59] *G* 248-9, and *GKPO* 160; *VPP* 39, and *MEW* XVI. 131-2.
[60] 'Gotha', p. 530, and *MEW* XIX. 20.
[61] 'Gotha', pp. 530-1, and *MEW* XIX. 21.

point.[62] I cannot agree with Brenkert and Wood here. It seems to me that the second stage of communism embodies a transformed concept of equality. Aristotle, for example, distinguished between arithmetic and geometric equality. Arithmetic equality requires that individuals receive strictly equal shares. The way A is treated is the same as the way B is treated. Geometric equality only requires equal proportionality, as when A is to B as X is to Y. Individuals of greater worth are due more, but equally in proportion to their worth. So the share of A is to the share of B as X is to Y, that is, as the worth of X is to the worth of Y, where X and Y are qualities of, respectively, A and B. This, it seems to me, is the principle adopted by Marx for the second stage of communism. However, for Marx, it is not a person's class, status, wealth, or even virtue which determines the amount due them, but simply their needs.

Thus, in the second stage of communist society, the bourgeois form of equal right will be transcended. Marx also speaks of equal right as being among 'ideas which in a certain period had some meaning but have now become obsolete verbal rubbish'.[63] It is clear that this general concept is determined differently in different periods and that the concept becomes more abstract, in the sense of being applicable in a more universal way, as communist society is approached. However, it finally ceases to be abstract in the sense of considering only one aspect of the individual in isolation. Equality moves from being an abstract universal to being a concrete universal as it approaches communist society—just as the method moves from the consideration of abstract categories to a grasp of the concrete.

Marx has more to say about freedom. He distinguishes three stages in its historical development:

Relations of personal dependence (entirely spontaneous at the outset) are the first social forms, in which human productive capacity develops only to a slight extent and at isolated points. Personal independence founded on objective dependence is the second great form, in which a system of general social metabolism, of universal relations, of all-round needs and universal capacities is formed for the first time. Free individuality, based on the universal development of individuals and on their subordination of their communal, social productivity as their social wealth, is the third stage. The second stage creates the conditions for the third.[64]

62 Ibid. Brenkert, 'Freedom and Private Property', p. 91. 'Reply', p. 131. Elsewhere, Wood's view is that Marx is 'an opponent of the ideal of equality'. See 'Marx and Equality', *Issues in Marxist Philosophy*, 4. *Social and Political Philosophy*, ed. J. Mepham and D. H. Ruben (Brighton: Harvester, 1981), 196 ff.

63 'Gotha', p. 531, and *MEW* XIX. 21-2.

64 *G* 158, and *GKPO* 75-6.

Concerning the first stage, Marx says that in the ancient world 'the single individual seems to be developed more fully, because he has not yet worked out his relationships in their fullness, or erected them as independent social powers, and as relations opposite himself'. The individual stands out, not yet subordinated to complex social relations. Marx also says of these individuals that 'although their relations appear to be more personal, [they] enter into connection with one another only as individuals imprisoned within certain definitions, as feudal lord and vassal, landlord and serf, etc.' In the second stage, 'the ties of personal dependence . . . are in fact exploded, ripped up . . . and individuals seem independent (this is an independence which is at bottom merely an illusion . . .), free to collide with one another and to engage in exchange within this freedom'. These individuals are alienated—subordinate to and dominated by their own complex social relations,

The definedness of individuals, which in the former case appears as a personal restriction of the individual by another, appears in the latter case as developed into an objective restriction of the individual by relations independent of him and sufficient unto themselves . . . individuals are now ruled by abstractions, whereas earlier they depended on one another. The abstraction, or idea, however, is nothing more than the theoretical expression of those material relations which are their lord and master.[65]

For Marx, this shows the

insipidity of the view that free competition is the ultimate development of human freedom . . . It is nothing more than free development on a limited basis—the basis of the rule of capital. This kind of individual freedom is therefore at the same time the most complete suspension of all individual freedom, and the most complete subjugation of individuality under social conditions which assume the form of objective powers, even of overpowering objects—of things independent of the relations among individuals themselves.[66]

Again, freedom becomes increasingly abstract and subordinate to complex social processes.

Only in the third stage is true freedom finally realized. In socialism, individuals must control rationally their interchange with each other and with nature in order to achieve a society in which 'the full and free development of every individual forms the ruling principle'. Here again, freedom remains abstract in the sense that it is universal, but it ceases to be abstract in the sense of the individual only being free in

[65] *G* 162-4, also pp. 464-5, and *GKPO* 80-2, 368-9.
[66] *G* 652, and *GKPO* 545.

certain isolated or abstracted ways (for example, in free competition). Socialized individuals become free in a concrete sense—they control their social and natural world so as to achieve a 'full and free development' by providing for each in accordance with their needs.[67] We see here, as well as in the discussion of equal right, that as we move from capitalism to socialism, moral categories do not continue to become subordinate to complex social relations, but free themselves from them. We will discuss this at a later point.

Marx also discusses justice,

The justice of the transactions between agents of production rests on the fact that these arise as natural consequences out of the production relationships. The juristic forms in which these economic transactions appear as wilful acts of the parties concerned, as expressions of their common will and as contracts that may be enforced by law against some individual party, cannot being mere forms, determine this content. They merely express it. This content is just whenever it corresponds, is appropriate, to the mode of production. It is unjust whenever it contradicts that mode. Slavery on the basis of capitalist production is unjust; likewise fraud in the quality of commodities.[68]

It is also clear that as material conditions develop, conceptions of justice are transformed in the same way as other categories. In modern society, for Marx, justice becomes increasingly determined by and subordinate to abstract social processes. Marx tells us that in feudal society the difference between necessary labour (the labour necessary to reproduce the value of labour power or the value of the labourer's subsistence) for which the worker was paid and surplus labour (labour that goes beyond necessary labour and which is the source of surplus value) for which the worker was not paid stood out clearly and visibly, 'the labour of the worker for himself, and his compulsory labour for his lord differ in space and time in the clearest possible way'. Labourers even may perform the work on two distinct plots of ground, one their own and the other their lord's, or they may perform entirely different sorts of labour for themselves and for their lord. Such a clear distinction is not visible in capitalist society. The worker simply labours for a certain number of hours and is paid for a day's labour. The difference between necessary labour which is paid and surplus labour which is not is unclear. The worker appears to be paid simply for the whole day's labour. This appearance,

---

[67] *C* III. 820, and *MEW* XXV. 825. *C* I. 78-80, 592, and *MEW* XXIII. 92-4, 618. 'Gotha', p. 531, and *MEW* XIX. 21.
[68] *C* III. 339-40, also pp. 385-6, and *MEW* XXV. 351-2, 398-9.

forms the basis of all the juridical notions of both labourer and capitalist ...
The exchange between capital and labour at first presents itself to the mind in
the same guise as the buying and selling of all other commodities. The buyer
gives a certain sum of money, the seller an article of nature different from
money. The jurist's consciousness recognizes this, at most, as a material difference ...[69]

The juridical consciousness abstracts from all relations except those
between buyer and seller, and this forms the basis for all juridical
notions—which would include the notion of justice. Thus, under
capitalism, the concept of justice as free exchange of equivalents comes
to be determined by and subordinate to complex, obscure, and abstract
social processes.

We have seen that Marx's treatment of these categories follows the
method outlined in the *Grundrisse* at least in the sense that these
categories undergo development and transformation through history,
and that they become increasingly abstract and subordinate to complex
social processes. It is also clear that Marx has changed his mind on an
important issue. In the *Communist Manifesto*, he registered the
objection of a hypothetical bourgeois, '"Undoubtedly," it will be said,
"religious, moral, philosophical and juridical ideas have been modified
in the course of historical development. But religion, morality,
philosophy, political science, and law, constantly survived this
change."' Marx then went on to reject this claim and to hold that such
moral and legal notions would disappear in communist society.[70] It is
now clear that Marx no longer rejects the claim made in this quotation,
at least for moral or juridical ideas. They will not disappear. His very
method is based upon understanding the transformation of such
concepts; he works out a theory of this transformation; and he holds
that these concepts will be realized fully in communist society.

It is also clear that Marx applies the methodological principle of
distinguishing between surface phenomena and inner essence to his discussion of equality and freedom. In bourgeois society, these categories
belong to the realm of surface phenomena, 'This simple circulation,
considered by itself—and it is the surface of bourgeois society,
obliterating the deeper operations from which it arises—reveals no
difference between objects of exchange except formal and temporary
ones. This is the realm of freedom, equality, and of property based on

[69] *C* I. 539-40, and *MEW* XXIII. 562-3.
[70] *Manifesto*, *MECW* VI. 504, and *MEW* IV. 480.

labour.'[71] Moreover, this liberty and equality, which appear as surface phenomena, disappear at the level of essence, 'In present bourgeois society as a whole, the positing of prices and their circulation etc. appears as a surface process, beneath which, however, in the depths, entirely different processes go on, in which this apparent individual equality and liberty disappear.' This equality and freedom 'prove to be inequality and unfreedom'.[72]

Does the distinction between essence and appearance also apply to the capitalist's appropriation of surplus value and to justice?[73] Marx says,

we started with the supposition that labour-power is bought and sold at its value. Its value, like that of all other commodities, is determined by the working time necessary to its production. If the production of the average daily means of subsistence of the labourer takes up 6 hours, he must work, on the average, 6 hours every day, to produce his daily labour-power, or to reproduce the value received as the result of its sale.[74]

But this does not prevent the labourer at all 'from working a whole day. Therefore, the value of labour-power, and the value which that labour-power creates in the labour-process, are two entirely different magnitudes; and this difference of the two values was what the capitalist had in view, when he was purchasing labour-power.' This difference is the source of the capitalist's surplus value,

The owner of the money has paid the value of a day's labour-power; his, therefore, is the use of it for a day; a day's labour belongs to him. The circumstance, that, on the one hand the daily sustenance of labour-power costs only half a day's labour, while on the other hand the very same labour-power can work during the whole day, that consequently the value which its use during the day creates, is double what he pays for that use is, without doubt, a piece of good luck for the buyer, but by no means an injury (*Unrecht*) to the seller.[75]

It is not an injury or an injustice to the seller because the seller has received the value of his or her labour power. The exchange was an exchange of equivalents. Generally speaking, for Marx, a transaction is just in capitalist society if it is an exchange of equivalents and if the

---

[71] 'Marx to Engels on 2 Apr. 1858', *SC* 107, and *MEW* XXIX. 317. See also *C* I. 540, and *MEW* XXIII. 562.

[72] *G* 247-9, and *GKPO* 159-60.

[73] On this matter see also G. A. Cohen, 'Karl Marx and the Withering Away of Social Science', *MJH* 288-300.

[74] *C* I. 231, and *MEW* XXIII. 245.

[75] *C* I. 193-4, and *MEW* XXIII. 208.

transaction was entered into freely. Equality and freedom amount to justice.[76]

But when Marx says that this exchange involves no injustice (*Unrecht*) to the seller, we must ask if, like equality and freedom, this is so only at the level of surface appearance. Marx tells us that 'The wage-form . . . extinguishes every trace of the division of the working-day into necessary and surplus labour, into paid and unpaid labour. All labour *appears* as paid labour . . . the unrequited labour of the wage labourer [is concealed].'[77] Thus the appearance is that the worker is paid simply the value of a day's labour and that the capitalist gains profit by selling the product of the day's labour on the market for more than it cost to produce it. The reality, however, is that surplus value is derived, not in circulation, not in the market, but in production. By distinguishing between labour (or a day's labour) and labour power, we see that the capitalist pays the value of labour power in the form of a wage, but pockets the difference between it and the value of the product produced by a day's labour and sold on the market. The worker is paid for one part of the labour and is not paid for the other part. The capitalist's profit is realized in circulation in the sense that the capitalist must sell successfully the product to realize a profit, but nevertheless, for Marx, this profit is dependent upon the surplus value produced by the unpaid surplus labour of the worker in production. Thus, Marx says,

Surplus-value and rate of surplus-value are, relatively, the invisible and unknown essence that wants investigating, while rate of profit and therefore the appearance of surplus-value in the form of profit are revealed on the surface of the phenomena . . . Although the excess value of a commodity over its cost-price is shaped in the immediate process of production, it is realized only in the process of circulation, and appears all the more readily to have arisen from the process of circulation . . .[78]

Thus, the surface appearance is that the worker is paid an equivalent for a day's labour and that the capitalist's profit comes from selling the product on the market. But in essence, in reality, surplus value arises

[76] This is implied at *G* 241, and *GKPO* 153. See also *VPP* 39-40, and *MEW* XVI. 131-2. Compare *C* I. 84, 84 n., with 168-9; for the German, *MEW* XXIII. 99, 99 n., 182-3.

[77] *C* I. 539-40 (my emphasis), and *MEW* XXIII. 562.

[78] *C* III. 43, see also p. 209, and *MEW* XXV. 53, 219. See also *C* I. 542, and *MEW* XXIII. 564; *G* 255, and *GKPO* 166. Cohen argues that Marx's concept of exploitation need not be based on his labour theory of value, but that nevertheless exploitation is unjust; see G. A. Cohen, 'The Labor Theory of Value and the Concept of Exploitation', *MJH* 135-57, esp. pp. 138-41, 153.

from the unpaid surplus labour of the worker in production. When Marx argues that the contract between the capitalist and the worker was not an *Unrecht* to the latter, he was able to argue this because the contract was entered into 'freely' and it involved an exchange of equivalents. All other aspects of this relation are ignored in capitalist society.[79] But this relation between capitalist and worker was an exchange of equivalents *only* at the level of surface appearance. In fact, capitalist equality and freedom in general, we have seen, are surface phenomena. Thus, since equality and freedom in exchange amount to justice, the right or justice on the side of the capitalist also belongs only to the realm of surface appearance. Marx himself says,

we may understand the decisive importance of the transformation of value and price of labour-power into the form of wages, or into the value and price of labour itself. This phenomenal form, which makes the actual relation invisible, and, indeed, shows the direct opposite of that relation, forms the basis of all juridical notions of both labourer and capitalist, of all the mystifications of the capitalist mode of production, of all its illusions as to liberty . . .[80]

If all juridical notions are phenomenal forms, so then is the conception of justice. The actual relation is the opposite of the apparent one. And even more clearly, Marx says,

Living labour capacity belongs to itself, and has disposition over the expenditure of its forces, through exchange. Both sides confront each other as persons. Formally, their relation has the equality and freedom of exchange as such. As far as concerns the legal relation, the fact that this form is a mere semblance, and a deceptive semblance, appears as an external matter.[81]

[79] e.g. Marx says, 'In so-called retail trade, in the daily traffic of bourgeois life as it proceeds directly between producers and consumers, in petty commerce . . . in this movement, which proceeds on the surface of the bourgeois world, there and there alone does the motion of exchange values, their circulation, proceed in its pure form. A worker who buys a loaf of bread and a millionaire who does the same appear in this act only as simple buyers, just as, in respect to them, the grocer appears only as a seller. All other aspects are here extinguished. The content of these purchases, like their extent, here appears as completely irrelevant compared with the formal aspect.' (*G* 251, and *GKPO* 163.)

[80] *C* I. 540, and *MEW* XXIII. 562.

[81] *G* 464, and *GKPO* 368. Marx also says, 'In so far as surplus capital I was created by means of a simple exchange between objectified labour and living labour capacity—an exchange of equivalents as measured by the quantity of labour or labour time contained in them—and in so far as the legal expression of this exchange presupposed nothing other than everyone's right of property over his own products, and of free disposition over them—but in so far as the relation of surplus capital II to I is therefore a consequence of this first relation—we see that, by a peculiar logic, the right of property undergoes a dialectical inversion, so that on the side of capital it becomes a right to an

In general, 'in present bourgeois society as a whole, this positing of prices and their circulation etc. appears as the surface process, beneath which, however, in the depths, entirely different processes go on, in which this apparent individual equality and liberty disappear'.[82]

We can see now that the passage from the 'Notes on Adolph Wagner', where Marx said that the exchange between capitalist and worker was both a robbery and also fully in accord with right, means that this exchange accords with right at the phenomenal level of surface appearance and that it is robbery in essence.[83]

It now should be clear that Wood is correct when he argues that capitalism and the exchange between the worker and the capitalist are not unjust, and when he marshals evidence to show that this in fact is Marx's view. However, Wood does not recognize that capitalism is just for Marx only at the level of surface appearance. Wood is careful to point out that capitalism is only just on the basis of standards that arise out of and express the material conditions of capitalist society. For Wood, these are the only legitimate standards by which to judge that society, but he does not see that they belong only to the realm of surface appearance. Since he does not see the difference between essence and appearance here, he does not see that for Marx capitalism is also unjust by other standards, and is so in essence. Thus, for Wood, when Marx expresses his opposition to capitalism or calls for its overthrow, this cannot be based upon the view that capitalism is unjust.[84]

alien product, or the right of property over alien labour, the right to appropriate alien labour without equivalent, and, on the side of labour capacity, it becomes a duty of respecting the product of one's own labour and one's own labour itself, as values belonging to others. The exchange of equivalents, however, which appeared as the original operation, an operation to which the right of property gave legal expression, has become turned round in such a way that the exchange by one side is now only illusory, since the part of capital which is exchanged for living labour capacity, firstly, is itself alien labour, appropriated without equivalent, and, secondly, has to be replaced with a surplus by living labour capacity, is thus in fact not consigned away, but merely changed from one form into another. The relation of exchange has thus dropped away entirely, or is a mere semblance. Furthermore, the right of property originally appeared to be based on one's own labour. Property now appears as the right to alien labour, and as the impossibility of labour appropriating its own product.' (G 457-8, and GKPO 361-2.)

[82] G 247, and GKPO 159.

[83] 'Notes on Wagner', p. 186, and MEW XIX. 359-60.

[84] 'Critique', pp. 3-4, 13-16, 21 ff. Allen tries to defend Wood here, and he is aware that for Marx we must distinguish between essence and appearance (see D. Allen, 'Marx and Engels on the Distributive Justice of Capitalism', Marx and Morality, p. 241). He admits that the exchange between worker and capitalist seems to be unjust because it is not an equal exchange. But for Allen, there are two conditions which determine whether or not an exchange is just. The first is whether or not the exchange is equal. The second is whether or not each party 'has a right to the share of wealth he receives and receives the share to which he has a right'. Thus, Allen argues that the exchange between

On the other hand, when Husami argues that for Marx capitalism *is* unjust, and when he marshals quotations to show that Marx characterizes capitalist exploitation as ' "robbery," "usurpation," "embezzlement," "plunder," "booty," "theft" . . .',[85] Husami is also perfectly correct. There is, however, a certain ambiguity in his article. At times he tries to discount Wood's claim that, for Marx, capitalism is just, and he even argues that in some of the passages where Marx actually claims that capitalism is just, Marx is speaking satirically or ironically. Husami's tendency here would seem to be that capitalism is simply unjust. Nevertheless, at other times, Husami is willing to admit that capitalism appears just to capitalists though it will not appear so to the proletariat. Here, Husami is closer to the truth than Wood is. For Husami, moral norms are determined by two factors: the prevailing mode of production and class interest. Thus capitalism can be both just or unjust, depending on one's class interests and the conditions which determine them.[86]

However, Husami's view that moral norms depend upon a class perspective seems to derive more from Engels than from Marx. For Engels, as we have seen, we must distinguish between Christian-feudal, bourgeois, and proletarian morality, and these ethical outlooks are determined by the practical relations on which class positions are based.[87] This does not seem to be Marx's view as far as I can see. Rather, for Marx, the difference between capitalist and socialist morality stems from the difference between everyday experience of surface phenomena determined by the prevailing mode of production and a scientific analysis which goes beneath this surface to grasp an essence. Marx thinks that socialist morality will accord and ought to accord with this scientifically grasped essence. Despite a passage in which Husami seems to hint that he might be about to move in this direction,[88] he does not seem to grasp the significance of Marx's method, and especially the distinction between essence and appearance, for the analysis of moral categories.

capitalist and worker is just in capitalist society, despite the fact that it is unequal, because in capitalist society the capitalist has a right to this unequal share (ibid. 241-2, 225-6). We must add that this right also belongs to the realm of surface appearance (see *G* 457-8, and *GKPO* 361-2, quoted in n. 81; *C* I. 540, and *MEW* XXIII. 562). Thus, justice on the side of the capitalist is not at the level of essence.

85 Husami, 'Marx on Distributive Justice', *MJH* 43, 45.
86 Ibid. 44, 47, 50, 53, 63, 67, 77.
87 *AD* 103-5, and *MEW* XX. 86-8.
88 Husami, 'Marx on Distributive Justice', *MJH* 69. A. E. Buchanan, however, seems to come even closer to moving in the right direction: *Marx and Justice* (Totowa, NJ: Rowman & Littlefield, 1982), 54.

Proletarian morality, before the realization of the second stage of communist society, will not be shaped by everyday experience as Husami seems to suggest it will. Science must get beneath obscure experience to the level of essence. Only this scientifically derived essence should shape proletarian morality. Proletarian morality based on everyday experience is very likely not to be distinguished from capitalist morality with sufficient clarity. We have already quoted a passage in which Marx said that all the juridical notions—and this would have to include justice—of both capitalist and worker, are shaped by phenomenal appearance.[89]

In making his argument that capitalism is just, Wood also argues that we find in Marx 'explicit denunciations and sustained criticisms of social thinkers (such as Pierre Proudhon and Ferdinand Lassalle) who did condemn capitalism for its injustices or advocated some form of socialism as a means of securing justice, equality, or the rights of man'. It is quite true that Marx does criticize these thinkers, but he does not denounce them because they thought capitalism unjust or saw socialism as a means of achieving moral ends, but because of the way in which they did this:

Thus, what all this wisdom comes down to is the attempt to stick fast at the simplest economic relations, which conceived by themselves, are pure abstractions; but these relations are, in reality, mediated by the deepest antitheses, and represent only one side, in which the full expression of the antitheses is obscured.

What this reveals, on the other side, is the foolishness of those socialists (namely the French, who want to depict socialism as the realization of the ideals of bourgeois society articulated by the French Revolution) who demonstrate that exchange and exchange value etc. are originally (in time) or essentially (in their adequate form) a system of universal freedom and equality, but that they have been perverted by money, capital, etc. Or, also, that history has so far failed in every attempt to implement them in their true manner, but that they have now, like Proudhon, discovered e.g. the real Jacob, and intend now to supply the genuine history of these relations in place of the fake. The proper reply to them is: that exchange value or, more precisely, the money system is in fact the system of equality and freedom, and that the disturbances which they encounter in the further development of the system are disturbances inherent in it, are merely the realization of equality and freedom, which prove to be inequality and unfreedom . . . What divides these gentlemen from the bourgeois apologists is . . . the utopian inability to grasp the necessary difference between the real and the ideal form of bourgeois society, which is the cause of their desire

[89] *C* I. 540, and *MEW* XXIII. 562.

to undertake the superfluous business of realizing the ideal expression again, which is only the inverted projection of this reality.[90]

Marx objects to these socialists fastening upon general abstractions without paying attention to how they are transformed historically and determined in different periods. They take bourgeois concepts of equality and freedom from the phenomenal surface of bourgeois society and hope to realize them in a pure unperverted form, without understanding that in their essence they prove to be inequality and unfreedom.[91] Moreover, for Marx, as we have seen already, the categories of one period can neither explain nor promote the transition to a subsequent higher period. This is an objection to Proudhon's method of approaching moral categories, not to his desire to realize them in a socialist society.

Marx, I think, is making the same point in the 'Critique of the Gotha Program',

I have dealt more at length with the 'undiminished proceeds of labour,' on the one hand, and with 'equal right' and 'fair distribution,' on the other, in order to show what a crime it is to attempt, on the one hand, to force on our Party again, as dogmas, ideas which in a certain period had some meaning but have now become obsolete verbal rubbish, while again perverting, on the other, the realistic outlook, which it cost so much effort to instill into the Party, but which has now taken root in it, by means of ideological nonsense about right and other trash so common among the democrats and French Socialists.[92]

As in the previous quotation, Marx objects to fastening upon moral categories, the past meaning of which has been lost since they have now been transformed, and to seeing such categories as general unchanging abstractions and taking them as ideals. This undermines the realistic, that is, as Marx explains later, the scientific, tendency of the party, which, as we have seen, looks beneath surface ideals to an inner essence and which tries to understand the transformation of categories. Again, this is not a rejection of all appeals to morality, but rather of the approach to morality characteristic of socialists like Proudhon and Lassalle. Marx, himself, on the preceding page of the 'Critique of the Gotha Program', spoke of equal right in socialist society, in order to

90 'Critique', p. 3. *G* 248-9, and *GKPO* 160. See also 'Marx to Engels on 2 Apr. 1858', *SC* 107-8, and *MEW* XXIX. 317-18.
91 *G* 247, and *GKPO* 159. See also *VPP* 39-40, and *MEW* XVI. 131-2.
92 'Gotha', p. 531, and *MEW* XIX. 21-2. See also 'Marx to Engels on 4 Nov. 1864', *SC* 148, and *MEW* XXXI. 15.

contrast his views with Lassalle's notion of equal right and fair distribution.[93]

This indicates why proletarian morality cannot be based on the everyday experience of the proletariat as Husami seems to suggest it should. Surface appearance in capitalist society differs sharply from what is discovered at the deeper level of inner essence. Proletarian morality must be based upon the scientifically discovered essence of things, or else it is likely to agree simply with capitalist morality, as Wood seems to think it will, or at best differ from it only in the inadequate fashion that it does for Proudhon or Lassalle.

Husami holds that 'the Marxian method of ethical thinking consists primarily in the moral evaluation of social institutions . . . It examines their consequences for the individuals living under them and then measures these consequences against the Marxian conception (or ideal) of man.'[94] This may be an adequate description of Marx's approach in 1844, but not of that seen in the later writings. I myself will argue at a later point that Marx has a teleological ideal, but to describe Marx's approach simply as one which uses an ideal to measure social institutions does not tell us how the ideal originates, whether it differs from the ideal of 1844, or how the scientifically correct method establishes this ideal.

Next, we must attend to Wood's claim that for Marx it would be impossible to condemn as unjust the institutions of an earlier society because the only standards by which a society can be judged legitimately are those which arise from its own mode of production. Thus, 'the holding of slaves by the ancients would be a just practice; and the claim that ancient slavery was unjust, whether it is made by contemporaries of the institution or by modern men reading about it in history books, would simply be wrong'. In the same way, it would be impossible to condemn capitalism on the basis of a socialist standard of justice, 'any such standards would not be rationally applicable to capitalism at all, any such condemnations would be mistaken, confused, and without foundation'.[95] Wood is simply wrong here. He does not

---

[93] 'Gotha', pp. 527-30, and *MEW* XIX. 16-20; on 'realistic' meaning 'scientific', compare to 'Gotha', p. 535, and *MEW* XIX. 25-6.

[94] Husami, 'Marx on Distributive Justice', *MJH* 60.

[95] 'Critique', pp. 18-19, 29. Also 'Reply', pp. 108-9, 130-1. Brenkert also holds that moral standards are applicable only to the mode of production out of which they arise: see 'Freedom and Private Property', pp. 89-90. However, Brenkert admits elsewhere that for Marx we can use later standards to judge earlier conditions, but he sees this as only the case for standards of freedom, not for standards of justice (see *Marx's Ethics of Freedom*, pp. 72-5, 131-2, 150-5). This is a bit odd because it would seem quite easy to

understand the method which Marx outlined in the *Grundrisse*.

For Marx, we have seen, there are categories which all stages of production have in common. These characteristics develop and are determined differently in different historical periods. If these categories, once they are fully developed, are worked into a paradigm which grasps and expresses modern society, the same paradigm will allow insight into earlier society, just as human anatomy contains a key to the anatomy of the ape. There will be a difference between earlier and later categories—partly unconquered remnants will have been carried along into the modern category and nuances in the earlier categories will have developed explicitly—but since the modern category will be a transformation of the old, it can give us insight into the older category.[96] I can see no reason why this aspect of the method would not apply to ethics. Moreover, we actually find Marx making moral judgements of earlier societies.[97]

In the first place, as we have seen already, Marx judges ancient society superior to modern society in certain respects. This is true of ancient art and it is also true of the individual of the ancient world whose development had not been frustrated by alienation.[98] Moreover, it seems that the morality of the ancient world, at least in one sense, was the highest morality,

All the law-givers of antiquity, Moses above all, founded their success in commanding virtue, integrity and proper custom on landed property, or at least

judge earlier conditions of equality by later standards of equality. If we can do this for both equality and freedom, and if equality and freedom amount to justice, then we should be able to use later standards of justice to judge earlier conditions.

[96] *G* 105, 776, and *GKPO* 25-6, 662.

[97] In one place Marx says, 'There is here, therefore, an antinomy, right against right, both equally bearing the seal of the law of exchanges. Between equal rights force decides.' (*C* I. 235, and *MEW* XXIII. 249.) This might appear to substantiate Wood's claim that a moral standard cannot be used to judge another society. However, here both claims to right are equally based upon and justified by the *same* standard—the capitalist standard. Neither appeals to a higher morality. Marx also says, 'The minimum limit of the value of labour-power is determined by the value of the commodities, without the daily supply of which the labourer cannot renew his vital energy, consequently by the value of those means of subsistence that are physically indispensable . . . It is a very cheap sort of sentimentality which declares this method of determining the value of labour-power, a method prescribed by the very nature of the case to be a brutal method' (*C* I. 173, and *MEW* XXIII. 187). Nor does this passage substantiate Wood's claim. Marx merely is rejecting moral objections to the correct scientific procedure of understanding the value of labour power. The way in which capitalism establishes the value of labour power may well be morally objectionable, but the correct interpretation of this determination of value by the science of political economy cannot be either moral or immoral.

[98] *G* 110-11, 162, and *GKPO* 30-1, 80.

on secured, hereditary possession of land, for the greatest possible number of citizens . . . The individual is placed in such conditions of earning his living as to make not the acquiring of wealth his object, but self-sustenance, his own reproduction as a member of the community . . . Antiquity unanimously esteemed agriculture as the proper occupation of the free man, the soldier's school.[99]

Thus the old view, in which the human being appears as the aim of production . . . seems very lofty when contrasted to the modern world, where production appears as the aim of mankind and wealth the aim of production . . . In bourgeois economics—and in the epoch of production to which it corresponds—this complete working-out of the human content appears as a complete emptying-out, this universal objectification as total alienation, and the tearing-down of all limited, one-sided aims as the sacrifice of the human end-in-itself to an entirely external end. This is why the childish world of antiquity appears on the one side as loftier. On the other side, it really is loftier in all matters where closed shapes, forms, and given limits are sought for.[100]

In one sense, Marx is suggesting that both ancient morality and modern bourgeois morality are one-sided. Ancient morality deals only with closed shapes, forms, and given limits, whereas bourgeois economics breaks down these closed forms and given limits. It develops human powers and capacities beyond them and completely works out the human content. In this sense the modern world is superior. But in doing so it produces alienation and uses the individual as a means towards the end of production, whereas the ancient world took individuals to be ends in themselves and production as a means to their realization. Here the morality of the ancient world is superior. In this passage Marx is certainly comparing moral standards and using one to judge the other.

Again, in discussing the opium trade in China, Marx is quite willing to judge pre-capitalist Chinese society as ethical and the capitalist policies of England as unethical. He says, 'the representative of the antiquated world appears prompted by ethical motives, while the representative of overwhelming modern society fights for the privilege of buying in the cheapest and selling in the dearest markets'. Later, he says, 'John Bull, however, used to plume himself on his high standard of morality, prefers to bring up his adverse balance of trade by periodical war tributes, extorted from China on piratical pretexts.'[101]

---

[99] *G* 476-7, and *GKPO* 379-81.

[100] *G* 487-8, and *GKPO* 387-8.

[101] 'History of the Opium Trade', *MECW* XVI. 16, and *MEW* XII. 552. 'The Anglo-Chinese Treaty', *MECW* XVI. 32, and *MEW* XII. 569.

We also can find passages where Marx does specifically what Wood prohibits. He judges capitalist society by socialist standards. In the following passage, we see a very good example of how Marx's method allows him both to explain the development of social institutions and to judge them morally:

> It was not, however, the misuse of parental authority that created the capitalistic exploitation, whether direct or indirect, of children's labour; but, on the contrary, it was the capitalist mode of exploitation which, by sweeping away the economic basis of parental authority, made its exercise degenerate into a mischievous misuse of power. However terrible and disgusting the dissolution, under the capitalist system, of the old family ties may appear, nevertheless, modern industry, by assigning as it does an important part in the process of production, outside the domestic sphere, to women, to young persons, and to children of both sexes, creates a new economic foundation for a higher form of the family and of the relations between the sexes. It is, of course, just as absurd to hold the Teutonic-Christian form of the family to be absolute and final as it would be to apply that character to the ancient Roman, the ancient Greek, or the Eastern forms, which, moreover, taken together form a series in historical development . . . the fact of the collective working group being composed of individuals of both sexes and all ages, must necessarily, under suitable conditions, become a source of humane development; although in its spontaneously developed, brutal, capitalistic form, where the labourer exists for the process of production, and not the process of production for the labourer, the fact is a pestiferous source of corruption and slavery.[102]

Here Marx is comparing the capitalist form of the family to other forms and measuring, judging, the capitalist form by a 'higher form', which is certainly the socialist form of the family that capitalism is preparing the ground for. Marx seems to be doing much the same thing when he says, 'From the standpoint of a higher economic form of society, private ownership of the globe by single individuals will appear quite as absurd as private ownership of one man by another.'[103]

Indeed, we can judge social institutions in accordance with higher standards. In the *Grundrisse*, Marx suggests that the illusion that we cannot is created by capitalism. Capitalism, as it arises and develops, creates conditions so that 'there appears nothing higher in itself, nothing legitimate for itself, outside the circle of social production and exchange', and on the following page Marx makes it clear that capitalism accomplishes this ideally but not really.[104]

[102] *C* I. 489–90, and *MEW* XXIII. 514.
[103] *C* III. 776, and *MEW* XXV. 784.
[104] *G* 409–10, and *GKPO* 313.

Moreover, we have already seen that Marx thinks that individuals can transcend their times. As soon as the modern worker recognizes the product as his own or the ancient slave sees that he is a person, then (contrary to Wood) this sounds the death knell of those economic systems. In *Capital*, Marx says, 'My standpoint, from which the evolution of the economic formation of society is viewed as a process of natural history, can less than any other make the individual responsible for relations whose creature he socially remains, however much he may subjectively raise himself above them.'[105] Individuals can transcend the moral values which arise out of the prevailing material conditions of society, but what effect does this have? Not enough for us to hold individuals responsible for social relations because for Marx moral insights alone are unable to transform society, and certainly individuals alone are unable to do so. The task is much more than a moral one. Society and its institutions would have to be radically changed for these higher moral insights to develop fully, for them to become widespread, and for them to come to be reinforced by new social institutions and thus realized.

Nevertheless, this moral transcendence does seem to have some effect. It sounds the death knell of the existing system. But how can morality both be so ineffective that we cannot hold the individual responsible, yet at the same time be effective enough that we can say that the death knell of the existing system has been sounded? This seems to be a contradiction. In *Capital*, Marx says, 'Political economy can remain a science only so long as the class-struggle is latent or manifests itself only in isolated and sporadic phenomena.' As class struggle developed in France and England, 'It sounded the knell of scientific bourgeois economy.' Why was this the case? Marx suggests that, as soon as a class struggle develops, capitalism no longer can be 'looked upon as the absolutely final form of social production instead of as a passing historical phase'. He goes on to say,

It was thenceforth no longer a question, whether this theorem or that was true, but whether it was useful to capital or harmful, expedient or inexpedient, politically dangerous or not. In place of disinterested inquirers, there were hired prize-fighters; in place of genuine scientific research the bad conscience and the evil intent of apologetics.

With the rise of class struggle, scientific political economy of the classical sort becomes impossible (although this will be noticed only by other scientists, and only by rather acute ones at that). What remains

[105] *G* 463, and *GKPO* 366-7. *C* I. 10, and *MEW* XXIII. 16.

possible at the scientific level is only the *critique* of political economy, and that, after all, is the subtitle of *Capital*.[106] Thus, moral transcendence, and even the early stages of the socialist movement, are not sufficient to cause the actual collapse of capitalism, but can cause collapse at the level of scientific theory.

It is true that we do not find many passages in which, from the perspective of a higher socialist morality, Marx condemns as unjust the institutions of other societies. I suspect, however, that the reasons for this are quite different from the ones that Wood gives. Marx says that to oppose the welfare of the individual to the welfare of the species,

> is to assert that the development of the species must be arrested in order to safeguard the welfare of the individual, so that, for instance, no war may be waged in which at all events some individuals perish. . . . Apart from the barrenness of such edifying reflections, they reveal a failure to understand the fact that, although at first the development of the capacities of the human species takes place at the cost of the majority of human individuals, and even classes, in the end it breaks through this contradiction and coincides with the development of the individual; the higher development of individuality is thus only achieved by a historical process during which individuals are sacrificed for the interests of the species . . .[107]

Marx, like Hegel and Kant, thinks that the development of humanity as a whole has proceeded at the expense of individuals.[108] If this is a true description of what has actually occurred in history, then despite the fact that past societies have been immoral and unjust, can be and have been condemned as such, this immorality and injustice must be accepted if the species is to develop. In Marx's view, the only real hope for humanity is to reach the end of history where finally the contradiction between the individual and the species will come to an end. Even in the passage concerning the family quoted above, Marx both condemns the dissolution of the family caused by capitalism and argues that capitalism is laying the foundation for a higher form of the family. Look at the language employed by Marx in that passage, 'However terrible and disgusting' the dissolution of the family under capitalism, 'nevertheless', capitalism creates the 'basis for a higher form of the family'.[109] The dissolution of the family under capitalism *is* immoral but it creates the basis for a higher form of the family. Any condemnation of past society must also recognize that that society is laying the

---

106 *C* I. 14-16, and *MEW* XXIII. 19-22.
107 *TSV* II. 118, and *MEW* XXVI, part ii. 111.
108 *PH* 25-7, *SW* XI. 54-7. Kant, *IUH* 13-16, and *KGS* VIII. 19-22.
109 *C* I. 489-90, and *MEW* XXIII. 514.

foundation of a higher society. If historical development were to stop, this would make impossible a final end to the conflict—the final reconciliation of the individual and the species. One refrains from a simple condemnation of past society not because there are no rational grounds for doing so, as Wood claims, but because it would show a lack of realism and a blindness to the moral end of history.

While Marx often may refrain from condemning past society, though he does not do so always, Wood is completely wrong to claim that Marx would hold that within ancient society slavery *actually* would 'be a just practice'.[110] Perhaps Wood gets this from Engels. However, Engels does not say that slavery is just but only that it constitutes a step forward.

It is very easy to inveigh against slavery and similar things in antiquity, and to give vent to high moral indignation at such infamies, namely that these institutions of antiquity are no longer in accord with our present day conditions and our sentiments, which these conditions determine . . . we are compelled to say—however contradictory and heretical it may sound—that the introduction of slavery at that time was a great step forward.[111]

At any rate, I do not think that Marx would agree with Wood that ancient slavery was simply just any more than he would agree that the capitalist form of the family is simply just. We have seen that he distinguishes between essence and appearance. At most he would hold that ancient slavery was just only at the level of appearance. Marx himself tells us that the slave's realization that he is a person sounds the death knell of an economic system based upon slavery, just as the modern worker's realization that the product belongs to him sounds the death knell of capitalism. Here, certain moral judgements do not retard the course of historical development, but hasten it. This might well be a criterion for distinguishing between hopeless and worthwhile forms of moral judgement. However, it does not follow from this, as we have seen Isaiah Berlin claim, that agreement or disagreement with the advance of history determines whether or not something is moral.[112] For Marx, things are moral or immoral independently of whether or not they will retard or hasten historical development. He does not decide that the dissolution of the family under capitalism should be considered

---

[110] 'Critique', p. 18.

[111] *AD* 200, and *MEW* XX. 168. See 'Reply', p. 117.

[112] I. Berlin, *Karl Marx: His Life and Environment*, pp. 154-5. This passage has been quoted above; Ch. 3, sect. v.

moral because it is laying the foundation for a higher form of the family. It *is* laying this foundation; nevertheless it is immoral.

Thus, when one claims that capitalism is unjust, this cannot mean that capitalism should or could have different standards than the ones which correspond to its mode of production. Nor does it imply that history should or could come to a standstill. Nevertheless, one does not want to argue that one thing is just for capitalism and another thing is just for socialism, and that there is no way to judge the former by the latter's standards. One wants to be able to say that socialism involves a higher standard of justice, one which capitalism cannot realize or fulfil, but which the historical development of capitalism prepares the ground for. Moreover, the development of this higher standard provides the key to understanding the earlier standard. It allows us to see the short-comings of capitalism as well as the way in which it is preparing the ground for a higher form of society.

Thus, in the 'Critique of the Gotha Program', where Marx says that present day distribution is the 'only "fair" distribution on the basis of the present-day mode of production', he is not claiming that no higher standard of justice can be envisioned or appealed to, but that no other form of distribution can be *realized* on the basis of capitalist production. A new mode of production would have to be brought about first. It is in this sense also that we must understand Marx's claim a few pages later that 'Right can never be higher than the economic structure of society and its cultural development conditioned thereby.'[113] This cannot mean that one is unable to envision a higher system of right, as Marx himself, a page earlier in the 'Critique of the Gotha Program', envisions and appeals to a higher system of right under socialism. The point is that moral transcendence is not equivalent to the full realization of a new system of values and that the former can occur before the latter is possible.

Marx, however, does not think that appeals to morality are a proper strategy for a socialist party. They are not sufficient to realize socialism. The main concern of a socialist party must be the actual transformation of society, which must occur before more than a few individuals will be able to morally transcend existing values in an acceptable way and certainly before these new values can be realized. If, as Marx says, between two equal rights within the same system of right, only 'force

---

[113] 'Gotha', pp. 528, 531, and *MEW* XIX. 18, 21. It is true that Marx is discussing the first stage of communist society when he makes this claim about rights. But clearly he makes it as a universal claim applicable even to capitalist society.

decides',[114] then this is even more likely between a right established on the basis of the existing mode of production and a higher right derived by science. This is so, for Marx, because consciousness is simply not powerful enough on its own to influence large masses of people against their interests as solidified in and reinforced by the prevailing mode of production. This is not to say that one cannot appeal legitimately to a higher morality, just that it is not strategically effective to do so. For Marx, a transformation of society will produce a new morality far more effectively than a new morality will transform society.

It is also the case that Wood's views saddle him with peculiar difficulties. It would seem that a socialist party, seeking a revolution, to act morally would have to act in accordance with capitalist morality. On these grounds, it might well be argued that such a party would have no moral right to revolt at all. If, on the other hand, this revolutionary party chooses not to act in accordance with capitalist standards of morality, then the actions of this party would be amoral or, by capitalist standards—which are the only standards in capitalist society for Wood—immoral. One might then be led to argue that there are not and should not be any moral constraints on the party's actions at all, and Wood comes very close to holding this view himself.[115] It may be that such thinking goes a long way towards explaining the behaviour of some leftist parties. At best, Marx would be put in the position of Kant, who argued that if a better constitution is realized through revolution, it would be wrong to try to overthrow the new constitution and return to the old, but, nevertheless, anyone caught in the act of revolt would deserve justly—by capitalist standards—the punishment received:[116] a position which Marx clearly did not hold.

Many of those who write on Marx seem to assume, whether they are fully aware of it or not, that Marx is primarily, or even exclusively, a theorist of revolution. From this assumption it might seem to follow that everything that Marx says, all areas that he investigates, must in some fairly direct way be connected with the promotion of revolution or the realization of socialism. If not, then something is wrong: either Marx has been misinterpreted or Marx made an error and must be revised. This assumption is especially important with regard to consciousness and it has special significance for ethics. It can lead in radically different directions depending upon whether or not one thinks that consciousness is *capable* of promoting revolution, but in any case it

---

[114] *C* I. 235, and *MEW* XXIII. 249.
[115] *Karl Marx*, pp. 141-2.
[116] *PP* 120, and *KGS* VIII. 372-3.

causes a misreading of Marx. Some theorists, like Lukács and Marcuse, are led to argue that consciousness—including ethics and aesthetics—does promote revolution, if not in a crude and immediate way.[117] Others, like Stanley Moore, think that morality is incapable of promoting social transformation, and argue that when Marx does appeal to morality he violates his own principles of historical materialism. Moore views Marx's thought as an unstable conflict between a dialectic of liberation involving moral prescriptions and a historical materialist sociology of change which is exclusively scientific and descriptive. He correctly points out that, in the 'Critique of the Gotha Program', when Marx discusses the transition from the first to the second stage of communism he does not argue that historical materialist causes produce this transition. Marx says,

In a higher phase of communist society, after the enslaving subordination of the individual to the division of labor, and therewith also the antithesis between mental and physical labour, has vanished; after labour has become not only a means of life but life's prime want; after the productive forces have also increased with the all-round development of the individual, and all the springs of co-operative wealth flow more abundantly—only then *can* the narrow horizon of bourgeois right be crossed in its entirety and society inscribe on its banner: From each according to his ability, to each according to his needs!

In this passage, the material transformation which occurs in the first stage of communist society does not *cause* us to move on to the second stage. It only makes it *possible* for us to do so. Why then would we? Moore argues that the reasons for doing so are moral.[118] Since the argument is moral, it is unacceptable to Moore and contradicts the principles of historical materialism.

Wood, too, seems to operate with a similar set of assumptions. He says,

To create a 'proletarian morality' or 'proletarian concept of justice' by disseminating a set of ideas which working-class agitators find politically advantageous would strike Marx as a shortsighted and self-defeating course for the movement to adopt. It is far safer and more efficacious in the long run to rely simply on the genuine (non-moral) reasons people have for wanting an obsolete and inhuman social system to be overthrown and replaced by a higher form of society. . . .

[117] G. Lukács, *History and Class Consciousness*, trans. R. Livingstone (Cambridge, Mass.: MIT Press, 1971), 2, 19-21, 42, 52-3, 70. H. Marcuse, *An Essay on Liberation* (Boston: Beacon, 1969), 37-8; *The Aesthetic Dimension* (Boston: Beacon, 1978), pp. xi-xiii, 1.

[118] S. Moore, 'Marx and Lenin as Historical Materialists', *MJH* 212 ff., 232-3. 'Gotha', p. 531 (my emphasis); and *MEW* XIX. 21.

Changes in the prevailing standards of right and justice do not cause social revolutions but only accompany them. This, of course, is not to deny that bringing about changes in the moral, legal, and political superstructure of society is for Marx an important subordinate moment of revolutionary practice. But on Marx's theory, new standards of right come to be valid because revolutionary changes occur in economic relations; it is not the case that revolutions do occur or should occur because post-revolutionary standards of right are already valid for pre-revolutionary society.[119]

For Wood, the fact that a higher socialist morality cannot promote revolution is connected closely with the claim that there can be no valid socialist morality until socialism is established and that capitalism cannot be judged by socialist standards.

I cannot accept the widespread assumption that Marx is primarily or exclusively a theorist of revolution, nor the consequences which this has for morality, namely, that if morality does not promote revolution it is illegitimate to appeal to it. Marx's thought certainly involves a theory of revolution, and his doctrine of historical materialism would make little sense without such a theory, but Marx's thought involves much more than this. His theory of historical materialism, which was set out first in the *German Ideology*, as well as the revised version of it first outlined in the Introduction to the *Grundrisse*, makes very general claims about the relationship of material conditions to all forms of consciousness. It is a general theory which demands that Marx develop, or at least be able to develop, theories of art, religion, law, psychology, morality, and indeed of all other forms of consciousness—even, one would assume, theories of the sciences and mathematics. He is obliged to develop these theories whether or not the forms of consciousness they describe will serve to promote revolution. If there is some connection between material conditions and consciousness, he must show that connection, and it is not in the least obvious that in all cases this will promote revolution. For Marx, religious consciousness will not promote revolution. Must psychology? Must art? Must mathematics? I do not think, for Marx, that ethics is expected to promote revolution. Nevertheless, he is obliged to have a theory of ethics. Marx says that the proletariat should 'vindicate', not reject, 'the simple laws of morals and justice which ought to govern the relations between individuals'. In *Capital*, he also says that individuals 'may subjectively raise themselves above' their social conditions, yet at the same time he does not hold that the individual can

---

[119] 'Reply', pp. 132-3. 'Critique', p. 30. Also, *Karl Marx*, pp. 126 ff. Here, if he is talking about communist revolution, Wood seems to contradict his earlier claim that for Marx in communist society there would be no concept of justice at all ('Critique', p. 30).

be held 'responsible for relations whose creature he socially remains'.[120] Morality is quite possible and has an important place despite the fact that it alone is not responsible for social conditions nor can it transform them or promote revolution.

The version of historical materialism found in the *German Ideology* saw ethics as ideological illusion that would disappear eventually. The method of the *Grundrisse* allows Marx to develop a theory of a higher socialist morality. He is obliged to have this theory; he can use it to make moral judgements; it may even be the case that making a revolution may inevitably involve appealing to morality, as we shall see in Chapter 5, section ii; but morality alone will not promote or cause revolution. There is nothing wrong with this unless you hold that historical materialism is only a theory of revolution and so everything must promote or contribute to causing revolution or lose its legitimacy.

We must also see that the relationship of consciousness to material conditions is transformed with the coming of socialist society. As we have seen, for the later Marx moral consciousness certainly plays a role in pre-socialist society, but it is unable independently to transform social conditions. On the other hand, socialism might almost be defined as a form of society in which for the first time consciousness is able to predominate over material conditions. Consciousness, as we shall see in the following chapter, will be able to control these conditions and begin to realize its own purposes.[121] Socialist morality will have real effect. It will be able to mould and transform material conditions with a degree of independence which was not possible in capitalist society. Thus, I think that Moore is wrong when he criticizes Marx on the ground that the only reason for the transition from the first to the second stage of communism is a moral one and that this is in conflict with his own claims concerning historical materialism.[122] Moral concerns would be quite capable of promoting the development of the second stage of

---

[120] *CWF* 35, and *MEW* XVII. 3. *C* I. 10, and *MEW* XXIII. 16.

[121] *C* I. 78-80, and *MEW* XXIII. 92-4.

[122] Moore suggests that, when Marx discusses the transition to the second stage of communism, he is making a scientific prediction about the coming of communism ('Marx and Lenin as Historical Materialists', *MJH* 233). I think that it is merely a moral prescription—the statement of an ideal. In fact, Moore himself, as we have seen, also suggests that it is a moral prescription (ibid.). It might be possible to hold that Marx is predicting what the ideals of communist society will be, but if so these moral ideals would have to be determined by material conditions. However, if Moore is holding that for Marx moral prescriptions *rather* than material conditions bring about the second stage, and that this violates the principles of historical materialism, then this would imply that moral ideals are independent of material conditions. If so, the transition to the second stage could not both be produced by moral ideas and predicted.

communism. Material conditions will not continue to predominate in communist society as Marx might have thought they would in the more determinist days of the *German Ideology*. Moore is operating with a notion of historical materialism that derives more from the *German Ideology* than from the *Grundrisse*.

5

The Transcendence of Morality

I

Marx's discussion of justice in the 'Critique of the Gotha Program' is worth special attention. There, Marx examines several models of distributive justice. He begins by telling us that the present day distribution of the proceeds of labour is the only fair distribution on the basis of the present day capitalist mode of production. He holds that legal relations arise from economic ones and denies that the former can regulate the latter. In the same vein, he also denies that higher principles of right can be realized on the basis of the capitalist mode of production.[1]

When the first stage of communist society emerges from capitalism, it will be 'economically, morally, and intellectually, still stamped with the birth marks of the old society from whose womb it emerges'.[2] The individual worker will receive a certificate from society indicating that he or she has contributed a certain amount of labour, from which, however, there will have been deducted a certain sum for a common fund (a fund for the replacement and expansion of the means of production, insurance funds, costs of administration, schools, health services, disability, and so forth). This certificate will be exchangeable for means of consumption which cost the same amount of labour. Marx says that here

the same principle prevails as that which regulates the exchange of commodities as far as this is exchange of equal values . . . a given amount of labour in one form is exchanged for an equal amount of labour in another form. Hence, equal right here is still in principle—bourgeois right, although principle and practice are no longer at loggerheads . . .[3]

In the first stage of communism, then, we have a principle of distributive justice to the effect that 'The right of the producers is

---

[1] 'Gotha', pp. 528, 531-2, and *MEW* XIX. 18, 22.
[2] 'Gotha', p. 529, and *MEW* XIX. 20.
[3] 'Gotha', pp. 528-30, and *MEW* XIX. 18-20.

proportional to the labour they supply; the equality consists in the fact that measurement is made with an equal standard, labour.' This is the same principle which prevails in capitalist society—that of equal right, the exchange of equivalents—though the contradictions of bourgeois society have been overcome, and, moreover, here there is common ownership and co-operative control of the means of production. Nothing can 'pass to the ownership of individuals except means of consumption'.[4]

However, the equal right of stage one is not fully acceptable to Marx. In practice it still involves a principle of *inequality*,

But one man is superior to another physically or mentally and so supplies more labour in the same time, or can labour for a longer time; and labour, to serve as a measure, must be defined by its duration or intensity, otherwise it ceases to be a standard of measurement. This equal right is an unequal right for unequal labour. It recognizes no class differences because everyone is only a worker like everyone else; but it tacitly recognizes unequal individual endowment and thus productive capacity as natural privileges. It is therefore, a right of inequality, in its content, like every right. Right by its very nature can consist only in the application of an equal standard, but unequal individuals (and they would not be different individuals if they were not unequal) are measurable only by an equal standard in so far as they are brought under an equal point of view, are taken from one definite side only, for instance, in the present case, are regarded only as workers and nothing more is seen in them, everything else being ignored. Further, one worker is married another not; one has more children than another, and so on and so forth. Thus, with an equal performance of labour, and hence an equal share in the social consumption fund, one will in fact receive more than another, one will be richer than another, and so on. To avoid all these defects, right instead of being equal would have to be unequal.

Only in a higher phase, the second stage of communist society, 'can the narrow horizon of bourgeois right be crossed in its entirety and society enscribe on its banners: From each according to his ability, to each according to his needs!'[5]

How are we to interpret this movement beyond the horizon of bourgeois equal right? Wood claims that Marx

believes that the end of class society will mean the end of the social need for the state mechanism and the juridical institutions within which concepts like 'right' and 'justice' have their place. If, therefore, one insists on saying that Marx's 'real' concept of justice is the one he would deem appropriate to a fully

---

4 'Gotha', p. 530, and *MEW* XIX. 20.
5 'Gotha', pp. 530-1, and *MEW* XIX. 20-1.

developed communist society, one's conclusion probably should be that Marx's 'real' concept of justice is no concept at all.

Brenkert, too, thinks that in the second stage of communist society, there will be no principles of justice; justice will be left behind. Buchanan holds a similar position. Schedler also thinks that this view is correct and he tries to explain why: for Marx, 'the second stage of communism is neither just nor unjust, because Marx's conception of it was such that the problem of justice or injustice could not arise'. For Schedler, justice (or at least distributive justice) is of concern only in conditions of moderate scarcity where we are handling conflicting claims concerning the division of social advantages and goods.[6] Thus, in a society which is wealthy enough to provide for each in accordance with their needs, that is, in a society without scarcity, there would be no need for a principle of justice.

It is not at all clear to me that this is correct. Even if one accepts the view that where scarcity is eliminated totally principles of justice will no longer be of concern, is it the case that *all* forms of scarcity can be eliminated? In communist society, will all, for example, have free and unrestricted access to *all* jobs? Marx does not say so. He claims that jobs will be rotated.[7] Thus, there could be disputes over the timing of the rotation or the order in which one comes up for the specific job. Questions of justice could arise also over the character of the decision-making procedures, rules at the work place, or even over the procedures for handling and arbitrating complaints. Conflicts of interest could arise between different age groups, sexes, and perhaps even races.

However, there is another and more important issue at stake here. What exactly does it mean to pass beyond the narrow horizon of bourgeois right? In the *Communist Manifesto*, as we saw in Chapter 3, Marx thought that morality was ideological illusion and that it would disappear in communist society.[8] Is this what Schedler, Buchanan, Brenkert, and Wood have in mind? As far as I can tell, it seems that it is. But in the *Grundrisse* and *Capital*, Marx certainly does not think that morality is mere ideological illusion to be rejected. There is, however, another way to move beyond right and justice. Instead of merely rejecting them, one can transcend them. How would this be different

----

[6] A. W. Wood, 'The Marxian Critique of Justice' ('Critique'), *MJH* 30. G. G. Brenkert, 'Freedom and Private Property in Marx', *MJH* 91. A. E. Buchanan, *Marx and Justice*, pp. 50, 57-60. G. Schedler, 'Justice in Marx, Engels, and Lenin', *Studies in Soviet Thought*, 18 (1978), 223-4.

[7] *C* I. 421, 487-8, and *MEW* XXIII. 443-4, 511-12.

[8] *Manifesto, MECW* VI. 504, and *MEW* IV. 480.

from merely rejecting them? In the *German Ideology*, Marx thought that material conditions so thoroughly determined consciousness, perhaps even in communist society, that it was illusion to appeal to some higher, independent source of moral obligation to regulate behaviour. We have seen that in the later writings Marx rejects such a strict view of the determination of consciousness by material conditions and thus allows, especially in communist society, for the influence of consciousness and therefore morality. What then can transcending such morality mean? Perhaps that individuals simply act justly without there being a principle which obligates or constrains them to do so. When Aristotle says that between friends justice is unnecessary, he is talking, I think, about transcending justice without rejecting it. Here, Aristotle does not mean what Marx meant in the *Manifesto* when he said that morality was ideological illusion that should disappear, but that friends fulfil the claims of justice without feeling constrained to do so. He holds that friendship is a truer and higher form of justice, and that friendship is more important than ordinary justice in holding a community together. In fact, the expectations of friendship are stricter than those of ordinary justice. For example, it would be worse to defraud a comrade than someone else. Ordinary rules of justice specify what we owe to others and what we are obliged to give them as their due. Friends fulfil the principles of justice and move beyond them. They give freely without constraint and perhaps more than is due. Aristotle even sounds like Marx in several places when he suggests that it is need which determines what is due between friends.[9]

Aristotle, as we have seen, also distinguished between arithmetic and geometric equality. We find what seems to be a version of arithmetic equality in Marx's first stage of communism, where each receives precisely equal shares (at least in so far as they contribute equal labour time). Actually this is already a form of geometric equality in that the share of A is to the share of B in the same proportion as the labour time of A is to the labour time of B. But in so far as the labour time of A and B are equal, their shares would be strictly equal. When Marx objects to the principle of equal right in the first stage of communism, his objection is that using labour time to determine the proportionality of shares between A and B produces inequality, or, we might say, an undesirable form of geometric equality. Shares are distributed not in

[9] Aristotle, *NE* 1155ᵃ, 1160ᵃ, 1163ᵃ-1163ᵇ. For a view in some ways similar to mine, see S. Lukes, 'Marxism, Morality, and Justice', *Marx and Marxisms*, ed. G. H. R. Parkinson (London: CUP, 1982), 177-205, esp. 195-203.

proportion to need, but in proportion to labour time, and this comes too close to arithmetic equality or, at most, varies from it only in ways which do not correspond to need.

With geometric equality, shares are not strictly equal. They are distributed in proportion to the worth or merit of individuals. Individuals of equal merit get equal shares. For Marx, in stage two, they are distributed geometrically in proportion to need.

We might also say that for Aristotle the relationship between friends is based on geometric rather than arithmetic equality. One gives to the friend not a mere arithmetic due, but in proportion to the friend's worth—in proportion to one's feeling about the friend or to the friend's need. There is good reason to think that Marx is transcending equal right and justice in this way, not simply rejecting them. In the 'Critique of the Gotha Program', he does not treat equal right as an ideological illusion. He takes it seriously; he shows how it can be realized in the first stage of communist society; and he suggests that this is an improvement over capitalism. In moving on to stage two, he suggests that he is moving on to something higher—a higher form of morality. Moveover, four years earlier, his view was that the proletariat should 'vindicate', not reject, 'the simple laws of morals and justice which ought to govern the relations between individuals'. In the same text, he said that communism, 'far from creating individual "moral constraints", will emancipate the "morals" of the individual from its class constraints'. It certainly seems to me that stage two involves a conception of justice. For example, it would certainly be unjust to try to return to the earlier principles of bourgeois right, or, even more so, to serfdom or slavery. It also seems a higher conception of justice much like the geometric equality Aristotle envisions between friends. The absence of a principle of justice which constrains our behaviour or obligates us in the normal way does not mean that we have done away with all morality and justice. For example, it is not the case that we would be unable to evaluate the morality of actions in communist society, nor, as Buchanan argues, that we would be unable to condemn the practices or institutions of earlier societies.[10] The justice of communist society appears as an ideal which we seek to realize. One can easily evaluate institutions, practices, or

[10] 'Gotha', pp. 530-1, and *MEW* XIX. 20-1.*CWF* 35, 168-9, and *MEW* XVII. 3, 563. Buchanan, *Marx and Justice*, pp. 50, 57-60. See also G. W. F. Hegel, *On Christianity: Early Theological Writings*, trans. T. M. Knox (Gloucester, Mass.: Peter Smith, 1970), 209-14, and *Hegels theologische Jugendschriften*, ed. H. Nohl (Frankfurt-on-Main: Minerva, 1966), 264-8.

behaviour in communist society as well as in earlier society by seeing how far short of that ideal they fall.

I must point out that a certain amount of what I have just said and of what will follow in this chapter, when I liken Marx's views to those of other philosophers, is a bit speculative. In the relatively few passages of the later writings where Marx discusses ethical issues, I cannot always find hard evidence for the parallels to other philosophers that I will discuss. At the same time, I cannot find evidence to the contrary. Such a procedure is necessary, I think, if we are to try to answer the questions that arise from Marx's texts themselves and to assess the interpretations of Marx's commentators. The test of my views can only be whether or not they illuminate Marx's thought and give a plausible and consistent interpretation of what Marx says and implies. The question as to whether or not Marx himself had such parallels in mind when he wrote must be left open.

To further understand the transcendence of morality we must discuss an aspect of Marx's distinction between essence and appearance which we have left aside until now. The concept of essence which we find in *Capital* and the *Grundrisse* differs radically from the concept of essence found in 1844. In 1844, the essence of a thing was its inner reality, its truth, and this inner metaphysical essence had to be realized so that existence corresponded to essence. Marx's early ethical views were built upon this conception of essence. Morality *was* the realization of essence in existence. In the *Grundrisse* and *Capital*, Marx does not seek to realize essence in existence or bring about a harmony between the two. He wants essences to disappear and thus for the whole opposition between essence and appearance to evaporate. Essences, strange as it may sound, are now thought of as types of appearance, but not as mere subjective appearances nor as surface phenomena. Essences allow us to grasp a fact about social reality, not a fact about our subjective perceptions. Essences, Marx says, have a 'purely social mode of existence'.[11] They arise out of social processes and will disappear when these disappear. They allow us to grasp social reality as it is and appears to science as long as that social reality lasts. They are, we might say, appearances-for-science. They are the scientifically coherent concrete for thought which organizes the otherwise chaotic appearance of surface phenomena. They are accurate reflections of reality gained only by

---

[11] *TSV* I. 171, and *MEW* XXVI. part i. 141.

science. Surface phenomena, on the other hand, appear to everyday experience, but differ from, even contradict, reality.[12]

Essences are *social* realities—they have no independent metaphysical existence of their own. They themselves do not produce surface phenomena or generate the actual concrete as essences did in 1844. Essences allow us to grasp social relations, structures, or processes which link the concrete to its surface phenomena and which allow the concrete to generate and transform surface phenomena. The actual concrete causes surface phenomena; essences grasp and describe how it does so. Essences are real in the sense that they describe real processes as long as those processes continue to exist.

Exchange value, for example, is an essence behind the surface phenomena of bourgeois society, and certainly it cannot be said that Marx wants to realize this essence. He wants to eliminate it. Marx says in the *Grundrisse* that as industry develops,

the creation of real wealth comes to depend less on labour time and on the amount of labour employed than on the power of the agencies set in motion during labour time, whose 'powerful effectiveness' is itself in turn out of all proportion to the direct labour time spent on their production, but depends rather on the general state of science and on the progress of technology, or the application of science to production . . . As soon as labour in the direct form has ceased to be the great well-spring of wealth, labour time ceases and must cease to be its measure and hence exchange value [must cease to be the measure] of use value.[13]

In the 'Critique of the Gotha Program', Marx says, 'Within the co-operative society based on common ownership of the means of production, the producers do not exchange their products; just as little does the labour employed on the products appear here as the value of these products, as a material quality possessed by them'.[14] Thus, exchange value, the essence grasped by science, disappears.

To know the actual concrete world, we must take into account the totality of its processes which are reflected in the categories and their interconnection—the essence. In this sense science allows us to understand reality. We understand a fact about capitalism, not a fact about our subjective perceptions. Yet, in grasping reality as it is given, we can still say in a sense that we know mere appearance, because in coming to know reality scientifically we see through it critically. We recognize that

---

[12] For a similar view of the development of Marx's views on essence, see J. Seigel, *Marx's Fate: The Shape of a Life* (Princeton University Press, 1978), 195, 201-2, 212, 304, 317-24, 359-61.

[13] *G* 704-5, and *GKPO* 592-3.   [14] 'Gotha', p. 529, and *MEW* XIX. 19-20.

in earlier periods of development the scientific appearance, the essence, produced was quite different, and we begin to see how it may be changed in the future. In other words, the natural and eternal appearance which reality possesses due to fetishism or alienation in capitalist society is *mere* appearance, which, nevertheless, is precisely the appearance actually and unavoidably belonging to reality as it exists,

> The categories of bourgeois economy consist of such like forms. They are forms of thought expressing with social validity the conditions and relations of a definite, historically determined mode of production, viz., the production of commodities. The whole mystery of commodities, all the magic and necromancy that surrounds the products of labour as long as they take the form of commodities, vanishes therefore, so soon as we come to other forms of production.[15]

Capitalism is marked by fetishism or alienation. This is caused by the fact that individuals produce independently and then bring their products to a market in which exchange is uncontrolled. Market laws set in and come to control the exchange of products independently of the will or consciousness of the producers. What is actually a particular set of relations between persons comes to appear as an abstract set of relations between things—the products. This abstract process will seem to have a life of its own above and beyond the control of individuals, and will come to dominate them.[16] To begin to understand these impersonal, and seemingly natural relations, science must go behind surface appearance to grasp capitalist reality. This is necessary only in an alienated or fetishized economy. Were fetishism to be overcome, as in communist society, social relations would appear as clear, intelligible, directly experienced relations between human beings who consciously organize and control their social interaction in specific ways. Here, 'the practical relations of everyday life [will] offer to man none but perfectly intelligible and reasonable relations with regard to his fellowmen and to Nature'. There would be no longer a gap between essence and appearance and, as Marx says, 'all science would be superfluous if the outward appearance and the essence of things directly coincided'. Theoretical social science would wither away and science would be necessary only as practical science—as purposeful control of production for the realization of practical objectives.[17]

[15] For further discussion, see my *Marx' Method, Epistemology, and Humanism* ch. 3, sect. vi. *C* I. 76, and *MEW* XXIII. 90.

[16] *C* I. 71-80, and *MEW* XXIII. 85-94.

[17] *C* I. 79, and *MEW* XXIII. 93. *C* III. 817, and *MEW* XXV. 825. Also see G. A. Cohen, 'Karl Marx and the Withering Away of Social Science', *MJH* 288-309. For further discussion, see my *Marx' Method, Epistemology and Humanism*, ch. 3, sect. viii.

As we have seen, Marx's view is that bourgeois morality and its concepts of freedom, equality, and justice are based upon, derive from, and express the alienated surface appearance of capitalist society. The concepts of freedom, equality, and justice proper to proletarian morality, on the other hand, derive from the scientific study of the essence of society (which contradicts surface appearance), and science allows for the beginnings of a new, higher morality. We must notice now that the concepts of morality to be found in a developed communist society arise with the overcoming and collapse of the distinction between essence and appearance. We have said that proletarian morality cannot be based on everyday experience. If it were, socialists very likely would end up like Proudhon trying to realize the ideals of bourgeois morality without seeking to change fundamentally the prevailing mode of production. On the other hand, once communism has been achieved, morality *would* be based on everyday experience which would be perfectly intelligible and would not differ from a deeper essence. Science would be unnecessary at this level.

To say that essences have been eliminated would be to say that fetishism had been overcome, and with fetishism overcome the transcendence of morality would be possible. With fetishism overcome, individuals no longer would confront an independent, abstract, and autonomous set of processes which they could not control and which dominated them. Nor would they need science to penetrate behind the surface appearance of these processes in order to understand them. All social relations would appear as clearly understood relations between human beings and these relations would be under the control of these human beings. In such a society, Marx thinks, morality no longer would be a morality of constraint.[18] As we have seen, he claims that communist morality would emancipate the individual from a morality of class constraint. With no classes, there would no longer be a ruling class which inevitably would impose its interests upon other classes with divergent interests. Moreover, to the extent that scarcity would be overcome, individual behaviour would not have to be constrained in ways which run counter to the needs of individuals. For Marx, morality arises from and corresponds to the prevailing mode of production. This morality will constrain individuals if the prevailing mode of production gives rise to fetishism, classes, or scarcity. But if individuals clearly understand their social interactions and are in control of them, then it seems at least possible that the morality which would arise would not

18 *CWF* 168-9, and *MEW* XVII. 563.

constrain them. If individuals control the processes of production which give rise to morality, they would be at least indirectly in control of their morality rather than dominated by it.

In the uncontrolled exchange of capitalist society the common good is realized behind the back of individuals and through an invisible hand. No one sees the common good and consequently no one seeks it or pays any special attention to it. Each seeks their own private interests and ends up treating others as means to the realization of this interest.[19] In fully developed communist society, exchange will have been abolished. Production will be co-operative and consciously regulated according to a social plan. Communist society would be able to seek the common good and order society so as to realize individuals as ends in themselves. The common good, the good of the species, would be no longer at odds with the interests of the individual. They would agree.[20]

In certain ways, communist society resembles the ideal state that Schiller envisioned at the end of his *Letters on the Aesthetic Education of Man*. He contrasted three forms of the state. In the natural or dynamic state, each person clashes with others and only in this way is activity restricted and order kept. In the ethical state, individuals are confronted by a general will and with rational duties to which they must subordinate their will. In the aesthetic state, individuals confront each other as ends in themselves, and the will of the whole is carried out spontaneously through the natural inclinations of the individuals.[21] The individual need not submit to a higher moral authority. Rather, the needs, inclinations, and interests of the individual spontaneously accord with duty, reason, and morality. There would be no tension or constraint here. Very roughly speaking, Marx's description of capitalist society resembles Schiller's natural or dynamic state, a state in which the common good is realized through an invisible hand and where individuals are coerced by processes which they can neither understand nor control. The first stage of communist society resembles the ethical state. In the first stage of communism, as we recall, Marx claimed that labour would be a social duty and suggested that principles of equal right would constrain individuals.[22] The second stage of communism resembles the aesthetic state.[23] Here, morality and constraint have been transcended.

[19] *G* 243-5, and *GKPO* 155-6.

[20] *C* I. 78-80, and *MEW* XXIII. 92-4. *TSV* II. 118, and *MEW* XXVI. part ii. 111.

[21] *AE* 215, and *SWN* XX. 410.

[22] *TSV* III. 257, and *MEW* XXVI. part iii. 253. 'Gotha', pp. 530-1, and *MEW* XIX. 20-1.

[23] Of course, Schiller is not proposing a communist mode of production. For a fuller discussion see my *Schiller, Hegel, and Marx*, pp. 25 ff.

We must explain further how it is possible to speak of morality in the absence of principles which constrain or obligate us. Communist society would seem to involve what Hegel called *Sittlichkeit*, morality based on custom and tradition so that 'is' replaces 'ought'. Here, for Hegel, individuals do not perceive moral laws as constraints, as obligations, or as duties to be fulfilled. Their behaviour is rooted in ethical custom which permeates their interests and inclinations. They *are* moral; they do not view morality as something they *ought* to be. For Hegel, this form of *Sittlichkeit* was found in the ancient world. Aristotle's discussion of friendship which is higher than justice could be taken as a good example. Hegel, however, sought a higher *Sittlichkeit* for the modern world which preserved the character of ancient *Sittlichkeit* but also included *Moralität*, morality based on conscious reflection and rationality.[24] Marx's second stage of communism would have to involve this higher form of *Sittlichkeit*. Marx admits that custom and tradition play an important role in earlier forms of society:

> it is evident that traditions must play a dominant role in the primitive and undeveloped circumstances on which these social production relations and the corresponding mode of production are based. It is furthermore clear that here as always it is in the interest of the ruling section of society to sanction the existing order as law and to legally establish its limits given through usage and tradition . . . And such regulation and order are themselves *indispensable elements of any mode of production* . . .

Elsewhere, as we have seen, Marx claims that such custom and tradition actually 'shapes, limits, or forbids the actual direction of society by its Sovereign'.[25]

Communist society will transcend principles of right and justice. What will remain, however, will be custom and tradition which are 'indispensable elements of *any* mode of production'. Moreover, the communal relations which give rise to custom and tradition will be subordinate to conscious and rational control.[26] This will be the higher form of *Sittlichkeit*.

II

As we have seen, Marx is willing to admit that individuals can subjectively raise themselves above, morally transcend, their social

[24] *PH* 35-6, 39-40, 104, 251-3, 269, and *SW* XI. 66-7, 71-2, 150-1, 328-31, 350. See also *PR* 11-13, 36, 91-2, 103-9, and *GPR* 15-17, 49-50, 122-3, 140-8.

[25] *C* III. 793 (my emphasis), and *MEW* XXV. 801. *Ethnological Notebooks of Karl Marx*, pp. 329, 334; this text contains Marx's original MS.

[26] *G* 158, 162-3, and *GKPO* 75-6, 80-1.

conditions, and he accepts the view that we can condemn one society by using the higher moral standards of another society. Nevertheless, in part at least, Marx's approach to ethics is descriptive and empirical. Values are to be treated as facts. Morality and justice are held to 'arise as natural consequences out of . . . production relationships'. They correspond to these relations. They do not determine, they reflect and express, the prevailing mode of production.[27] For the scientist studying justice or morality in, say, capitalist society, these phenomena must be treated as facts which the scientist must approach descriptively and be able to confirm empirically—it even seems to be Marx's view that for the scientist there should be no difference between ethical statements and the ordinary statements of empirical science. He writes in *Capital*,

Proudhon begins by taking his ideal of justice . . . from the juridical relations that correspond to the production of commodities . . . Then he turns round and seeks to reform the actual production of commodities, and the actual legal system corresponding thereto, in accordance with this ideal. What opinion should we have of a chemist, who, instead of studying the actual laws of the molecular changes in the composition and decomposition of matter, and on that foundation solving definite problems, claimed to regulate the composition and decomposition of matter by means of the 'eternal ideas' of 'naturalité' and 'affinité'?[28]

While individuals in capitalist society actually may appeal to higher standards or ideals, the scientist, for Marx, must not import such ideals into the study of capitalist society in the way that Proudhon does. Moreover, the approach which the party of the proletariat must take to morality should also be scientific in this sense.

On the other hand, in communist society, where consciousness finally comes into its own and can predominate in determining material conditions, and where individuals can become self-determined, morality, for Marx, is to be understood teleologically. In pre-socialist society, historical development occurred behind the back of individuals and the development of morality was determined, by and large, by the development of material conditions. With the coming of communist society, individuals will be able to understand and consciously control their social development. Morality and custom still will arise from and express the prevailing mode of production, but if the latter can be

---

[27] 'Notes on Adolph Wagner', in *Texts on Method*, p. 186, and *MEW* XIX. 359-60. *C* III. 339-40, and *MEW* XXV. 352. 'Gotha', p. 531, and *MEW* XIX. 20.

[28] *C* I. 84-5 n., and *MEW* XXIII. 99-100 n.

controlled consciously and purposefully, so can the customs and morality generated by these material conditions. Moreover, custom and morality themselves can come to play a role in controlling and transforming these conditions. Morality can begin to play a role in purposefully seeking a teleological goal. It follows, then, that the prescriptive ideals which arise in this society must have a place in Marx's scientific study of morality.

After communism has been established, science will become super-fluous, but until then the moral views of the proletariat must be based upon science. It follows that science will have to involve an understanding of the ideal that will arise in communist society—an ideal, moreover, which can begin to regulate society and be used to judge other societies. Yet, at the same time, the scientific study of this ideal must be empirical and descriptive. We must try to sort out how Marx's approach can be both descriptive and prescriptive. But first we must ask what the telos or goal of communist society will be.

Much as for Aristotle and the ancient world, the highest end, for Marx, is the full realization of individuals as ends in themselves. In *Capital*, Marx speaks of creating the material conditions 'which alone can form the real basis of a higher form of society, a society in which the full and free development of every individual forms the ruling principle'. He also speaks of shortening the work day so as to create a realm of leisure time in which 'begins that development of human energy which is an end in itself, the true realm of freedom'.[29]

If individuals are to be realized as ends in themselves, production must not be the end which individual activity serves as a means. Marx says, 'the old view, in which the human being appears as the aim of production . . . seems to be very lofty when contrasted to the modern world, where production appears as the aim of mankind and wealth the aim of production'. And also,

In bourgeois economics . . . this complete working-out of the human content appears as a complete emptying-out, the universal objectification as total alienation, and the tearing down of all limited, one-sided aims as sacrifice of the human end-in-itself as an entirely external end. This is why the childish world of antiquity appears on one side as loftier. On the other side, it really is loftier in all matters where closed shapes, forms, and given limits are sought for.[30]

---

[29] *C* I. 592, and *MEW* XXIII. 618. *C* III. 820, and *MEW* XXV. 828. See also *G* 162, 706, and *GKPO* 80, 593.
[30] *G* 487-8, and *GKPO* 387.

To realize individuals as ends in themselves, individuals must control their production and be self-determined. The goal is 'Free individuality, based on the universal development of individuals and on their subordination of their communal social productivity as their social wealth'.[31]

In *Capital*, Marx called Aristotle's vision a dream,

if every tool, when summoned, or even of its own accord, could do the work that befits it, just as the creations of Daedalus moved of themselves, or the tripods of Hephaestos went of their own accord to their sacred work, if the weaver's shuttles were to weave of themselves, then there would be no need either of apprentices for the master workers, or of slaves for the lords.[32]

We can see that in socialist society, given a reduced work day, increased productivity, and common control over production, this dream finally could be realized.

In stage two of communism the principle of distributive justice which is based on geometric equality and involves the transcendence of morality is absolutely necessary if we seriously want to achieve the very *highest* realization of individuals as ends in themselves. The principle here is, 'From each according to his ability, to each according to his needs!'[33]

If we really expect to achieve the highest realization of individuals as ends in themselves, it would be necessary to realize the first part of this slogan, 'From each according to his ability', not simply for the good of society, or to ensure that each contributes a fair share towards the benefit of others, but for the benefit of the individual contributors themselves. For Marx, individuals only develop by being active, as he says in the *Grundrisse*,

Free time—which is both idle time and time for higher activity—has naturally transformed its possessor into a different subject, and he then enters into the direct production process as this different subject. This process is then both discipline, as regards the human being in the process of becoming, and, at the same time, practice, experimental science, materially creative and objectifying science as regards the human being who has become, in whose head exists the accumulated knowledge of society.[34]

For individuals to be realized as ends in themselves, they must develop their powers and capacities through objectification and control their

[31] *G* 158, also p. 476, and *GKPO* 75, 379-80.
[32] *C* I. 408, and *MEW* XXIII. 430.
[33] 'Gotha', p. 531, and *MEW* XIX. 20.
[34] *G* 712, and *GKPO* 599-600.

world so as to make it serve their ends. Only by objectifying themselves in their world will their world reinforce and develop them rather than frustrate their development.

On the other hand, the second part of the slogan, 'to each according to his needs', also would be necessary because the strict equality of stage one of communism would frustrate the highest development of the powers and capacities of individuals.[35] Human development, for Marx, is understood in terms of the generation and satisfaction of needs. Only if individuals develop and satisfy higher and increasingly more complex needs can individuals develop to their very highest potential. Thus, freedom as self-determination and geometric equality based on need, the two factors which produce the form of distributive justice found in stage two, are necessary for the highest realization of individuals as ends in themselves. Contrary to the understanding of Wood, Brenkert, Buchanan, and Schedler, then, justice, far from disappearing, plays a crucial role in the moral realization of the teleological end which communist society seeks to bring about.

Furthermore, to realize individuals as ends in themselves in the highest sense would mean, just as for Aristotle's discussion of friends, Schiller's aesthetic state, and Hegel's concept of *Sittlichkeit*, that individuals must not be subordinate to anything—certainly not to production, but not even to constraining moral principles. Individuals must not be subordinate to moral principles which are seen as the highest ends in themselves. Individuals must fulfil but transcend moral principles. In the absence of constraining moral principles, custom based on community and spontaneous co-operation would replace the antagonistic and constrained interaction of individuals characteristic of pre-communist society. Communal solidarity or friendship must replace the constraints of justice, spontaneous inclination must replace duty, and 'is' must replace 'ought' if individuals are to be realized as ends in themselves in the very highest sense.

To further understand the transcendence of morality, let us look a bit more carefully at Aristotle. For him, the good life is understood as a life of activity, and the highest kind of activity proper to a human being—which is contemplation or wisdom—produces the highest happiness. The question that must be asked here is why contemplation will produce happiness. Even if we grant that contemplation is the highest and best activity, it does not follow obviously from this that contemplation necessarily would have anything to do with happiness, let alone produce the

---

[35] 'Gotha', pp. 530-1, and *MEW* XIX. 20-1. See also *G* 91-2, and *GKPO* 12-14.

highest happiness.[36] Why should the highest and best sort of activity proper to a human being make them happy? True wisdom, for some, might mean that we look into the horror of existence—into a cosmos which is an empty, alien, and hostile void. Far from producing happiness, this simply would produce terror, or at best resignation and acceptance. We must notice that there is a hidden step in Aristotle's argument, something which perhaps he never says explicitly, but which is implicit in almost everything he writes, namely, that human beings *fit* their world. The human essence, when realized, is at home in the cosmos. Thus, the best life, the life which realizes our essence, *would* be a life of happiness because the contemplative life would be at least in part a contemplation of this proper fit between human beings and their world. If it were the case that humans were alienated from the cosmos, as seems to be the case for Nietzsche and perhaps even in Sophocles' *Oedipus Rex*, the best life, even the life of virtue, would not lead to happiness.[37]

For Marx also, the highest life arises when there finally occurs a fit between humans and their world. For Marx, however, this fit has not existed hitherto in history. Individuals have been alienated from their world. Only through socially organized labour have human beings transformed nature, society, and themselves so that there finally can occur a fit between their world and their needs—and not just basic needs but higher needs. With the development of a society that can satisfy these higher needs, we would have a fit between humans and their world. In a society where this process of development were directed consciously and purposefully, individuals would be able to realize themselves as ends in themselves. The interests of individuals no longer would have to be sacrificed to the interests of the species.[38]

For Wood, I have argued, Marx ultimately abandons a concept of justice rather than transcends it. Wood likens Marx to Nietzsche, who, he thinks, rejects all morality because moral values are detrimental to certain other goods like strength and creativity.[39] Perhaps this is partly true of Nietzsche, but I think that Nietzsche rejects morality for another

[36] Aristotle, *NE* 1177a-1179a.

[37] Nietzsche quotes Silenus as saying that the cosmos is so terrifying for human beings that 'what is best of all is utterly beyond your reach: not to be born, to be nothing. But second best for you—is to die soon.' (*Birth of Tragedy*, trans. W. Kaufmann (New York: Vintage, 1967), sect. 3). Compare to Sophocles, *Oedipus the King*, in *Sophocles I*, trans. D. Green (University of Chicago Press, 1954), 69, also p. 64.

[38] *TSV* II. 118, and *MEW* XXVI. part ii. 111.

[39] A. W. Wood, 'Marx on Right and Justice: A Reply to Husami', *MJH* 124-5. Also 'Critique', p. 30.

and more important reason: he believes that there is no fit between human beings and the cosmos. We live in an alien, meaningless, and valueless world. Nietzsche rejects morality because it is sheer illusion. To see that it is illusion, allows us, if we are strong enough, to create our own values on no authority but our own.[40] This is not Marx's view at all. Like Aristotle, he hopes to bring about a fit between humans and their world so as to realize human beings as ends in themselves, and he sees this as a goal which transcends morality but does not reject it. Marx himself tells us in the *Civil War in France* that the task of the proletariat is to vindicate the simple principles of morality and justice and that communist society will realize a morality without constraint.[41]

However, if the morality of communist society is teleological, if it seeks an end or ideal, how can this ideal legitimately arise for science, if, as we have already seen, Marx denies that scientists should import ideals into the study of capitalist society and even that morality itself can be effective in transforming society? If Marx's approach to capitalist morality is empirical and descriptive, how and why, when we move to communist society, does it legitimately become prescriptive and teleological?

In the *Civil War in France*, Marx says,

The working class did not expect miracles from the commune. They have no ready-made utopias to introduce *par décret du peuple*. They know that in order to work out their own emancipation, and along with it that higher form to which present society is irresistably tending by its own economical agencies, they will have to pass through long struggles, through a series of historic processes, transforming circumstances and men. They have no ideals to realize, but to set free the elements of the new society with which the old collapsing bourgeois society itself is pregnant.[42]

This progress towards communist society is not envisioned as a process motivated by a moral yearning for an ideal. It is a process which occurs whether individuals attend to ideals or not. It is a process which is brought about by the development of material conditions—by irresistible economic tendencies. Thus, it can be treated simply in a descriptive and empirical manner. Yet it is a process tending towards a certain result or end, though not seeking this end itself and certainly not seeking it *consciously*. Nevertheless, due to the social contradictions involved in capitalism, it is tending irresistibly towards this end. The

---

[40] See my 'Nietzsche, Skepticism, and Eternal Recurrence', *Canadian Journal of Philosophy*, 13 (1983), 365-87.

[41] *CWF* 168 n., 169, and *MEW* XVII. 563.

[42] *CWF* 77, and *MEW* XVII. 343.

individuals involved are transformed during this process. They can come to understand it, to work along with it, and to shorten and lessen the birth pangs of the new society.[43] Moreover, these individuals are capable of having ideals. They should avoid the sorts of ideals we find among socialists like Proudhon; they should confine themselves to the ideals with which existing society is itself pregnant; and they should realize that these ideals alone and of themselves are ineffective. But nevertheless, they do have ideals. Marx says that they have 'no ideal . . . *but* to set free the elements of the new society' emerging from the old.[44] This is to say that their ideal *is* to set free these elements. When the new society finally has emerged, then moral ideals or teleological ends can come into their own.

An empirical and descriptive approach to ethics is not incompatible with a teleological approach. The empirical and descriptive approach to ethics claims that values can be treated as facts, that they arise from facts, and that this process can be understood empirically. A teleological approach to ethics need not deny that values arise from facts or that values can be treated as facts. In other respects, however, these approaches do differ. In Marx's view, at least in the later writings, the teleological approach implies that values, ends, or ideals can have some effect in determining facts or material conditions, while the empirical and descriptive approach, certainly in the *German Ideology* but also in the later writings, implies that at least in capitalist society facts or material conditions predominate in determining values or ideals.

We must explain then how values arise from facts—how the ideals of communist society arise from material conditions. Marx suggests that these ideals arise from setting free the elements of the new society with which the old is pregnant. This can be explained by focusing on Marx's concept of need. What drives us to transform present day society and to realize socialism are the needs generated by the existing mode of production—basic needs concerned with obtaining the necessities of life. But in the process of changing society, individuals and their needs are also transformed. Marx discusses the transformation of needs in the *Grundrisse,*

Production mediates consumption; it creates the latter's material; without it, consumption would lack an object. But consumption also mediates production, in that it alone creates for the products the subject for whom they are products . . . A railway on which no trains run, hence which is not used up, not

---

[43] *C* I. 10, and *MEW* XXIII. 16.
[44] *CWF* 77 (my emphasis), and *MEW* XVII. 343.

194   *The Transcendence of Morality*

consumed, is a railway only potentially, and not in reality . . . consumption creates the need for new production, that is it creates the ideal, internally impelling cause for production, which is its presupposition . . . consumption ideally posits the object of production as an internal image, as a need, as drive and as purpose . . . Production also gives consumption its specificity, its character, its finish . . . Firstly, the object is not an object in general, but is a specific object which must be consumed in a specific manner, to be mediated in turn by production itself. Hunger is hunger, but the hunger gratified by cooked meat eaten with a knife and fork is a different hunger from that which bolts down raw meat with the aid of hand, nail, and tooth . . . Production thus creates the consumer . . . Production not only supplies a material for the need, but it also supplies a need for the material. As soon as consumption emerges from its initial stage of natural crudity and immediacy—and, if it remained at that stage, this would be because production itself had been arrested there—it becomes itself mediated as a drive by the object. The need which consumption feels for the object is created by the perception of it. The object of art—like every other product—creates a public which is sensitive to art and enjoys beauty.[45]

For Marx, needs call forth development in production—they are the ideal, internally impelling cause of production—and developments in production transform needs. At a lower stage of the development of production we can be dominated by very crude needs—hunger can be satisfied by raw meat. At higher levels of development we can enjoy having and satisfying the need—we need cooked meat eaten with knives and forks. Production can create even a need for art and beauty. Higher needs call forth more complex production and more complex production produces higher needs. Such needs even can be ends in themselves—their tendency certainly is to move far beyond the stage of crudity and immediacy. In the *Economic and Philosophic Manuscripts* of 1844, Marx said,

It will be seen how in the place of the wealth and poverty of political economy come the rich human being and the rich human need. The rich human being is simultaneously the human being in need of a totality of human manifestations of life—the man in whom his own realization exists as an inner necessity, as *need*.[46]

This is to say that as higher needs develop, the realization of individuals as ends in themselves would be felt as a *need*. It seems to me that this is still Marx's view in the later writings. For example, he speaks of a need for art and beauty, and when in the 'Critique of the Gotha Program', Marx describes a society wealthy enough to establish the principle 'to

45 *G* 91-2, and *GKPO* 12-14.
46 *EPM, MECW* III. 304 (Marx's emphasis), and *MEW*, suppl. I. 544.

each according to his needs', I do not think that Marx is talking merely about basic needs. He has in mind a society which has understood that needs call forth production and that production transforms needs—a society that thus would begin to experience a need to control production consciously so as to produce in individuals higher needs, needs which would be ends in themselves, needs for a totality of human manifestations of life, or for the full development of the powers and capacities of the individual. The teleological goal of communist society, its ideals, would arise from and come to be felt as needs. Thus, as needs are transformed and higher needs realized, the shift to teleology, to the ideal of realizing individuals as ends in themselves, would be a natural development.

Individuals always will be motivated by needs. In a society marked by fetishism, constraint, and scarcity, we would expect individuals to be dominated by their needs. But what sorts of needs would be likely to arise in a society which had overcome these problems and which was under the control of free individuals? We might well expect that the needs that would arise here, especially if these individuals were in control of the processes which generated needs, would be the sorts of needs which those individuals would desire—needs which eventually would be ends in themselves, needs for the full and free development of these individuals.

This would be a development which could be studied in a purely descriptive and empirical fashion, and for Marx the scientist must study it in this fashion. But at the same time this development would involve the emergence of an ideal, and an ideal which itself would come to play a role in regulating the very development involved. The task of science, for Marx, is to understand social development so as to guide practice in assisting the realization of that development and in setting free the elements of the new society with which the old is pregnant, to shorten and lessen its birth pangs.[47] In this sense the task of science would be merely descriptive and empirical. But in so far as social development eventually gives rise to a moral ideal, which itself begins to regulate this development, the task of science also will involve a prescriptive and evaluative function.

It is not legitimate to dismiss either the prescriptive or the descriptive side of this approach, or to confuse them. If we were to dismiss the prescriptive and teleological side, we would reduce Marx's approach to the approach of the *German Ideology*, where all was exclusively descript-

[47] *CWF* 77, and *MEW* XVII. 343. *C* I. 10, and *MEW* XXIII. 16.

ive and where moral values perhaps were emotive preferences. On the other hand, if we were to dismiss the descriptive side, we would run the risk of returning to the position of 1844, where morality was able to play a direct role in transforming the material conditions of capitalist society and in realizing socialism, or, short of that, of importing ideals into science like Proudhon, and thus ceasing to be scientific. Science, for Marx, preserves the difference between facts and values. We must understand the development of communist morality in a descriptive and empirical way, without importing our own values into it, if morality is to be correctly used to evaluate earlier development and to assist the practice of a political party.

Moral ideals should not influence the process of scientific discovery and analysis. Rather, science must give rise to an understanding of these moral ideals—especially since they will eventually come to play a role in determining social development. Moral ideals alone—and for that matter, scientific theory alone—will not produce social transformation in pre-capitalist society.[48] Nevertheless, morality and custom serve an important function in stabilizing social relations. Marx also said that the General Council of the International maintains its power only through 'moral influence and moral authority'. Moreover, he held that when workers raise themselves above, morally transcend, their social conditions, they sound the death knell of the existing system—they cause the collapse of the bourgeois science of political economy.[49] In other words, while morality alone is incapable of producing social transformation, it can influence the minds of individuals. In this sense, proletarian morality, which is based on science, is absolutely necessary in order to prevent proletarian consciousness from falling back to the moral outlook prevailing in capitalist society, which, as we have seen, would be its normal tendency, or to prevent the proletariat from adopting inadequate ideals like those found in Proudhon and Lassalle. In other words, morality based on science is necessary to reinforce, stabilize, and guide proletarian consciousness along the right road. If, as we have seen, Marx no longer holds that consciousness is strictly determined by material conditions, then the reinforcing of proletarian consciousness by scientific morality becomes necessary and most important. On the other hand, as we approach fully developed communist society, morality will become increasingly capable of regulating the transformation of material conditions in a more direct way.

[48] *G* 100-2, and *GKPO* 21-2. *C* I. 19, 75, and *MEW* XXIII. 27, 89.
[49] *C* III. 793, and *MEW* XXV. 801. 'Amsterdam Speech', in *Marx-Engels Reader*, p. 523, and *MEW* XVII. 160. *C* I. 14-16, and *MEW* XXIII. 19-22.

Elsewhere, I have argued that Marx's science is incapable of making long-term predictions and that Marx does not intend it to predict in this way.[50] This can be seen most clearly in those passages where Marx tells us that categories are transformed in each historical period and that the categories which allow us to understand one period will neither explain nor promote the categories which will allow us to understand a subsequent period. We have also seen that needs are transformed historically. Thus it would follow that the needs characteristic of one period would not give us a basis from which to predict the needs of a subsequent period, nor to predict what these needs would lead individuals to do. If this is so, a serious problem arises. If an understanding of communist moral ideas is necessary to Marx's science, how can we gain this understanding if Marx's science is unable to predict these ideals? It seems to me that when Marx describes communist morality, he is not predicting. Instead, he is giving us a moral prescription as to what ought to occur in communist society. He says that the slogan 'From each according to his ability, to each according to his needs' can replace the narrow horizon of bourgeois right.[51] He is not predicting that this *will* occur; he is saying that it *can* occur and is suggesting that it *ought* to occur. The task of science in capitalist society is to allow the proletariat to understand the tendency of capitalist society so that the proletariat can begin to transform society intelligently in response to its needs. With the collapse of capitalist society and thus the collapse of a society marked by fetishism, constraint, and scarcity, with the end of a situation in which individuals are dominated by their needs, individuals will be able to regulate consciously their society and ought to do so to realize themselves. Marx's views on morality in communist society are prescriptions concerning what individuals ought to do or perhaps what it is likely that they would choose to do under conditions where it is no longer impossible for them to generate the sorts of needs which they would desire—needs which are ends in themselves.

In this sense moral prescription becomes a necessary and integral part of scientific method. If the method cannot predict the transformations that will occur under communism, then the only way we can proceed is morally. We can indicate what ought to occur. Then, of course, science itself finally withers away. The key here is that as communism arises, the conditions which obstruct freedom and which prohibit morality from having real effect in transforming material conditions are no longer expected to obtain. This is crucial. If communist society were

[50] See my *Marx' Method, Epistemology, and Humanism*, ch. 3, sect. iv.
[51] 'Gotha', p. 531, and *MEW* XIX. 21.

strictly determined as Marx perhaps thought it would be in the *German Ideology*, then, according to the view that from the categories of one period we cannot derive those of the next, we could neither predict nor prescribe communist conditions. We would be able to foresee nothing of communist society. We can foresee something only if the individuals of communist society are free. If they are, then we can say a little about what they would be likely to do or what they ought to do to realize the sorts of ideals that would be possible under such conditions.

Marx's views resemble those of Epicurus. In his Dissertation, Marx told us that for Epicurus the task of science was to rid the world of determinism so as to make *ataraxia*, or peace of mind, possible. For Epicurus, it was not at all necessary that science achieve an absolutely correct understanding of natural phenomena. Any interpretation that accorded with appearances and allowed for *ataraxia* was acceptable. Clearly, for Epicurus, the highest end was the moral ideal of peace of mind, not science. Science was to serve merely as a means towards the achievement of this ideal.[52] Marx's views are similar. Science cannot make long-term predictions; it cannot be certain about what will occur in fully developed communist society. But if science can guide practice to the point where capitalist society collapses, where freedom becomes possible, where there can be a society in which humans are in control of their material conditions, then science has achieved its goal. At that point theoretical science can wither away and consciousness, including moral consciousness, can take over, and that, after all, is all Marx is after. That, we can almost say, is the definition of communist society.

As I argued in the Introduction, for Althusser science is opposed to humanism and the later Marx is a scientist, not a humanist. I cannot agree with this view. Science is not incompatible with humanism and the later Marx is a humanist as well as a scientist. For Althusser, humanism reduces the forces and relations of production to human relations, whereas he sees the forces and relations of production as responsible for structuring human relations and thinks science's task is to study this social structure. But for Marx, as I have tried to show, science of this sort is only necessary in pre-communist, fetishized society where the forces and relations of production do dominate and determine human relations and where science must go behind abstract

---

[52] *Dissertation*, MECW I. 45, 67-73, and *MEW*, suppl. I. 227, 297-305. For further discussion of this matter see *Marx' Method, Epistemology, and Humanism*, ch. 3, sect. viii.

and obscure surface appearance to understand reality. With the end of
fetishism and the rise of communist society, human relations will be
dominated no longer by obscure and powerful social structures.
Instead, human beings will come to control their social relations and
these will appear as clear, intelligible, directly experienced relations
between human beings and between human beings and nature. Abstraction and mystification will disappear. Contrary to Althusser, the forces
and relations of production *will be reduced* to clearly understood human
relations and will be controlled by human beings so as to produce a
world which fits them, develops higher needs, and satisfies those needs.
Furthermore, moral values will come to play a role in determining these
material conditions. Morality is not incompatible with science, and
morality is not set to one side so that science can be pursued as our main
end. Science, for Marx, is merely the means to realize these humanistic
ideals—that is science's ultimate purpose. And then theoretical science
which was necessary to pierce through the fetishized surface appearance
of capitalist society will wither away as the gap between essence and
appearance is overcome. Moreover, morality is certainly not confined to
the ideological realm in communist society, and I even doubt whether
such a realm exists in communist society for the later Marx. Morality,
like all social consciousness, will arise from the everyday experience of
an unfetishized world—experience which, far from being a distortion of
reality, will reflect it accurately. Nor would moral principles constrain
individuals or stand over and dominate them. Rather, individuals in
control of their forces and relations of production would be able to
mould their own customs, traditions, and morality. Individuals would
become ends in themselves and their moral values would be means to
realize this ideal. This undoubtedly humanistic ideal is very definitely
Marx's ideal in the later writings. It is different from the humanistic
ideal of 1844, in that it does not employ a concept of human essence and
it does not understand morality as the realization of this essence in
accordance with a categorical imperative, but it is still a humanistic
ideal.

Moreover, we do not find an ongoing contradiction between science
and ethics in Marx's thought as the contradiction theorists argue. If we
recognize that Marx's views undergo shifts in the different periods of
his thought, we see that in the *German Ideology* science *is* incompatible
with ethics and that this leads Marx to reject the possibility of ethics. In
the later writings there is no incompatibility as I have tried to show.

III

At the end of Chapter 2, we noticed that in the writings of 1843 Marx rejected rights. There were two main reasons for this. In the first place, a right against the state would presuppose the separation of state from society, with the former standing over the latter to enforce such rights. In the later writings, there is some evidence to indicate that Marx would no longer make this sort of objection. In the earlier drafts of the *Civil War in France*, he argues that the task of a citizen militia, besides seeing to the defence of the citizens, would be to ensure that the governing body did not become a state standing over society.[53] If an armed militia would not presuppose, if in fact it would prevent, the re-establishment of a state standing over society, then it would be hard to imagine how rights could be objectionable in this regard.

In the second place, Marx's rejection of rights in 1843 followed from his concept of essence. The realization of the human essence required that individuals consciously work for the universal—the common good of the species. A concern with rights was thought to involve a concern with particular interests against the particular interests of others, against the universal, and against the common good of the community. Rights certainly were compatible with a competitive market economy regulated by an invisible hand where individuals sought their particular interests and only contributed to the common good unconsciously. But if realizing the species essence required *conscious* work for the benefit of the species, rights which reinforced particular interests would frustrate this realization and thus were to be rejected. While it was definitely the case that Marx wanted something higher than rights, nevertheless, I do not think we can say that in the early writings Marx wanted to transcend rights. He wanted to reject them from the start. A transitional society based on rights would not prepare for the transcending of rights. It would frustrate the realization of the human essence. As we have seen, Marx abandoned this concept of human essence in the *German Ideology* and he does not return to it in the later writings. The question we must ask, then, is whether in the later writings Marx still could make this sort of objection to rights.

Buchanan argues that the later Marx *does* reject rights because 'any society in which the potential for interpersonal conflict is serious enough to warrant the establishment of rights to serve as limits on conflict is a deeply divided society'.[54] In Buchanan's view, to say of a

---

[53] *CWF* 73-4, 152, 199, and *MEW* XVII. 338-40, 543, 595-6.
[54] Buchanan, *Marx and Justice*, pp. 64, also p. 77.

society that it has or needs rights is, for Marx, to make a serious and fundamental criticism of that society. I do not think this interpretation is tenable. If Marx holds that an armed and coercive citizen militia does not promote but even can prevent social division, I cannot see how he could hold that rights could promote divisions. In fact, they too might be able to assist in preventing divisions. It seems to me that the view of the later Marx is that social divisions are produced by material conditions, not by citizen militias or rights, and that this is a view which he had not come to yet in 1843, which, after all, was several years before the development of his doctrine of historical materialism. In 1843, Marx's view was quite clearly that forms of consciousness could play a role in transforming material conditions. In the later writings he does not think that this can occur before the full realization of communist society.

In the 'Critique of the Gotha Program', Marx tells us that in the first stage of communist society the same principle would prevail as in bourgeois society, namely, the principle of equal right. Here, it is true, Marx is speaking only about a principle of distributive justice. He does not mention civil rights like freedom of speech or of the press, but it certainly would seem that such rights would be present. Marx tells us that we must understand the first stage of communism 'just as it emerges from capitalist society, which is thus in *every* respect, economically, morally, and intellectually, still stamped with the birth marks of the old society from whose womb it emerges'.[55] It would seem to follow from this that since civil rights were present in capitalist society they would be present still in the first stage of communist society and perhaps even that here too 'principle and practice would no longer be at loggerheads'.[56]

We must notice that Marx's approach to rights in the 'Critique of the Gotha Program' is fundamentally different from his approach in 1843. In the 'Critique of the Gotha Program', rights are realized first, and only then, in the second stage of communism, do we pass beyond the 'narrow horizon of bourgeois right'. Moreover, it is clear that the existence of rights in stage one will not frustrate the development of the second stage of communist society—in fact, rights prepare the ground for this higher stage. Marx does not argue here that rights cause individuals to turn away from the common good towards particular interests. Instead, rights are held to serve a very important function—they firmly

---

[55] 'Gotha', pp. 529 (my emphasis), 530, and *MEW* XIX. 20, 21.
[56] 'Gotha', p. 530, and *MEW* XIX. 20.

establish a strict form of equality. Only once this equality is established, does it become possible to transcend the narrow horizon of bourgeois right and to move on to a higher stage where individuals are treated as equals not merely in terms of specific isolated qualities abstracted out of their real lives but concretely, in accordance with their needs.[57]

Here, rights are not being rejected from the start. They are realized first, and only then transcended. This is crucial because it means that the rights which were realized in stage one would have shaped custom and tradition and thus as stage one was transcended rights would continue on in stage two where they would no longer appear as formal constraining principles but would be embedded in the customs and traditions of stage two. They would take the form of *Sittlichkeit*, not *Moralität*—'is' would replace 'ought'. Here, in a real sense, rights would be transcended, not rejected. Moreover, if the second stage of communism were to falter during its development, its tendency might be to slip back towards the rights it had transcended rather than towards the absence of rights which had been rejected. There would be no guarantee of this. We cannot predict what will occur in stage two. But if rights were firmly established in the customs and traditions of stage two and had never been viewed as things to be rejected, there would be some tendency not to fall beneath the level of rights.

On the other hand, I do not think that, in the later writings, formal rights would be compatible with the realization of the highest ideals of communist society. Just as we have seen that the highest realization of individuals as ends in themselves is incompatible with subordination to constraining moral principles, so it would be incompatible with the constraints of formal rights. Moreover, as consciousness came into its own and began to predominate in determining material conditions, formal rights, in so far as they would now be in a position to have a more powerful effect on consciousness, might hinder the realization of the higher form of equality which, contrary to the principle of equal right, distributes goods in accordance with needs. Nevertheless, the ideals of stage two would tend to move beyond rights in the way that friendship moves beyond justice, to respect the claims of justice and rights as minimal claims in so far as they were embedded in custom and tradition. And any slippage would be a slippage back to rights and justice. In this respect, I would be inclined to say that the later Marx is more of a humanist than the early Marx was.

But even so, given the experience of twentieth-century communist

---

[57] 'Gotha', p. 531, and *MEW* XIX. 21.

societies, I would at least hesitate before wanting to transcend rights, despite the fact that the highest ideals of communist society would require this transcendence. The promise of what could be gained would have to be weighed against the risk of what could be lost. But such would be the inevitable dilemmas of a free society.

Bibliography

Works by Marx and Engels

Marx, K. *Capital*. Ed. F. Engels. 3 vols. New York: International, 1967.
—— *Civil War in France*. In *Writings on the Paris Commune*. Ed. H. Draper.
New York: Monthly Review Press, 1971.
—— *Critique of Political Economy*. Ed. S. W. Ryazanskaya. London: Lawrence &
Wishart, 1971.
—— 'Critique of the Gotha Program.' In *The Marx-Engels Reader*. 2nd edn. Ed.
R. C. Tucker. New York: Norton, 1978.
—— *Ethnological Notebooks of Karl Marx*. Ed. L. Krader. Assen: Van Gorcum,
1972.
—— *Grundrisse*. Trans. M. Nicolaus. London: Allen Lane, 1973.
—— *Grundrisse der Kritik der politischen Ökonomie*. Frankfurt: Europäische
Verlagsanstalt, 1953.
—— *Texts on Method*. Trans. T. Carver. New York: Barnes & Noble, 1975.
—— *Theories of Surplus Value*. Ed. S. Ryazanskaya. 3 vols. Moscow: Progress,
1969.
—— *Value, Price, and Profit*. Ed. E. M. Aveling. New York: International, 1935.
—— and Engels, F. *Marx and Engels: Basic Writings on Politics and Philosophy*.
Ed. L. S. Feuer. Garden City, New York: Doubleday, 1959.
—— *Marx Engels Collected Works*. 28 vols. to date. New York: International,
1975- .
—— *Marx Engels Gesamtausgabe*. Ed. Institut für Marxismus-Leninismus.
Berlin: Dietz, 1975- .
—— *Marx Engels historisch-kritische Gesamtausgabe*. Ed. D. Rjazanov. Berlin:
Marx-Engels Verlag, 1927- .
—— *Marx Engels Selected Correspondence*. Ed. S. Ryazanskaya. Moscow:
Progress, 1965.
—— *The Marx-Engels Reader*. 2nd edn. Ed. R. C. Tucker. New York: Norton,
1978.
—— *Marx Engels Werke*. 41 vols. Berlin: Dietz, 1972- .
Engels, F. *Anti-Dühring*. Trans E. Burns. New York: International, 1939.
—— *Dialectics of Nature*. Ed. C. Dutt. New York: International, 1939.
—— *Origin of the Family, Private Property, and the State*. New York:
International, 1942.

General Works

Acton, H. B. *The Illusion of the Epoch*. Boston: Beacon, 1957.
— *What Marx Really Said*. New York: Schocken, 1971.
Adler, M. *Kant und der Marxismus*. Berlin: E. Laub'sche Verlags-buchhandlung, 1925.
Allen, D. 'Does Marx Have an Ethic of Self-Realization? Reply to Aronovitch.' *Canadian Journal of Philosophy*, 10 (1980), 377-86.
— 'Marx and Engels on the Distributive Justice of Capitalism.' *Marx and Morality*. Ed. K. Nielsen and S. C. Patten. *Canadian Journal of Philosophy*, supplementary vol. 7 (1981), 221-50.
— 'Reply to Brenkert's "Marx and Utilitarianism."' *Canadian Journal of Philosophy*, 6 (1976), 517-34.
— 'The Utilitarianism of Marx and Engels.' *American Philosophical Quarterly*, 10 (1973), 189-99.
Althusser, L. *Essays in Self-Criticism*. Trans. G. Lock. London: NLB, 1976.
— *For Marx*. Trans. B. Brewster. London: NLB, 1977.
— *Lenin and Philosophy*. Trans. B. Brewster. New York: Monthly Review Press, 1971.
— and Balibar, E. *Reading Capital*. Trans. B. Brewster. London: NLB, 1970.
Aristotle. *The Basic Works of Aristotle*. Ed. R. McKeon. New York: Random House, 1941.
Aronovitch, H. 'Marxian Morality.' *Canadian Journal of Philosophy*, 10 (1980), 357-76.
— 'More on Marxian Morality: Reply to Professor Allen.' *Canadian Journal of Philosophy*, 10 (1980), 387-93.
Avineri, S. *The Social and Political Thought of Karl Marx*. Cambridge: Cambridge University Press, 1970.
Ayer, A. J. *Language, Truth and Logic*. New York: Dover, 1942.
Bauer, O. 'Marxismus und Ethik.' *Die Neue Zeit*, 24 (1905-6), 485-99.
Beck, L. W. *A Commentary on Kant's Critique of Practical Reason*. Chicago: University of Chicago Press, 1960.
Berlin, I. *Karl Marx: His Life and Environment*. 3rd edn. Oxford: Oxford University Press, 1963.
Brandt, R. B. *Ethical Theory*. Englewood Cliffs, NJ: Prentice Hall, 1959.
Brenkert, G. G. 'Freedom and Private Property in Marx.' *Marx, Justice, and History*. Ed. M. Cohen, T. Nagel, and T. Scanlon. Princeton: Princeton University Press, 1980.
— 'Marx and Utilitarianism.' *Canadian Journal of Philosophy*, 5 (1975), 421-34.
— 'Marx, Engels, and the Relativity of Morals.' *Studies in Soviet Thought*, 17 (1977), 201-224.
— 'Marx's Critique of Utilitarianism.' *Marx and Morality*. Ed. K. Nielsen and S. C. Patten. *Canadian Journal of Philosophy*, supplementary vol. 7 (1981), 193-200.

—— *Marx's Ethics of Freedom*. London: Routledge & Kegan Paul, 1983.

Buchanan, A. E. *Marx and Justice*. Totowa, NJ: Rowman & Littlefield, 1982.

Burke, J. P., and Crocker, L., eds. *Marxism and the Good Society*. Cambridge: Cambridge University Press, 1981.

Callinicos, A. *Althusser's Marxism*. London: Pluto, 1976.

Cohen, G. A. 'Karl Marx and the Withering Away of Social Science.' *Marx, Justice and History*. Ed. M. Cohen, T. Nagel, and T. Scanlon. Princeton: Princeton University Press, 1980.

—— *Karl Marx's Theory of History*. Princeton: Princeton University Press, 1978.

—— 'The Labor Theory of Value and the Concept of Exploitation.' *Marx, Justice, and History*. Ed. M. Cohen, T. Nagel, and T. Scanlon. Princeton: Princeton University Press, 1980.

—— 'More on Exploitation and the Labour Theory of Value.' *Inquiry*, 26 (1983), 309-31.

Cohen, M., Nagel, T., and Scanlon, T., eds. *Marx, Justice and History: A 'Philosophy and Public Affairs' Reader*. Princeton: Princeton University Press, 1980.

Colletti, L. *Marxism and Hegel*. Trans. L. Garner. London: NLB, 1973.

Collier, A. 'Scientific Socialism and the Question of Socialist Values.' *Marx and Morality*. Ed. K. Nielsen and S. C. Patten. *Canadian Journal of Philosophy*, supplementary vol. 7 (1981), 121-54.

—— 'The Production of Moral Ideology.' *Radical Philosophy*, 9 (1974), 5-15.

—— 'Truth and Practice.' *Radical Philosophy*, 5 (1973), 9-16.

DiQuattro, A. 'Alienation and Justice in the Market.' *Marxism and the Good Society*. Ed. J. P. Burke and L. Crocker. Cambridge University Press, 1981.

Easton, S. M. 'Facts, Values and Marxism.' *Studies in Soviet Thought*, 17 (1977), 117-34.

—— *Humanist Marxism and Wittgensteinian Social Philosophy*. Manchester: Manchester University Press, 1983.

Ebbinghaus, J. 'Interpretation and Misinterpretation of the Categorical Imperative.' *Kant: A Collection of Critical Essays*. Ed. R. P. Wolff. Garden City, NY: Doubleday, 1967.

Evans, M. *Karl Marx*. Bloomington, Ind.: Indiana University Press, 1975.

Ewing, A. C. *Ethics*. New York: Free Press, 1953.

Falk, W. D. 'Morality and Nature.' *The Australasian Journal of Philosophy*, 28 (1950), 69-72.

Feinberg, J., and Gross, H. *Justice*. Encino, Calif.: Dickenson, 1977.

—— *Law in Philosophical Perspective*. Encino, Calif.: Dickenson, 1977.

—— *Punishment*. Encino, Calif.: Dickenson, 1975.

Fetscher, I. *Marx and Marxism*. New York: Herder & Herder, 1971.

—— 'The Young and the Old Marx.' *Marx and the Western World*. Ed. N. Lobkowicz. Notre Dame: University of Notre Dame Press, 1967.

Feuer, L. S. 'Ethical Theories and Historical Materialism.' *Science and Society*, 6 (1942), 242-72.

Feuerbach, L. *The Essence of Christianity*. Trans. G. Eliot. New York: Harper and Row, 1957.

—— *The Fiery Brook: Selected Writings of Ludwig Feuerbach*. Trans. Z. Hanfi. Garden City, NY: Doubleday, 1972.

—— *Sämtliche Werke*. Ed. W. Bolin and F. Jodl. 13 vols. Stuttgart-Bad Cannstatt: Frommann, 1959- .

Fleischer, H. *Marxism and History*. Trans. H. Mosbacker. London: Allen Lane, 1973.

Frankena, W. K. *Ethics*. 2nd edn. Englewood Cliffs, NJ. Prentice Hall, 1973.

Fried, A., and Sanders, R., eds. *Socialist Thought*. Garden City, NY: Doubleday, 1964.

Fromm, E. *Marx's Concept of Man*. New York: Ungar, 1973.

Fuchs, W. W. 'The Question of Marx's Ethics.' *Philosophical Forum*, 7 (1976), 237-45.

Garner, R. T., and Rosen, B. *Moral Philosophy*. New York: Macmillan, 1967.

Gilbert, A. 'Historical Theory and the Structure of Moral Argument in Marx.' *Political Theory*, 9 (1981), 173-205.

Golding, M. P. *Philosophy of Law*. Englewood Cliffs, NJ: Prentice Hall, 1975.

Goldmann, L. *Immanuel Kant*. Trans. R. Black. London: NLB, 1971.

Gould, C. *Marx's Social Ontology*. Cambridge, Mass.: MIT Press, 1978.

Gouldner, A. *The Two Marxisms*. New York: Seabury, 1980.

Green, M. 'Marxist Ethics: II, Marx, Utility and Right.' *Political Theory*, 9 (1983), 433-46.

Greer, P. T. *Marxist Ethical Theory in the Soviet Union. Sovietica*, 40. Dordrecht: D. Reidel, 1978.

Habermas, J. *Knowledge and Human Interests*. Trans. J. Shapiro. Boston: Beacon, 1971.

—— *Theory and Practice*. Trans. J. Viertel. Boston: Beacon, 1974.

Hamilton, A., Jay, J., and Madison, J. *The Federalist*. New York: Random House, n.d.

Hare, R. M. *The Language of Morals*. New York: Oxford University Press, 1964.

Hegel, G. W. F. *Enzyklopädie der philosophischen Wissenschaften im Grundrisse*. Ed. F. Nicolin and O. Pöggeler. Hamburg: Felix Meiner, 1969.

—— *Grundlinien der Philosophie des Rechts*. Ed. J. Hoffmeister. Hamburg: Felix Meiner, 1955.

—— *Hegel's Philosophy of Nature*. Trans. J. Petry. 3 vols. London: Allen & Unwin, 1970.

—— *Hegel's Science of Logic*. Trans. A. V. Miller. London: Allen & Unwin, 1969.

—— *Hegels theologische Jugendschriften*. Ed. H. Nohl. Frankfurt-on-Main: Minerva, 1966.

—— *The Logic of Hegel.* Trans. W. Wallace. London: Oxford University Press, 1968.

—— *On Christianity: Early Theological Writings.* Trans. T. M. Knox. Gloucester, Mass.: Peter Smith, 1970.

—— *Phänomenologie des Geistes.* Ed. J. Hoffmeister. Hamburg: Felix Meiner, 1952.

—— *Phenomenology of Spirit.* Trans. A. V. Miller. Oxford: Oxford University Press, 1978.

—— *Philosophy of History.* Trans. J. Sibree. New York: Dover, 1956.

—— *Philosophy of Right.* Trans. T. M. Knox. Oxford: Oxford University Press, 1967.

—— *Sämtliche Werke.* Ed. H. Glockner. 26 vols. Stuttgart: Frommann, 1927- .

—— *Science of Logic.* Trans. W. H. Johnston and L. G. Struthers. 2 vols. London: Allen & Unwin, 1966.

—— *Wissenschaft der Logik.* ed. G. Lasson. 2 vols. Hamburg: Felix Meiner, 1969.

Heller, A. 'The Legacy of Marxian Ethics Today.' *Praxis International,* 1 (1982), 346-64.

—— *The Theory of Need in Marx.* New York: St Martin's, 1976.

Hess, M. *Moses Hess: Philosophische und Sozialistische Schriften.* Ed. A. Cornu and W. Mönke. Berlin: Academie, 1961.

—— 'The Philosophy of the Act.' *Socialist Thought.* Ed. A. Fried and R. Sanders. Garden City, New York: Doubleday, 1964.

Hobbes, T. *English Works of Thomas Hobbes.* Ed. W. Molesworth. 11 vols. Scientia Aalen, 1962.

Hodges, D. C. 'Historical Materialism in Ethics.' *Philosophy and Phenomenological Research,* 23 (1962-3), 1-22.

—— *Socialist Humanism.* St Louis: Warren H. Green, 1974.

Holstram, N. 'Marx and Cohen on Exploitation and the Labor Theory of Value.' *Inquiry,* 26 (1983), 287-307.

Hook, S. *Revolution, Reform, and Social Justice: Studies in the Theory and Practice of Marxism.* New York: New York University Press, 1975.

Husami, Z. I. 'Marx on Distributive Justice.' *Marx, Justice, and History.* Ed. M. Cohen, T. Nagel, and T. Scanlon. Princeton: Princeton University Press, 1980.

Kain, P. J. 'Estrangement and the Dictatorship of the Proletariat.' *Political Theory,* 7 (1979), 509-20.

—— 'Marx, Engels, and Dialectics.' *Studies in Soviet Thought,* 23 (1982), 271-83.

—— 'Marx's Dialectic Method.' *History and Theory,* 19 (1980), 294-312.

—— *Marx' Method, Epistemology, and Humanism.* Dordrecht: D. Reidel, 1986.

—— 'Nietzsche, Skepticism, and Eternal Recurrence.' *Canadian Journal of Philosophy,* 13 (1983), 365-87.

—— *Schiller, Hegel, and Marx.* Montreal: McGill-Queen's University Press, 1982.

Kamenka, E. *Marxism and Ethics*. London: Macmillan, 1969.

—— *The Ethical Foundations of Marxism*. 2nd edn. London: Routledge & Kegan Paul, 1972.

Kant, I. *Critique of Judgment*. Trans. J. Bernard. New York: Hafner, 1966.

—— *Critique of Practical Reason*. Trans. L. W. Beck. Indianapolis: Bobbs-Merrill, 1956.

—— *Critique of Pure Reason*. Trans. N. K. Smith. New York: St Martin's, 1965.

—— *Foundations of the Metaphysics of Morals*. Trans. L. W. Beck. Indianapolis: Bobbs-Merrill, 1959.

—— *Kant's gesammelte Schriften*. Ed. Royal Prussian Academy of Science. 26 vols. Berlin: Reimer, 1910- .

—— *Kant's Political Writings*. Ed. H. Reiss. Cambridge: Cambridge University Press, 1970.

—— *On History*. Ed. L. W. Beck. Indianapolis: Bobbs-Merrill, 1963.

—— *The Metaphysical Elements of Justice: Part I of the Metaphysics of Morals*. Trans. J. Ladd. Indianapolis: Bobbs-Merrill, 1965.

—— *Religion Within the Limits of Reason Alone*. Trans. T. M. Greene and H. H. Hudson. New York: Harper & Row, 1960.

Kautsky, K. *Ethics and the Materialist Conception of History*. 4th edn. Trans. J. B. Askew. Chicago: Charles Kerr, 1918.

Kellner, D. 'Marxism, Morality, and Ideology.' *Marx and Morality*. Ed. K. Nielsen and S. C. Patten. *Canadian Journal of Philosophy*, supplementary vol. 7 (1981), 93-120.

Kline, G. L. 'Was Marx an Ethical Humanist?' *Studies in Soviet Thought*, 9 (1969), 91-103.

Kolakowski, L. *Main Currents of Marxism*. Trans. P. S. Falla. 3 vols. Oxford: Clarendon Press, 1978.

Kuhn, T. S. *The Structure of Scientific Revolutions*. 2nd edn. Chicago: University of Chicago Press, 1970.

Lerner, M. P. 'Marxism and Ethical Reasoning.' *Social Praxis*, 2 (1974), 63-88.

Lobkowicz, N., ed. *Marx and the Western World*. Notre Dame: University of Notre Dame Press, 1967.

Lukács, G. *History and Class Consciousness*. Trans. R. Livingstone. Cambridge, Mass.: MIT Press, 1971.

Lukes, S. 'Can a Marxist Believe in Human Rights?' *Praxis International*, 1 (1982), 334-45.

—— 'Marxism, Morality and Justice.' *Marx and Marxisms*. Ed. G. H. R. Parkinson. London: Cambridge University Press, 1982.

Lyons, D. *Rights*. Belmont, Calif.: Wadsworth, 1979.

McBride, W. L. 'Marxism and Natural Law.' *American Journal of Jurisprudence*, 10 (1974), 127-53.

—— 'The Concept of Justice in Marx, Engels, and Others.' *Ethics*, 85 (1974-5), 208-18.

—— *The Philosophy of Marx*. London: Hutchinson, 1977.

210 *Bibliography*

210 *Bibliography*

MacIntyre, A. *After Virtue*. Notre Dame: University of Notre Dame Press, 1981.

—— *A Short History of Ethics*. New York: Macmillan, 1966.

McMurtry, J. 'Is There a Marxist Personal Morality?' *Marx and Morality*. Ed. K. Nielsen and S. C. Patten. *Canadian Journal of Philosophy*, supplementary vol. 7 (1981), 171-92.

—— *The Structure of Marx's World-View*. Princeton: Princeton University Press, 1978.

Marcuse, H. *An Essay on Liberation*. Boston: Beacon, 1969.

—— *The Aesthetic Dimension*. Boston: Beacon, 1978.

Marković, M. 'Marxist Humanism and Ethics.' *Inquiry*, 6 (1963), 18-34.

Merleau-Ponty, M. *Humanism and Terror*. Trans. J. O'Neill. Boston: Beacon, 1969.

Meynell, H. *Freud, Marx, and Morals*. London: Macmillan, 1981.

Mill, J. S. *Utilitarianism*. Indianapolis: Bobbs-Merrill, 1957.

Moore, S. 'Marx and Lenin as Historical Materialists.' *Marx, Justice, and History*. Ed. M. Cohen, T. Nagel, and T. Scanlon. Princeton: Princeton University Press, 1980.

—— *Marx on the Choice between Socialism and Communism*. Cambridge, Mass.: Harvard University Press, 1980.

—— *Three Tactics: The Background in Marx*. New York: Monthly Review Press, 1963.

Myers, D. B. 'Marx and Transcendence of Ethical Humanism.' *Studies in Soviet Thought*, 21 (1980), 319-30.

Nielsen, K. 'Conventionalism in Morals and the Appeal to Human Nature.' *Philosophy and Phenomenological Research*, 23 (1962), 217-31.

—— 'Marxism, Ideology, and Moral Philosophy.' *Social Theory and Praxis*, 6 (1980), 53-68.

Nielsen, K., and Patten, S. C., eds. *Marx and Morality*. *Canadian Journal of Philosophy*, supplementary vol. 7 (1981).

Nietzsche, F. *Birth of Tragedy*. Trans. W. Kaufmann. New York: Vintage, 1967.

—— *Nietzsche Werke: Kritische Gesamtausgabe*. Ed. G. Colli and M. Montinari. Berlin: DeGruyter, 1967- .

Nowell-Smith, P. H. *Ethics*. Harmondsworth: Penguin, 1964.

Ollman, B. *Alienation: Marx's Conception of Man in Capitalist Society*. 2nd edn. Cambridge: Cambridge University Press, 1976.

O'Malley, J. 'History and Man's Nature.' *Review of Politics*, 28 (1966), 508-22.

Peffer, R. G. 'Morality and the Marxist Concept of Ideology.' *Marx and Morality*. Ed. K. Nielsen and S. C. Patten. *Canadian Journal of Philosophy*, supplementary vol. 7 (1981), 67-91.

Phillips, D. Z., and Mounce, H. O. *Moral Practices*. London: Routledge & Kegan Paul, 1967.

Plamenatz, J. *Karl Marx's Philosophy of Man*. Oxford: Clarendon Press, 1975.

Plato. *The Collected Dialogues of Plato*. Ed. E. Hamilton and H. Cairns. Bollingen Series LXXI. New York: Pantheon, 1961.

Popper, K. R. *The Open Society and its Enemies*. 4th edn. 2 vols. Princeton: Princeton University Press, 1963.

Rader, M. *Ethics and the Human Community*. New York: Holt, Rinehart, and Winston, 1964.

— *Marx's Interpretation of History*. New York: Oxford University Press, 1979.

Rosdolsky, R. *The Making of Marx's Capital*. Trans. P. Burgess. London: Pluto, 1977.

Ross, W. D. *Foundations of Ethics*. Oxford: Clarendon Press, 1960.

Rousseau, J. J. *Émile*. Trans. B. Foxley. New York: Dutton, 1966.

— *OEuvres complètes*. 4 vols. Paris: Gallimard, 1959-

— *The Government of Poland*. Trans. W. Kendall. Indianapolis: Bobbs-Merrill, 1972.

— *The Social Contract and Discourses*. Trans. G. D. H. Cole. New York: Dutton, 1950.

Rubel, M., ed. *Pages choisies pour une éthique socialiste*. Paris: M. Rivière, 1948.

Ryan, C. C. 'Socialist Justice and the Right to the Labor Product.' *Political Theory*, 8 (1980), 503-24.

Sadurski, W. 'Marxist Ethics: I, To Each According to His (Genuine?) Needs.' *Political Theory*, 11 (1983), 419-31.

Schaff, A. *Marxism and the Human Individual*. New York: McGraw Hill, 1970.

Schedler, G. 'Justice in Marx, Engels, and Lenin.' *Studies in Soviet Thought*, 18 (1978), 223-33.

Schiller, F. *Essays Aesthetical and Philosophical*. London: Bell, 1879.

— *On Naive and Sentimental Poetry and On the Sublime*. Trans. J. A. Elias. New York: Unger, 1966.

— *On the Aesthetic Education of Man*. Trans. E. M. Wilkinson and L. A. Willoughby. Oxford: Oxford University Press, 1967.

— *Schillers Werke: Nationalausgabe*. Ed. J. Petersen and G. Fricke. 43 vols. Weimar: Böhlaus, 1943- .

Schmidt, A. *History and Structure*. Trans. J. Herf. Cambridge, Mass.: MIT Press, 1981.

Seigel, J. *Marx's Fate: The Shape of a Life*. Princeton: Princeton University Press, 1978.

Sève, L. *Man in Marxist Theory and the Psychology of Personality*. Trans. J. McGreal. Sussex: Harvester, 1978.

Shaw, W. H. 'Marx, Morals, and Philosophy.' *Social Praxis*, 8 (1981), 137-51.

— *Marx's Theory of History*. Stanford: Stanford University Press, 1978.

Singer, M. G. *Generalization in Ethics*. New York: Knopf, 1966.

Skillen, T. 'Marxism and Morality.' *Radical Philosophy*, 13 (1974), 11-15.

— *Ruling Illusions*. Brighton: Harvester, 1977.

Smith, A. *The Wealth of Nations*. Ed. E. Cannan. New York: Random House, 1937.

Soper, K. *On Human Needs*. Brighton: Harvester, 1981.

Sophocles. *Oedipus the King. Sophocles I*. Trans. D. Green. Chicago: University of Chicago Press, 1954.

Stevenson, C. L. *Ethics and Language*. New Haven: Yale University Press, 1944.

Stojanović, S. *Between Ideals and Reality*. Trans. G. S. Sher. New York: Oxford University Press, 1973.

Taylor, C. 'Marxism and Empiricism.' *British Analytical Philosophy*. Ed. B. Williams and A. Montifiore. London: Routledge & Kegan Paul, 1966.

Toulmin, S. C. *An Examination of the Place of Reason in Ethics*. Cambridge: Cambridge University Press, 1958.

Trotsky, L. *Their Morals and Ours*. New York: Pathfinder, 1969.

Tucker, R. C. *Philosophy and Myth in Karl Marx*. Cambridge: Cambridge University Press, 1964.

— *The Marxian Revolutionary Idea*. New York: Norton, 1970.

Vandeveer, D. 'Marx's View of Justice.' *Philosophy and Phenomenological Research*, 33 (1972-3), 366-86.

Vázquez, A. S. *The Philosophy of Praxis*. Trans. M. Gonzalez. London: Merlin, 1977.

Venable, V. *Human Nature: The Marxian View*. New York: Knopf, 1945.

Vorländer, K. *Kant und der Sozialismus*. Berlin: Reuther und Reichard, 1900.

Wallimann, I. *Estrangement: Marx's Conception of Human Nature and the Division of Labor*. Westport, Conn.: Greenwood Press, 1981.

Wellmer, A. *Critical Theory of Society*. Trans. J. Cumming. New York: Herder and Herder, 1971.

Wolff, R. P., ed. *Kant: A Collection of Critical Essays*. Garden City, NY: Doubleday, 1967.

Wood, A. W. *Karl Marx*. London: Routledge & Kegan Paul, 1981.

— 'Marx and Equality.' *Issues in Marxist Philosophy, 4. Social and Political Philosophy*. Ed. J. Mepham and D. H. Ruben. Brighton: Harvester, 1981.

— 'Marx on Right and Justice: A Reply to Husami.' *Marx, Justice, and History*. Ed. M. Cohen, T. Nagel, T. Scanlon. Princeton: Princeton University Press, 1980.

— 'The Marxian Critique of Justice.' *Marx, Justice, and History*. Ed. M. Cohen, T. Nagel, and T. Scanlon. Princeton: Princeton University Press, 1980.

Young, G. 'Doing Marx Justice.' *Marx and Morality*. Ed. K. Nielsen and S. C. Patten. *Canadian Journal of Philosophy*, supplementary vol. 7 (1981), 251-68.

Yovel, Y. *Kant and the Philosophy of History*. Princeton: Princeton University Press, 1980.

Zelený, J. *The Logic of Marx*. Trans. T. Carver. Oxford: Blackwell, 1980.

Zoolalian, D. E. 'Marx, Man, and Methodology: Some Remarks on Marx's Theory of Human Nature.' *Social Praxis*, 7 (1980), 41-57.

Index

10ﾝ

surplus value (*contd*)
  appropriation of as robbery 138
  rate of 157
symbol
  of the morally good 68
synchronic relations 140
synthetic connections 72

talents 29 n., 53 n., 63
teleology 65, 163, 187-95 *passim*
theology 23, 89
theory and practice 26, 59, 76
thing-in-itself 20 n.
tools 57
tradition
  see custom, and tradition
transcendence
  of justice 179-80, 186
  of morality 176, 178-92 *passim*
  of rights 186, 202-3
transcendental self 20
trustworthiness 52, 148
Tucker, R. C. 136

unhappy consciousness 24
universal class 38, 41, 77, 80-1, 107-11
universality 19-50 *passim*, 64, 76, 111,
  114, 131, 150-1, 153, 200
universalization 1, 5, 9, 15-16, 24 n.,
  28-9, 34-5, 60, 62, 65, 75, 78, 107,
  110, 113, 150 n.
unpaid labour 154, 157-8
Unrecht 156, 158
unsocial sociability 44
use value 145, 182
utilitarianism 72, 102-3

value 142, 145-6, 156, 158, 164, 182
valuelessness 192
Vergegenständlichung 56
  see also objectification
vindication
  of morality and justice 128, 173, 180,
  192
violence 48, 101
Vorländer, K. 15 n.
voting 81
Vulcan 147

wage labour 53, 61, 139
wages 52, 62, 72, 151, 157-8
  equality of 151
wants and desires 60
war 44, 168
wealth 148, 165, 172, 182, 189
wealth-getting 52, 67 n.
Wellmer, A. 9
will 154
  determined 115, 119
  divine 127
  see also choice; free will
wisdom 190-1
women
  in labour market 166
  as possessions 67
  relation to men 26 n.
Wood, A. W. 10, 135-8, 151-2, 159-78
  passim, 190-1
wood theft 35
world-historical individuals 35 n.
World Spirit 48

Young, G. 137 n.
Yovel, Y. 45 n., 74 n.